INFERIOR COURTS, SUPERIOR JUSTICE

Contributions in Legal Studies
Series Editor: Paul Murphy

Stability, Security, and Continuity: Mr. Justice Burton and Decision-Making in the Supreme Court, 1945-1958
Mary Frances Berry

Philosophical Law: Authority, Equality, Adjudication, Privacy
Richard Bronaugh, editor

Law, Soldiers, and Combat
Peter Karsten

Appellate Courts and Lawyers: Information Gathering in the Adversary System
Thomas B. Marvell

Charting the Future: The Supreme Court Responds to a Changing Society, 1890-1920
John E. Semonche

The Promise of Power: The Emergence of the Legal Profession in Massachusetts, 1760-1840
Gerard W. Gawalt

John R. Wunder

INFERIOR COURTS, SUPERIOR JUSTICE

A History of the Justices
of the Peace on the Northwest
Frontier, 1853-1889

Contributions in Legal Studies,
Number 7

GREENWOOD PRESS
Westport, Connecticut • London, England

Library of Congress Cataloging in Publication Data

Wunder, John.
    Inferior courts, superior justice.

    (Contributions in legal studies ; no. 7 ISSN 0147-
1074)
    Bibliography: p.
    Includes index.
    1.   Justices of the peace—Northwest, Pacific—
History.   I.   Title.   II.   Series.
KF8800.W9   347'.795'016   78-66720
ISBN 0-313-20620-1

Library of Congress Catalog Card Number: 78-66720
ISBN: 0-313-20620-1
ISSN: 0147-1074

First published in 1979

Greenwood Press, Inc.
51 Riverside Avenue, Westport, Connecticut 06880

Printed in the United States of America

10 9 8 7 6 5 4 3 2 1

for SUSAN

CONTENTS

TABLES

FIGURES

ACKNOWLEDGMENTS

This book is the product of many people who have helped in countless ways. Of primary importance is Vernon Cartensen of the University of Washington who first suggested the topic to me and who meticulously read the original manuscript and guided its conceptual organization. Also at the University of Washington were Arthur Bestor and Dauril Alden of the History Department who gave so generously of their time and energy to analyze critically the original drafts.

Collection of manuscript material involved the assistance of many persons, especially Andy Johnson of the University of Washington Library's Pacific Northwest Collection, Robert Whitner of Whitman College, and Jimmie Jean Cook, Island County auditor.

Many thanks must go to Mikel Aickin of Arizona State University for his excellent histostatistical consultation; to Lorin Anderson of Portland State University for his skillful drafting and reproduction of a variety of illustrations; and to Jan Webster of the Newberry Library, Antoinette Wills of Seattle, Washington, and Richard White of Michigan State University for their very constructive technical help, comments, and criticisms.

I am indebted also to Malcolm Rohrbough of the University of Iowa for encouraging me very early in my formative college years to combine my frontier and legal history interests; to Robert Ireland of the University of Kentucky for his very valuable reading of my completed manuscript; and to David Van Tassel and Carl Ubbelohde, present and past chairmen of the Department of History of Case Western Reserve University, for their sustenance and support of this project.

Of my parents, Mary and Arnold Wunder, I am constantly re-
minded of their unswerving dedication to education and ideas and
their inculcation in their son of a profound respect for history—no
mean achievement in rural Iowa.

And to Susan, Amanda, and Nell, I offer my devotion, respect,
gratitude, and love.

John R. Wunder
Texas Tech University
Lubbock, Texas

INTRODUCTION

The justice of the peace has been an important local legal institution of the common law world since its inception, providing communities with the administrative and judicial leadership necessary for the development of an orderly society. Local justices were first conceived in twelfth-century England as a means by which the Crown could gain influence in local affairs. Gradually, the office of justice of the peace evolved into courts with significant criminal and civil jurisdiction. In addition, many administrative duties were placed on local justices.

At the time of the migration to the American colonies, justices of the peace had reached a high point in their judicial and administrative evolution, and, therefore, a thriving, powerful English institution was easily transplanted to the American frontier. Here the colonists perceived a need for order and laws, and justices of the peace readily filled colonial demands.

The American Revolution did not deter the extension of local justices to settlements in the West. People continued to migrate and they brought justices of the peace to their new communities, a process that was officially sanctioned by the Northwest Ordinance of 1787 and succeeding organic acts. On the United States frontier, justices of the peace were described as an arch-symbol of the American emphasis on local autonomy, as powerful potentates who violated the separation of powers doctrine, and as the one institution preventing "barbarism" from conquering "civilization."[1] Indeed, JPs have been universally portrayed by their contemporaries and historians as important members of American and English society for over eight centuries.[2]

The recognition of the significance of justices of the peace has not, however, resulted in a multitude of historical analyses, especially of American JPs. Lawrence M. Friedman in his excellent survey of American legal history, *A History of American Law*, has noted that "very little work has been done on the personnel of lower courts, and their impact on society . . . little about form, function, and staff is definitely known." Generally, scholars of American history have not answered the questions "Who served as justices of the peace? What was their background and influence? . . . what was the quality of J.P. justice? How much of the justice's work was social control of the English type—autocratic guidance through democratic forms?"[3] In fact, only in Robert M. Ireland's recent book, *The County Courts of Antebellum Kentucky*, have these questions and several others been answered with detail and accuracy.

Because of the inattention given to American lower courts, legal historians have had to be content with mere speculation or with decrying the lack of knowledge available concerning justices of the peace in American history. But until more information is forthcoming, we must be careful not to "overspeculate." This is not to imply that new ideas should be discouraged or withdrawn; rather, the argument generated by new ideas is an essential part of the interpretive historical process. In order to obtain a more accurate picture of America's past, society's closest relationships to law must be fully explored; therefore, a history of the justice of the peace courts on the American frontier is needed. However, before a frontier survey can be compiled, many case studies, such as Ireland's on Kentucky, must be completed.[4] This work focuses on one such case study, a history of justices of the peace in Washington Territory, 1853-1889.

part I

THE JUSTICE OF THE PEACE AS A DEVELOPING ANGLO-AMERICAN LEGAL INSTITUTION

In the years after the American Revolution and before the statutory extension of territorial status to the far Northwest in 1853,[1] the institution of the justice of the peace developed in the United States under law and custom. It coalesced into a judiciary that became a regular member of the federal judicial system and a responsive agent to residents of new communities. How justices of the peace reached this stage in their historical development is the subject of this first section. Beginning with a short description of their English genesis, this section traces the growth, maturation, and extension of justices of the peace to the trans-Appalachian west where American institutional modifications transformed frontier magistrates into vital contributors to constitutionalism and to social and political stability.

This historical growth was marked by three important characteristics. First, the establishment of justices of the peace, whether in twelfth-century Kent or in nineteenth-century Alabama, met so strong a societal desire for judicial decision-making that the men who became magistrates exercised power before it was statutorily bestowed. Thus, the strength of the office of justice of the peace as a legal institution was inherent within society itself.

Second, the transplantation of English law and JPs to America was a relatively simple and comprehensive process that would withstand the assaults of the American Revolution and the New World frontier. On board the first ships carrying English colonists to the New World was an enormous supply of institutional baggage, and of major significance to the colonies' future was the cargo of law. English legal institutions came onto American soil with the first Britishers, and Anglo-Saxon legalisms clung to life so skillfully that they remain a dominant feature of the United States' legal heritage.

The successful grafting of English law to the Americas was particularly evident with the justice of the peace. This legal mainstay of England's developing judicial hierarchy came to the colonies in the very first settlement, and it grew in stature and strength with subsequent migrations. Local justices made major administrative decisions as well as criminal and civil determinations that affected the daily lives of most colonists.

Third, justices of the peace in the new U.S. territories migrated across the continent, but not without modification. Americans certainly desired these bulwarks of societal order, but they wanted them to be responsible to the local community. No longer would JPs be the patrons of an outsider. They would serve frontier America as a distinctive part of frontier tradition, and they would serve it quite well.

In addition to a brief history of justices of the peace prior to the creation of Washington Territory, this section addresses two very important questions that must be answered in order to discern the contributions of justices of the peace to an American social and legal heritage. Who were these important American dispensers of the law? And what was the quality of their justice? To suggest a means by which these questions might be resolved and to provide a vehicle for the case study of Washington Territory that follows, a prosopographical or collective biographical model is introduced, and the quality of justice is defined for a limited sample of frontier justices of the peace prior to 1853.

1
From England to the American Pacific Northwest: A Brief History of Justices of the Peace

JPs in Britain: Conception, Nurture, and Transplantation

The justices of the peace originated during the twelfth century when the English Crown sought to inject royal influence into local community life. Because of King Richard I's absenteeism, his brother John's subsequent rebellion, and the restive nature of many shire leaders, administrators for the king instituted a policy of rewarding local informants, usually knights, who were then settling down to become rural gentry, for loyalty and information.[1]

The duties of the knights quickly expanded from those of royal supporter and listener to the king's representatives in the local judicial process. They acted as coroners and kept the pleas of the Crown.[2] Under Henry III in the thirteenth century, they were used for informal police and administrative work until internal strife, pitting the Crown against the English barons, again consumed England.[3] Once this struggle was concluded, a writ was issued calling for peace within the realm. The barons and the king appointed the knights as "conservators of the peace" (*custodes pacis*) for each shire, thereby legitimatizing the functions the knights performed prior to and during the conflict.

They were publicly and firmly to forbid homicide, incendiarism, robbery, extortion, bearing of arms without license, and to repress all other offences against the peace under pain of disinheritance and peril of life and members. They were ordered to arrest all malefactors and keep them in safe custody awaiting orders from the crown. If necessary, the conservators could take the *posse comitatus* and even that of an adjacent county, and furthermore they were to aid the conservators of the other counties on due occasion.[4]

The conservators of the peace continued to serve as the king's local troubleshooters until 1285. In that year, the Statute of Winchester was made the law of the realm. The statute provided a rudimentary design for maintaining order with its inclusion of articles specifying lawful behavior and authorizing conservators to receive presentments from constables accusing persons of violating the "king's peace." Although conservators were charged to accept complaints of criminal misconduct, they were not allowed to render formal decisions. In fact, the statute failed to specify any judicial machinery to enforce and interpret the act.[5]

From 1285 until Edward III's reign, conservators, appointed on an experimental individual basis, enforced and interpreted the Statute of Winchester, even though they clearly had no statutory grant of judicial power. The writs and orders coming before the local judicial officers became quite numerous. Then, in 1330 Edward III and Parliament authorized all *custodes pacis* to receive indictments and accusations preferred by juries and to imprison defendants for trial before the king's circuit judges.[6] Once again, the local legal institution had increased its functions and stature by independent action which was followed by statutory and royal ratification.

The forerunner to the justice of the peace had begun as an effort by the Crown merely to make its influence felt among the people, but by 1330 the conservators had developed so many community legal responsibilities that they were only one step away from becoming full-fledged members of the English judiciary. From 1330 to 1361, the year of the formulation of the Justice of the Peace Act, England experienced two events that caused tremendous upheaval and forced the consideration of new approaches to maintaining order.

Seven years after Edward III gave the conservators the powers to enforce the Statute of Winchester, the Hundred Years' War began. Although the war was fought on French soil for over one hundred years, it had a profound effect upon England. Not only did the war drain England of its wealth and men, but also it awakened a looter mentality in the populace. With the return of English troops in 1360, because of a temporary detente marked by the Treaty of Bretigny, an emergency situation quickly developed. Local leaders could not keep the rule of law; pillaging rapidly predominated over village life. Edward III needed new judicial machinery to bring peace back to his realm.[7]

During this same thirty-year period, England reeled under the attack of the Black Death. In 1348-1349, the plague devastated England. Prior to the Black Death, England's population was estimated at four million persons; by 1350, the number of inhabitants had fallen to two and a half million.[8] Entire populations of towns and villages were decimated, and panic swept the realm. The Black Death also had a profound economic influence upon British society. The tremendous loss of life meant a shortage of labor, increased wages, and rising prices. To meet a spiralling inflationary trend, Edward III issued an order to all employees and employers in 1349; this order was ratified by Parliament in the Statute of Laborers in 1351. Briefly stated, the Statute of Laborers imposed wage controls on workers and price controls on employers. Those not obeying the act were subject to summary punishment by the "Keepers or Conservators of the Peace." The keepers were to enforce the act and to set wage and price controls.[9] Edward III's drastic action marked the beginning of special jurisdictions and increased the duties of justices of the peace.

The Hundred Years' War and the Black Death were the catalysts that changed what was essentially a strictly local governing judiciary into a regular judicial institution. In 1361, Parliament ratified the Justice of the Peace Act, which vested two basic duties in the Crown's local judicial appointees: "to pursue, arrest, take" offenders, and "to chastize" offenders found guilty.[10] The first commission went from Edward III to eight JPs in Kent. They were to "beware of the disturbances in our kingdom" caused by the "many vagabonds who have congregated themselves in huge, evil multitudes and become disturbers of our peace."[11]

The statute of 1361 in effect transformed the *keepers* of the peace into *justices* of the peace. Not only could the justices apprehend potential criminals and indict them; they could also try persons accused of crimes. The JPs were authorized to hold two different courts. Justices of the peace of a shire met four times a year, each meeting being termed a quarter session. After grand juries issued indictments, the persons indicted were tried by this court. English quarter sessions courts tried capital cases until the eighteenth century.

Quarter sessions also had an appellate jurisdiction from petty sessions, which consisted of two or more JPs who tried lesser offenses. These cases were adjudicated without a jury.[12] Under Henry VII, all offenses less than a felony were made justiciable by JPs without a jury. This radical departure from the common law was an outgrowth of the first special summary jurisdiction given justices of the peace in the Statute of Laborers. Both quarter and petty sessions were ultimately responsible to the Court of Star Chamber, which could hear their proceedings on appeal; after the Star Chamber was abolished, JPs were positioned directly under the common law courts.[13]

Parliament seldom met without adding a new duty to the justices of the peace; hence, JPs rapidly became established, active judicial officers of the Crown. The ascendancy of the Tudors to the English throne did not curb their growing strength as major local judicial officials. Rather, the stability and importance of the institution were enhanced. The Tudors' general policy involved consolidating the Crown's power, and JPs naturally fitted into this arrangement.[14]

The duties of English justices of the peace under the Tudors included extensive local governmental and administrative functions in addition to "keeping the peace." JPs declared wage and price controls, monitored the care of the poor, provided for the elderly, and authorized the building and maintenance of roads and bridges. They informed the Crown of local economic conditions, prevented community monopolies from price-fixing, subsidized grain markets at parity by buying large amounts of corn and selling it to the poor for less than the purchase price, and licensed and inspected alehouses.[15]

The extension of power, which encouraged justices to continue to hear community criminal actions and also direct local administrative services, attracted civil disputes to their chambers. Just as they assumed their criminal jurisdiction before a legal delegation, JPs were quick to respond by including civil actions in their judicial repertoire. Wallace Notestein found that on the eve of migration to the American colonies justices of the peace in England were entertaining a variety of civil actions:

Two yeomen had a difference about the ownership of a lamb. Seventeen harvesters declared that they had not been paid for reaping, shearing, and inning the corn grown on a baronet's land. What the justices did in many cases was to name one, two or three of their number to look into the matter and arbitrate it.[16]

In essence, justices of the peace in seventeenth-century England "made local government work."[17] By 1620, JPs as a group were wealthy, educated, and very influential in English society. With their social, political, and judicial status solidified by custom and law, it would be a relatively easy matter to transplant successfully the English legal institution of the justice of the peace to the American colonies.

The earliest English settlers in America brought with them English JPs and subsequently English law. The first Anglo-Saxon settlement, that on Roanoke Island, was authorized by the Crown through a charter to Sir Walter Raleigh which stated that all settlers and their descendants "shall and may have all the privileges of free denizens, and persons native to England."[18] Similar charters were issued shortly thereafter to other proprietors who made rules and encouraged local government that conformed to English law as closely as possible.[19] Later, in South Carolina, JPs functioned "almost from the day on which the first settlement was made."[20] Even in the northern colonies, such as Massachusetts, which were more exempt from English supervision, justices of the peace quickly assumed local judicial powers. In fact, the Massachusetts judicial system which relied heavily upon justices of the peace was inspired chiefly by Governor John Winthrop, a man who had served as a justice of the peace in England and had had administrative and criminal jurisdiction in quarter and petty sessions courts.[21] Like Winthrop, many of the judges had prior legal training, and some had been English justices of the peace before their immigration to New England. The JPs readily took to their New World environment.

Any notion that the office of justice of the peace that developed in the United States was a uniquely American legal institution, the opposite of the JP of England, is inaccurate. In all colonies at the beginning of the colonial period, including those of New England, deference was paid to English legal institutions and in particular to justices of the peace. When the Crown eventually took firm control over all the colonies in the eighteenth century, it pursued with a special interest the policy of molding colonial judicial systems in an English cast. Colonial law "was to provide for a judicial system modeled on that of the mother country," and in carrying out this mandate, the cementing of the English legal institution of the justice of the peace into the American colonies was reinforced.[22] By the time of the American War for Independence, all of the colonies had state-centralized court systems; the justices of the peace were serving both singularly and collectively, and they were being appointed by royal governors, two structural characteristics that would be altered by the successful American union.

The powers, jurisdiction, and duties of the colonial justices of the peace were as extensive, if not more so, than those of their contemporaries in England. By 1700, a recognizable body of American law had been created on the coast of North America that England could easily live with rather than change. Modifications to English law had occurred, but the legal base was solidly anchored in Anglo-Saxon tradition. By the mideighteenth century, the colonists had reached the first eastern mountainous areas, and by the late eighteenth century, justices of the peace controlled by the coastal regions extended into the backcountry.[23]

Here for the first time since the inception of the JPs, communities seriously questioned the basic powers and structure of that office. Local justices could no longer cater solely to their benefactors; their constituents meant to be heard. Because of the American local judiciary's independent development and later inclusion within the colonial legal system, frontier Americans strongly felt that JPs should be members of the community and subject to local sanctions. While the Crown and the moneyed interests of the colonies disagreed and ultimately triumphed, the deficiencies which the malcontents identified would be corrected. Basic judicial institutional modifications occurred which would allow for a further transplantation and adaptation of JPs under the aegis of the United States once it gained its own colonial empire.

Magistrates on the American Frontier: A Demand for Local Justice

The contributions and developments of the first U.S. justices of the peace can best be described by observing the trans-Appalachian west shortly after 1776. Land north of the Tennessee River had been settled during the 1780s, and by 1784, the settlers felt the area was ready and deserving of statehood. Congress, however, viewed eastern Tennesseans as Carolinians. When the residents of this area called a convention and agreed upon a constitution creating the state of Franklin, the federal solons remained unimpressed.[24] The most significant aspect of this extralegal activity was the form of institutions the frontiersmen chose. In particular, to adjudicate their legal problems, the Franklinites created justices of the peace, and unlike their formal counterparts in the thirteen original states, Franklin JPs "were selected for life . . . were required to be 'scholars to do the business,' and were to receive no remuneration."[25]

From 1784 to 1853, Americans migrating to other portions of what became the United States picked justices of the peace to act as local judicial officials. In Florida, Louisiana, and New Mexico, the transition from Spanish to American hegemony required military rule and justice of the peace appointments.[26] In Iowa, lead miners agreed upon their own laws and their own JPs to interpret the law.[27] In Alabama, JPs took office before the Tombigbee settlements were officially recognized. Marion County residents chose their own JPs, "for a number of years there being no acting Justice of the peace . . . and the citizens thereof put to great inconvenience . . ."[28]

In Utah, Mormon bishops settled local disputes before the Mormons created the extralegal state of Deseret in which persons of each precinct could elect a justice of the peace. The Mormons simply took over the ecclesiastical machinery and transformed it into a local judiciary.[29] In the Oregon Country, a group of Americans created an unrecognized provisional government in 1843. Motivated by the lack of clear rules to administer estates, the need to protect their farm animals from predators, and a general dislike of British influence, Oregonians organized their own government and court system. From 1843 until 1849, when Oregon was officially granted territorial status, justices of the peace served Oregon's settlers. JPs under the Oregon provisional government performed the same basic functions that they would under federal law. In addition, two judges chosen by the legislature and a justice of the peace chosen by the people made up the supreme court of the provisional government.[30]

Justices of the peace, then, became an established institution throughout the new settlements of the West before Congress statutorily authorized their presence. In most emerging communities, Americans recognized a need for law and order, and JPs were created to satisfy that need.

In order to legitimatize existing local judiciaries, the Northwest Ordinance of 1787 and succeeding territorial organic acts provided for the legal extension of justices of the peace to the new western communities.[31] The Ordinance was basically a conservative document that extended rudimentary government to those Americans already on the trans-Appalachian lands. It provided for three stages of colonial territorial development. A governor, a secretary, and three supreme court judges to be appointed by Congress guided the *district*, with the governor and judges adopting laws from those of the states. Once the district population reached five thousand free male inhabitants, it would pass into the second stage, that of a *territory*. A governor, secretary, and three judges continued to be appointed, but they no longer adopted laws. The Ordinance provided for a bicameral legislature, composed of a house and a council, which would formulate statutes. The third stage of territorial development was *statehood*. Whenever a territory held sixty thousand free inhabitants, it could apply for admission into the Union on an equal footing with all other states. Congress then set a time and place within the territory for a constitutional convention. The constitution was then submitted for approval to Congress and sometimes to the residents of the proposed state.[32]

The Ordinance created the continental colonial system of the United States. New government for the new settlements on the American frontier was imposed on territorial residents from the outside by outsiders. There was no self-government during the first stage, and even with representative government during the second stage, the governor held an absolute veto and property qualifications were required for suffrage rights.[33] Indeed, the government established by the Ordinance constrained rather than facilitated the development of representative institutions.

The historian Randolph Downes likened the Ordinance to a rental contract written by a property owner who was seeking the best way to maintain order without vesting power in the hands of unruly tenants. According to Downes, the Ordinance reflected the economic reality of a penniless, conservative national government in collusion with a profit-seeking land company, the product of which was "a highly autocratic frame of government for the inhabitants" of the frontier.[34] A later historian, John Barnhart, has maintained that the people of the territories were in worse shape than the colonists before the American Revolution. Territorial residents were under despotic rule; they were forced to pay taxes to a federal government without their consent and without representation at most governmental levels.[35] Reginald Horsman, who agrees in principle with both Barnhart and Downes, has found that frontier democracy was inhibited and repressed by the Ordinance. He contends that "the major complicating factor in the political development of the territories . . . was the conservative nature of the Northwest Ordinance."[36]

Indeed, the Northwest Ordinance was a conservative document. This law was designed to impose the forms of an established government upon frontier communities. At the same time, however, the ultimate aims of the Ordinance included representative government and equal governmental status for territorial residents.

A significant portion of the Ordinance related to the courts. For each new district and territory it provided for a court consisting of three judges to be appointed by the president of the United States. These judges were to reside in the district or territory of their appointment, and each had to have a freehold estate of five hundred acres to qualify for the appointment. Any two judges could meet to conduct judicial business; the court had common law jurisdiction; and each judge's appointment was to last during the individual's good behavior. Under the district stage, members of this court, acting in concert with the governor, adopted the criminal and civil laws applicable to the district. This court was originally dubbed the general court; later it was termed the superior court and finally the supreme court of the territory.[37]

In addition to its provision for a territorial supreme court, the Northwest Ordinance empowered the governor to "appoint such magistrates [a term synonymous with justices of the peace] and other civil officers in each county or township, as he shall find necessary for the preservation of the peace and good order of the same."[38] It was assumed that the governor and the district supreme court judges would shape and define the duties and powers of local judicial officials. However, once territorial status was achieved, the legislature was vested with the power to regulate JPs; until a state constitution provided otherwise, all magistrates were to continue to be appointed by the governor.[39]

The Ordinance made no other provisions for justices of the peace. Only the vague reference to "magistrates and other civil officers" extended the institution of the local judiciary to the American frontier. What type of court was intended? What powers, jurisdiction, and duties did it have? Who could be a JP? Congress ignored all of these questions. But in the limited references made to the local judiciary, one provision does stand out: there was no doubt that the office of justice of the peace was to be under the patronage of the territorial governor. Thus, the Ordinance specifically forbade communities from choosing their own JPs.

Once JPs had been formally extended to a territory by Congress, territorial legislative bodies had to determine what the local justices were to do. There was remarkably little federal intervention or direction. Not until the Wisconsin Territory Organic Act of 1836 and succeeding organic acts did Congress exhibit much concern about regulating the functions of frontier justices of the peace, and then the Wisconsin Act only regulated JP jurisdiction.[40]

In the first territory created, the Northwest Territory, one of the early statutes adopted by Governor Arthur St. Clair and two judges, John Cleves Symmes and George Turner, was a law concerning justices of the peace on the Ohio frontier.[41] St. Clair and his secretary, Winthrop Sargent, exercised great influence over the frontier settlements; they tried to force their basic autocratic beliefs on Ohio's rural residents through the use of the extensive powers given and implied in the office of territorial governor.[42]

St. Clair's Code vested in the JPs of the Northwest Territory, and subsequently in local judiciaries of many other territories, numerous administrative and judicial functions. In their administrative capacities, the local justices paid out bounties, supervised bridge and road building, and recorded lost canoes in the estray book. More important was their control over local governmental offices. JPs appointed assessors, constables, county commissioners, surveyors, overseers of the poor, and town clerks, and they divided counties into townships. The frontier justices had *complete* control over local taxation. They appointed constables who appraised the value of property, and they chose the commissioners who estimated county expenses and levied taxes accordingly. JPs sitting as a court reviewed the tax rates set by their appointees, the county commissioners.[43] Thus, frontier justices of the peace held sway over the local police and local moneys.

This system was not popular with frontier residents; they continually complained about the oppressive conduct of the JPs. The justices sometimes appointed themselves county commissioners; and a few forced local citizens, who were appearing before them with county commission business, to refer to them as "the worshipful Justice of the Peace."[44] The uproar generated by the administrative actions of some of the local justices brought reform to the Northwest Territory in 1802. In that year, the territorial assembly passed the Township Act which removed certain administrative powers from JPs and gave them to the people. Every first Monday in April, all free white males, twenty-one or over, who paid a territory or county tax were to meet in their township of residence and select one township clerk, three or more trustees, two property appraisers, a sufficient number of road supervisors, and one or more constables. As a result of this statute, the nonjudicial functions of the local judiciary were severely limited, but the justices' power to supervise tax returns, to determine where and what roads to build, and to lay out new townships remained intact. These last administrative duties were given to county commissioners shortly after Ohio became a state. The Township Act was part of a general reform movement that tried to place justices of the peace more in harmony with frontier community needs.[45]

In the South, the first JPs also possessed strong administrative powers. They laid out roads, authorized ferries and mills, issued liquor licenses, registered cattle brands, and paid bounties for wolf skins. They appointed clerks, surveyors, jailors, coroners, sheriffs, and constables. These powers likewise were abused. In frontier Kentucky, for example, local justices coerced voters by issuing summonses to be served on them on election day. Residents, viewing this action as oppressive and as a perversion of the grant of power to JPs, clamored for reform. The result was a curtailment of the justice's administrative functions.[46]

Whereas the JPs' administrative functions were limited to a large degree early in the territorial period, the judicial powers inherent in the office remained relatively stable. The first JPs north of the Ohio River were members of three courts: general quarter sessions of the peace court, court of common pleas, and individual justices of the peace court. The quarter sessions court, composed of all JPs in a county, met four times annually to consider all crimes—felonies and misdemeanors—in which the punishment was not death, loss of a limb, imprisonment for more than one year, or forfeiture of personal or real property. The court of common pleas, composed of three or more JPs (the number being determined by the governor), gathered four times annually at the same place as the quarter sessions court to hear all types of civil cases. Individual justices could issue writs and other process and make arrests, and they could hear cases involving fines or awards of up to $5.[47] Most, but not all, lower court territorial systems copied the system of the Northwest Territory. One major exception was the Territory of Orleans which was divided into twelve parishes; each parish had an "inferior" court composed of at least one justice of the peace.[48]

The quarter sessions and common pleas courts were the county or inferior courts, and in 1805 they were merged into one county court in Indiana Territory. Individual justices had the same jurisdiction as the inferior courts except in cases involving more than forty shillings. The decision of an individual justice of the peace could be appealed to the county courts. Cases before county courts could then be appealed to the territorial supreme court.[49] Until 1805, no cases could be appealed from the territorial supreme court; in that year, Congress in effect made the highest courts in the territory U.S. district courts, in order to bring the territorial court system under the federal court system.[50]

Territorial legislatures made few changes in the structure, jurisdiction, and functions of territorial justice of the peace courts. Only in Illinois Territory were major innovations adopted, and these were then incorporated into the judicial systems of many of the other territories. As mentioned above, in 1805, Indiana Territory's inferior courts were merged. Illinois Territory inherited this system and found it objectionable. Thus, in 1809, the Illinois territorial legislature repealed all laws related to courts of common pleas (the name given to the merged inferior courts) and gave its general or supreme court all original and final jurisdiction. Individual JPs could hear all civil cases not exceeding $20 and all non-felony cases. In 1810, justice of the peace decisions awarding no more than $4.16 2/3 were no longer subject to appeal. In order to serve Illinois residents closer to their homes and help take up some of the increased burden placed on the territorial supreme court by the abolition of the courts of common pleas, the territorial legislature provided for circuit courts of individual supreme court members, their decisions being appealable to the territorial supreme court meeting collectively.[51] In essence, the intermediate court composed of justices of the peace was replaced by individual territorial supreme court judges. The extra work did not sit well with the Illinois judges, and with the support of Governor Ninian Edwards, they protested against this judicial system to Congress.[52]

The federal lawmakers paid no attention to the territorial officers' pleas; instead, they reenacted the Illinois Territory statute.[53] This act passed by Congress marked the passage into a new stage in the development of territorial justices of the peace. The Illinois Territory judicial matrix was copied throughout the territorial system. Missouri, Indiana, Alabama, and Arkansas Territory judicial systems were brought into line with the system of Illinois, and the Wisconsin Territory Organic Act of 1836 copied it for implementation into future territorial systems.[54] Clearly, the justice of the peace had been incorporated within the regular judicial system, but the incorporation process had necessitated the elimination of its appellate jurisdictional powers.

Major efforts to change or reform the local judiciary were usually thwarted. In the Northwest Territory, Judges Turner and Symmes favored increasing the jurisdictional monetary limits of individual JPs from 40 shillings or $5 to a large amount. In 1790, they proposed an upward limit of $20. Turner and Symmes reasoned that an increase was needed to meet the needs of the masses who could not afford the money to travel long distances to county courts. St. Clair countered by arguing that local justices were stupid and ignorant of the law, to which Turner replied, "We may hope to find [in them] plain good sense and integrity."[55] Turner also proposed as an economic measure that litigants before a JP have the option to submit their case before a six-man jury. Jury trials previously either were denied or were composed of twelve persons. St. Clair saw this as discouraging plaintiffs from bringing an action. Turner felt that the six-man jury would be commonly used and that the jurors would help a justice in any case of extreme complexity. None of the reforms was approved; St. Clair, in alliance with conservative Judge Rufus Putnam, prevailed. Eventually, after the Northwest Territory moved from the district into the territorial stage, JP jurisdiction was increased from $5 to $12, but the change was only the result of piecemeal compromises. Further efforts to effect JP jurisdictional and procedural reforms during the existence of the Northwest Territory met with failure.[56]

A similar situation developed in Mississippi Territory in 1811. In that year, the Mississippi territorial legislature passed an act giving individual justices of the peace unlimited civil jurisdiction. To prevent repetitious, expensive, and extra jury trials, jury trials at the JP level in cases over $20 were prohibited, and cases over $20 were appealable to county courts where a jury trial could be requested by either litigant.[57] Acting Governor Henry Daingerfield was leery of this proposed law. He asked his attorney-general, William Shields, if this act could be vetoed on the grounds that it violated the Ninth Amendment of the Constitution. Shields assured Daingerfield that he could disapprove of the act on this basis, and Daingerfield promptly prevented an expansion of justice of the peace jurisdiction.[58] Thus, territorial changes in the judicial capacity of frontier justices of the peace were unusual. Territorial officials seldom permitted laws to alter significantly the operations of the lower courts.

Once a justice of the peace court had been set up in the territories, its judicial functions rather than its jurisdiction were usually expanded by special orders or legislation. In 1793, Acting Governor Winthrop Sargent informed the residents of the Northwest Territory that he would not tolerate continued cutting of the forests on the public domain. He issued a proclamation prohibiting

all persons from cutting down carrying away or barking any of the Trees upon the same [U.S. property]—or upon the Lots which have been appropriated for public purposes without proper authority for so doing as they shall answer the contrary at their Peril—And the Justices of the peace throughout the said County and all other civil Officers are hereby required to pay the due attention to this proclamation.[59]

Similarly, in 1816, William Clark, governor of Missouri Territory, ordered all of Missouri's local justices to aid in apprehending William Henderson, accused murderer and St. Louis County jail escapee. Clark further enticed the JPs by offering them $100 for delivering Henderson to the St. Louis County sheriff.[60]

Special legislation was also used to increase the responsibilities of local judiciaries. On the southern frontier, JPs were authorized to handle problems of slave identification and escape. For example, after 1807 no free blacks could enter Orleans Territory. All of those claiming to be free were required to appear before a justice of the peace and to prove their nonslave status. If a JP found that a black had entered Orleans after 1807 or was of a questionable free status, he could order the black to be sold into slavery.[61] In Florida, G. K. Walker, the acting governor of Florida Territory, was forced to reassure the chief of the Appalachicolas, John Walker, that any endeavor to steal or free the chief's slaves would be prevented by the proper authorities—the JPs. "Upon application to a Justice of the Peace in your neighborhood, should an attempt be made to carry them [slaves] off—every assistance will be given you that the Laws of the Territory can afford."[62]

Northern justices of the peace were also concerned with runaway black slaves. In November 1828, a slaveowner from Kentucky, Ezekiel Hudnell, was in Detroit pursuing two male runaway slaves. He was quite distressed over the possibility that his slaves would escape to Canada. Hudnell went to a local Michigan Territory JP, John McDonnell, and had the proper papers sworn out authorizing Sheriff Thomas C. Sheldon to arrest the slaves. Sheldon found Hudnell's runaways and promptly placed them in jail. However, not everyone was in sympathy with the slaveowners and the institution of slavery. The Michigan Territory supreme court issued a writ of habeas corpus to free the slaves based on the grounds that McDonnell's JP commission was defective. Hudnell was forced to show that the justice of the peace held a legal appointment and that the JP orders were lawful. The Kentuckian was successful in quashing the writ, but his troubles were not over. Secretary of the Territory James Witherell refused to release McDonnell's order to turn over the slaves to Hudnell, and so Hudnell went to McDonnell to obtain a second order of release. This was accomplished and Sheriff Sheldon honored the legal order.[63]

Hudnell had proposed to transport the slaves by water to Ohio and then by land to Kentucky. Because of the judicial delays, time had allowed a party of armed blacks from Canada to plan to capture the runaways. Sheriff Sheldon, hearing the rumors of the proposed liberation, moved to prevent it. He assigned a deputy to accompany Hudnell and his passengers to a river boat, but before the vessel left Detroit, and after the deputy had departed for shore, the two slaves overpowered Hudnell, escaped, and swam to freedom.[64]

Special legislation sometimes obliged the justice of the peace to alter his traditional role as a frontier community decision-maker. For instance, in New Mexico Territory, JPs were required to hire teachers and monitor the attendance of children in the schools from November to April. In essence, justices of the peace served as school boards and truant officers.[65] An even more fundamental example of extended JP roles occurred in Mormon settlements in the West. Utah Territory was created by Congress in 1850. Before this date local disputes in Utah were settled by bishops (termed "magistrates of the ward") who were appointed by the president of the Mormon church, Brigham Young. Once territorial status was achieved, local Mormon bishops continued in their JP roles; Mormons controlled the territorial assembly, and Brigham Young was installed as governor. The Mormons found that they could not influence a majority of the members of the territorial supreme court, and so to modify non-Mormon power, the Utah assembly, with the consent of Governor Young, instructed the JP and probate courts to become the courts of last resort. Justices of the peace were to prevent appeals and "to use all diligence and influence in their power to prevent litigation."[66] In effect, basic JP functions were expanded in Utah Territory by placing all cases within the jurisdiction of the local justices.

Thus, during the early territorial era, the territories themselves regulated most of the jurisdiction, powers, and functions of frontier justices of the peace. In the formative years, JPs exercised considerable power on the frontier through extensive administrative and judicial duties. By 1810, however, many of their traditional administrative functions had been given to other township or county officials. JPs nevertheless continued to discharge judicial functions, and they occasionally were used for special purposes. Throughout this period in American territorial history, justices of the peace developed into the primary judicial representatives of frontier residents in new communities.

* * * *

Five centuries spanned the development of the office of justice of the peace from its conception in medieval England to its adoption in post-Revolutionary America. It endured the neglect of its creator, the destructive forces of the Black Death and the Hundred Years' War, the hazardous voyage to the New World, and the colonial disorders culminating in the American War for Independence. What began as an effort by the English Crown to gather information and to consolidate favorable support among the common people evolved into a powerful, multifaceted, local legal institution.

The justice of the peace became a stable component of the Anglo-Saxon judiciary because of aggressive central governing forces, receptive local communities in need of laws and corresponding interpreters, and the initial momentum inherent in a wisely perceived and popularly received governmental agency. The exigencies of the times made this institution so necessary that often JPs assumed powers, developed jurisdictions, and settled disputes prior to royal or legislative sanction.

The central features in the development of the justice of the peace in England and early America also characterized the evolution of the office in the new settlements of the trans-Appalachian frontier. Justices came to communities whose members sensed a need for local judicial institutions. And just as early English justices of the peace frequently assumed powers before they had been bestowed, local American justices transcended the lag of statutory law. When Americans migrated beyond colonial boundaries, they carried their own institutions with them, and already imbedded in the American experience was the justice of the peace.

Unlike the early English, however, most frontier Americans viewed their local judiciary as an institution distinctly tied to the community. JPs had traveled to the new settlements with the first pioneers; therefore, settlers believed their local justices were subject only to local sanctions. When the law caught up with the nonstatutory development of the justices of the peace, controversy ensued between representatives of the parent American government and the settlers, and it focused on the dichotomy of the roles created. JPs under the law became powerful patronage devices used by an outside government to control its frontier population. According to custom JPs had been agents of the community that made decisions on the basis of the community's own conceptions of justice. By the 1850s, American justices of the peace under law and custom had solved their dual growth problems and had emerged as a necessary component of the American legal system.

2

Frontier Justices and Their Work

This inquiry has thus far been limited to an impersonal historical overview of justices of the peace, tracing the development of the office from its origins in twelfth-century England to its transplantation to the American colonies and its functioning in the initial settlement in the American West to its official establishment as part of the federal judiciary. In order to complete the discussion of the heritage of the JPs of Washington Territory, this chapter presents a more personal historical overview of the office, including a biographical profile of justices of the peace on the American frontier prior to 1853 and an examination of the quality of their justice.

Table 1

General Biographical Interrogatories Applied to American Frontier Justices of the Peace

1. What was the subject's life span?
2. Where was the subject born?
3. What was the occupation of the subject's father?
4. When did the subject migrate to an American territory?
5. When did the territory of migration exist as an American territory?
6. When was the subject first commissioned a justice of the peace?
7. Was the subject involved in politics?
8. Did the subject hold local political office(s) other than justice of the peace?
9. Did the subject hold an elective political office?
10. Did the subject hold other occupations than frontier JP? If so, what occupations?
11. Did the subject own land?

A Prosopographical Approach

Who were the justices of the peace in American territories? In order to answer this question with some historical precision, a prosopography or collective biography, using two samples of frontier justices, has been assembled.[1] Through this technique, past historical generalizations concerning frontier justices of the peace are examined and a more accurate picture of the Washington Territory JPs emerges. To construct a group biographical profile, the samples are examined in terms of general biographical data, which are analyzed, organized, and extrapolated from the questions posed in Table 1. From responses to the general biographical questions,

Table 2

Sample 1: Eighteen Frontier Justices of the Peace

Justice of the Peace	*Territory of JP Commission*
1. Boilvin, Nicholas	Illinois, Michigan
2. Boulhillier, Francis	Michigan
3. Brisbois, Martin	Michigan
4. Brown, Joseph R.	Wisconsin
5. Brown, William W.	Iowa
6. Campbell, John W.	Michigan
7. Carter, William A.	Utah
8. Clark, Lardner	Southwest
9. Dumoulin, John	Indiana
10. Dunbar, William	Mississippi
11. Goforth, William	Northwest
12. Johnson, John W.	Michigan
13. Lockwood, James	Michigan
14. McMillan, William	Northwest
15. Reame, Charles	Indiana, Michigan
16. Sibley, Henry	Northwest, Iowa
17. Wells, William	Northwest
18. West, Cato	Mississippi

several characteristics of JPs can be discerned, which allows a comparison to any previous notions of frontier judges.

The first of the two samples used in this study is a general sample consisting of eighteen justices from ten different territories. This sample is analyzed in terms of responses to all of the biographical questions. It should be emphasized that these justices were chosen on the basis of the accessibility of specific biographical data. This was not a random sample, and any quantitative analysis of data derived from the sample does not constitute proof of any proposition (see Table 2). The second sample is a more random and complete one, including all of the first justices of the peace commissioned in Mississippi Territory in 1798 and 1799. This sample indicates the political and economic status of specific JPs. Although it neither substantiates nor disproves generalizations about JPs, it does offer valuable information about the first justices of the peace in a newly organized area (see Table 3). In sum, thirty-nine justices of the peace are examined with reference to eleven general biographical questions in order to determine the political, social, and economic characteristics of frontier JPs.

Table 3

Sample 2: Justices of the Peace in Mississippi Territory, 1798-1799

1. Brashears, Tobias	13. Harrison, Richard
2. Calvet, Joseph	14. Howard, Joshua
3. Clarke, David	15. Humphreys, George
4. Collins, John	16. McIntosh, James
5. David, Hugh	17. Smith, John
6. Dixon, Roger	18. Smith, Philander
7. Dunbar, Robert	19. Throckmorton, Mordecai
8. Dunbar, William	20. Thomas, William
9. Ellis, Abraham	21. Vousden, William
10. Ellis, John	22. West, Cato
11. Gaillard, Isaac	23. Wilkins, Thomas
12. Gibson, Samuel	

Historian Francis S. Philbrick has concluded that, surprisingly, governmental and judicial officers on the frontier were very young, usually in their teens and early twenties. Based on this finding, Philbrick has suggested that these officers were new frontier residents who were "ambitious and talented," and anxious to assume economic and political leadership.[2] In contrast, Robert Ireland, in his comprehensive and quantitative study of Kentucky JPs from 1792 to 1850, has found that the average age of justices of the peace in Kentucky during this period was 49.2 years. This implies that JPs were established citizens of the frontier.[3] The conflict between Philbrick's and Ireland's findings can in part be explained by the fact that Ireland's study relies heavily upon the 1850 census, and it can be argued that Kentucky after 1812 was not a frontier society or was a frontier society in transition.

Questions 1, 4, 5, and 6 in Table 1 have been applied to the JPs of Sample 1. Of the eighteen justices in the sample, sufficient information was available to ascertain the age of thirteen of them at the time of their first JP commission in an American territory.[4] For example, Sir William Dunbar of Mississippi Territory was born in 1749, migrated to Philadelphia and later to Baton Rouge, and was commissioned a JP by Governor Winthrop Sargent in 1799.[5] For others, educated guesses had to be made. Martin Brisbois came to Prairie du Chien in 1781 as a fur trader, and his JP commission was first granted by Governor Lewis Cass of Michigan Territory in 1818. One must assume that Brisbois was at least twenty years old when he came to Prairie du Chien, which places his birth in approximately 1761.[6] Thus, he was probably over fifty-seven years old when first commissioned.

The average age of the justices of Sample 1 at the time of their first commission was 38.6 years. Over one-half of the ages were estimated at the lowest number, so the average age was computed at the youngest approximation. Thus, the data analyzed from Sample 1 show that frontier justices tended to be drawn from among older residents and thus give more credence to Ireland's than to Philbrick's generalization. Moreover, one justice in Sample 1 viewed youth as a deterrent to holding a commission. James Lockwood, a Michigan Territory JP, refused a commission to be a county court justice and had to be strongly persuaded by his neighbors before he would accept such an appointment. The twenty-five-year-old Lockwood considered himself too young and inexperienced to assume such an important office.[7]

Dunbar Rowland, in his history of Mississippi, found that JPs "were all representative men," ranging from poor mechanics to rich planters. He suggests that the economic condition of frontier county officers reflected that of the frontier residents. Similarly, James Willard Hurst categorically states that there were very few landholders among justices of the peace.[8] Other historians disagree with Rowland and Hurst. Anton-Hermann Chroust has noted that the earliest frontier justices were "usually wealthy farmers, squires, merchants, or landlords,"[9] and Francis Philbrick maintains that the justices were the economic "magnates of their counties, the 'county gentry.' "[10] In the only available quantitative examination of this economic characteristic, Robert Ireland concurs with Chroust and Philbrick. Ireland examined the tax records of JPs in antebellum Kentucky, and he recorded the holdings of JPs and non-JPs in terms of land acreage, slaves, and taxable chattel property (livestock, pianos, buggies, gold watches, and the like). Based on these data, he concluded that the general property holdings of JPs were "considerably higher than the average white adult male."[11]

Questions 2, 3, 10, and 11 have also been applied to the JPs of Sample 1. From questions 2 and 3, it can be determined that JPs were not born into wealth on the frontier. None of those justices was native to the frontier of their commission. There was not sufficient information available to determine whether most JPs brought wealth with them to the frontier. One who did was Lardner Clark. He and William Wycoff, Jr., were merchants and landowners in Kaskaskia, Illinois Territory. Clark migrated to Nashville in 1783 with enough capital to open a branch of the Wycoff-Clark General Store operations; later, he was commissioned a JP for the Southwest Territory.[12] Unlike Clark, James Lockwood came to the frontier with few holdings. After two false starts in law and medicine, he moved to Green Bay in 1815 to begin his career as a trader.[13]

It is also evident that all the JPs of Sample 1 had occupations other than that of local justice, and almost all were landowners. All of the southern local justices in Sample 1 owned slaves. Of the occupations held, politician, lawyer, farmer, and fur trader were most numerous. Cato West, a Mississippi JP, owned a large plantation and eventually became secretary of Mississippi Territory. Martin Brisbois and John Campbell were farmers, traders, and lawyers on the Michigan frontier.[14]

Several of the justices held a wide variety of positions. Henry Sibley was a bank president, a lawyer, and an American Fur Company trader, in addition to holding numerous political offices.[15] William Carter was a probate judge and a sutler for Livingston, Kinkead and Company at Fort Bridger, Utah Territory.[16] That justices had multifaceted careers is substantiated by Everett Dick in *The Dixie Frontier*, which describes the activities of an Arkansas Territory JP. The justice was the first mayor of Little Rock, a school teacher, bookkeeper, post office clerk, house and sign painter, glazier, and general tinker, as well as a local justice.[17] Clearly, then, JPs on the American frontier appeared to have had a higher economic status than the average frontier citizen; they held a variety of occupations and they owned land.

Political leadership as a characteristic of justices of the peace has also been much debated. Chroust, for example, believes that leadership in frontier military activities, rather than in politics, was the major criterion for JP selection. He states that local justices were usually Indian fighters who commanded authority among frontier inhabitants.[18] Philbrick, however, sees the JPs as fundamentally political animals, describing them as local political potentates with much power and influence.[19] Similarly, Ireland's study shows Kentucky JPs to have been very active politically. One of every three was a militia officer, a valued political appointment, and they were all much concerned with state politics. One-fourth of the state House and one-fifth of the state Senate were justices of the peace; eight of seventeen governors and seven of twenty-one senators had been JPs. The justices of the peace were politically powerful not only on the local level, but also in an entire region. They did not hold merely political appointments; they also held popularly elected political offices.[20]

In Sample 1, all justices examined were found to be politically active: eleven of the eighteen held political offices other than justice of the peace, and seven held elective office. Nicholas Boilvin was an Indian agent in addition to JP; John Johnson was a U.S. factor;

and Joseph Brown was a clerk of Wisconsin Territory's second district court, who organized the extralegal Stillwater Convention which elected a delegate from Minnesota to Congress under the assumption that land not included in Wisconsin State was still part of the formally organized Wisconsin Territory.[21] This small sample, then, suggests that frontier JPs were leaders in local politics.

Sample 1 is weakened by the possibility that JPs emerged from the sources examined simply because the materials primarily reflect political activity; any general conclusion about their political leadership is therefore suspect. Sample 2, however, does not suffer from this defect. All of the justices examined were appointed by Mississippi Territory Governor Winthrop Sargent in 1798-1799. They represent a complete set of the first JPs commissioned in an American territory.

Mississippi's first justices of the peace were overwhelmingly interested in frontier politics (nineteen of twenty-three); they held many political offices other than their initial justice of the peace appointment (nineteen of twenty-three); and some held elective offices (six of twenty-three). John Ellis was a militia officer, speaker of the Mississippi House, and president of the Mississippi Council; John Collins was a member of a law and order committee sanctioned by Governor Sargent, an election judge, and a JP in Adams and Wilkinson counties; and John Smith was arrested and imprisoned for inciting a revolt against the Spanish.[22] The justices of the peace in Mississippi Territory were definitely active in politics.

In summary, the evidence suggests that frontier justices of the peace were not apolitical, they were not poor, they were not young, and they were not ambitious men eager for their first economic and political successes. This partial profile of JPs shows that frontier justices were social, economic, and political leaders of their communities.

A Qualitative Approach

A second basic question that must be investigated in any examination of a legal system is, what was the quality of the justice produced? Before this question can be answered, the term *quality of justice* must be defined. For the purposes of this study, the term is defined by using four indicators. Two of these indicators are considered in terms of present-day evaluations of judicial systems, and the other two in terms of the standards of the nineteenth-century frontier community.

One indicator is whether the JPs' decisions were based upon intelligent, legal reasoning. A presumption has generally been made that judges make informed and fair decisions if attorneys are present in the courtroom and if judges have had an education. An even better decision can be reached if the judge has had a legal education and has access to or is familiar with written law. Thus, subject to the exception that education will not insure fairness, the judge needs some kind of legal training in order to be a good judge and thereby make fair decisions. The recent trend has been toward the elimination of so-called lay judges (judges who have had no formal legal training) because persons with legal training are more likely to make fair decisions.[23] The frontier JPs were not required to have an acquaintance with the law, but they still may or may not have had an education, legal training, or access to the written law. Whatever their conditions, the JPs' level of education and exposure to written law must be considered in evaluating the quality of their decisions.

The second indicator is the accessibility of the decision-making machinery. Accessibilty can be viewed in terms of geography, cost, and type of dispute. Were JPs readily available? Were the costs of going to justice of the peace courts within the economic range of most citizens of the frontier? Were the kinds of cases heard before justices of the peace representative of controversies indigenous to frontier life? Answers to these questions all touch on the notion of accessibility. If justice is convenient, its quality is enhanced; conversely, if justice is remote, its quality is diminished.

A third indicator is adjudication celerity. Chief Justice of the U.S. Supreme Court Warren Burger recently noted that high-quality justice is directly dependent on a speedy determination of the facts of a case and a speedy formation of an intelligent, judicial opinion.[24] The Constitution states, "In all criminal prosecutions, the accused shall enjoy the right to a speedy and public trial,"[25] and the right to a speedy trial has also been applied to civil disputes. If an adjudication is drawn out, evidence becomes stale and witnesses die or disappear; in short, what once was a clear, justiciable matter becomes a cloudy, confused disagreement, and it is more difficult, or in fact impossible, to render a fair decision. The best trained judge of a readily accessible court is incapable of constructing high-quality opinions if he is too busy. The more crowded a court docket and the longer a case languishes, the greater the probability that the quality of justice will be poor. Whether JPs handled a large number of cases and reached speedy determinations are important factors in discovering the quality of their justice.

The last indicator is the community's level of acceptance of a court and of its decisions. If JP courts were in moderate use, if few appeals were made from cases adjudicated in these courts, and if frontier residents were not deciding controversies outside the courtroom, then the community's reception of the justices' decisions was favorable. And if frontier residents accepted and employed justices of the peace, then the quality of justice disseminated must have been sufficient.

Thus, the analysis that follows deems frontier judicial excellence to be high or low depending upon (1) the training of the justices of the peace and the participation of attorneys in JP courtroom deliberations; (2) the accessibility of the JPs' judicial services to frontier inhabitants; (3) the speed and efficiency of JP decision-making; and (4) the level of community acceptance of frontier justice.

A complete analysis of JP justice depends primarily on records of court cases and other legal original sources. For Washington Territory, adequate samples of legal source material exist; therefore, a thorough study of the quality of justice on the Washington frontier, making use of all the techniques outlined in this chapter, is offered in later chapters. For the American frontier experience prior to the creation of Washington Territory, no regional works emphasizing JP justice have been completed. Until frontier legal sources have been culled for relevant data, the quality of the justice, as examined through the four indicators defined above, can only be partially illustrated and inconclusively described.

Historians have generally regarded frontier justices of the peace as untrained in the law. Chroust contends that they "were uneducated men: some were almost illiterate, and virtually none were grounded in the law or versed in its most fundamental technicalities"[26]; Philbrick describes them as without "qualifications, educational or moral, in any noticeable degree''; Dick too notes that they were entirely without legal training.[27] An examination of the educational and legal qualifications of the JPs in Sample 1, however, does not verify these beliefs. In this sample, 27.3 percent had a legal education, 36.4 percent a formal education of some type, and 86.4 percent access to law books to help make their decisions.

Cato West, one of the first JPs in Mississippi Territory, had no formal education, and his contemporaries described him as "by no means brilliant" and "a striking illustration of the success of mediocrity, in politics."[28] In contrast, Nicholas Boilvin was a lawyer before he became a justice of the peace in Illinois Territory. His library included one volume, respectively, of the Northwest Territory, Missouri Territory, and Illinois Territory statutes.[29] Lardner Clark never studied the law because the Revolutionary War interrupted his education, but his library collection included many books on the law.[30] Charles Reame, "an old Frenchman at Green Bay . . . who could read and write a little," had neither a classical nor a legal education. Still, Reame used Blackstone and the French Civil Code, as well as fur trapper custom, in reaching his judicial decisions.[31]

Whereas the percentages cited may be inflated because Sample 1 was not a random sample, the evidence cannot be refuted. Some JPs were well qualified for their positions, and many had legal texts available. Hence, assertions that JPs had no contact with the law are extremely vulnerable, if not inaccurate.

One problem that legal training could not allay was the frontier justice's knowledge of only one language. The American frontier was a focal point of interaction for many people who spoke a variety of languages, and some justices of the peace knew only one tongue. For example, on one occasion early in his career, John B. Brisbin of St. Paul, Minnesota Territory, a lawyer who took many cases before JPs, was called to Mendota to defend a client charged with trespassing ("jumping a claim"). Brisbin began by making eloquent arguments before the JP, who nodded with approval. Then the opposition lawyer, Jacob J. Noah, the first clerk of the Minnesota supreme court and a man known as Major, addressed the court in French. Brisbin objected, stating he knew only English. But Major quickly informed the young lawyer that his arguments had to be in French because that was the only language the JP could understand.[32] Obviously, then, the quality of justice of this Minnesota magistrate was limited by his inability to speak or understand languages other than French.

Sometimes language limitations caused greater problems than the mere embarrassment of a young, inexperienced lawyer. Frontier JPs were frequently called upon to settle disputes between whites and native Americans, a role which required delicate diplomacy and a respect and knowledge of alien cultures—two characteristics which many frontier justices lacked. Governor William Clark of Louisiana Territory received a petition from five militia officers from New Madrid illustrating this situation:

That all the Indian Tribes on the Ohio and Tennessee Rivers in their passage to and from the different tribes living in the South; pass through this place and the Village of the Little Prairie. And that in the intercourse which does necessarily take place between them & the white people many unpleasant disputes arise calculated to destroy Harmony and concord and to create suspicion & distrust.

In many cases the Justices of the peace endeavour to Settle those disputes. But they ignorant of the Indian language act in the Dark—are dissatisfied with their own decisions and probably the Indians (who do not know the reasons which operate to determine the Justices in these decisions) are much more so—[33]

Because of the troubles local justices were causing, the militia officers asked that an experienced Indian agent, skilled in communications with the Indians of the Missouri Bootheel, be appointed who would be vested with the power of a JP.

The geographical accessibility of justice of the peace courts to frontier residents depended upon settlement patterns and political organization. If the area in question had been organized into a geographically compact county, JPs were readily accessible. However, regions within territories were not always designated as counties, and JPs were not located near all citizens of the frontier.

The accessibility of JPs in terms of costs cannot be determined with any degree of specificity. In the 1840s in Wisconsin Territory, Vince Roberts, a JP from Dodge County, usually charged fees of $0.50 to $1.00. Charles M. Baker, a JP from Geneva, assessed only slightly higher fees during this same period. There were no local complaints about the costs of the justice courts during Wisconsin's territorial days.[34] Residents of other frontier areas did complain about the cost of going to JP court. In December 1831, a grand jury in Jackson County, West Florida, charged that JP court costs were unduly high. The jury represented

as oppressive, the Fee Bill of the officers of the Territory generally, but particularly those relating to Justices Courts, and respectfully recommend the Council to have them amended and reduced to similar rates of the adjacent States, also to confine the jurisdiction of Justices of the Peace in like manner, and confine Justices and Constables in civil business to their districts, without mileage to the latter.[35]

Some JPs in Florida, however, were appalled by the smallness of their fees. In a letter to Governor Andrew Jackson, David Shannon, a local justice in Escambia County, asked for more money for himself and his colleagues because the duties placed upon JPs forced them to neglect their private businesses:

I am the more solicitous on this subject as I find it will be impossible, if the Gov't does not make me some allowance, (altho' my whole time is devoted to the service of the public) for me to pay my expenses out of the proceeds of my industry, —which is the only means I have as support.[36]

No clear division of opinion emerged from frontier residents on court costs; some thought JP fees were excessive, others felt local judicial costs were fair, and still others concluded JP fees were inadequate. Until legal sources have been examined and more regional legal studies have been written, generalizations on JP cost accessibility on the American frontier cannot be made.

Similarly, it is difficult to draw any conclusions pertaining to JP case accessibility. Legal historian Anton-Hermann Chroust maintains that, "As a rule litigations on the frontier consisted of actions arising from disputed land claims, fraudulent titles, 'hog stealing,' horse thieving, slander, or similar instances of assault and battery (often with a deadly weapon)."[37]

But Chroust neglects to qualify his statement. Land title disputes were heard in federal courts or were settled locally without court intervention. He also fails to consider civil actions on the frontier. Other historians have recognized the pitfall of generalizing without sufficient data, and they have limited their observations. For example, Everett Dick has found that the first JP court sessions in frontier Kentucky mostly heard cases concerning debts and assaults in addition to nine cases of selling liquor without a license and eight cases of adultery and fornication. He identifies horse stealing and counterfeiting as the most hated crimes.[38] Moses Strong observes that the first JP session in what would become Wisconsin heard no criminal cases, decided a few civil cases, and granted two tavern licenses. Randolph Downes describes the first JP court case of record in an American territory in which Northwest Territory justice of the peace William McMillan was asked to hear a case concerning the theft of cucumbers. The party accused of the theft was found guilty and was given twenty-nine lashes.[39] William Davis, in his brief biographical study of Utah Territory JP William Carter, concludes that because Carter's court frequently heard cases involving horse and livestock stealing, JP justice in northern Utah was most attuned to rancher and business interests.[40]

The justices of the peace on the frontier also commented about their caseloads. Richard Claiborne, newly appointed JP in Orleans Territory in 1808, was warned that

the business transacted in courts of justice [in Orleans Territory] comes home to every man's feelings and fireside, and the petty contests and domestic brawls which arise in a village or neighborhood excite more interest than all the differences of whatever kind in which the rest of the world may be engaged.[41]

William Dunbar, a Mississippi Territory JP, was more specific in his judicial interests. Dunbar charged his first grand jury to pay particular attention to what he termed "a crime of heinous nature" —duelling.[42]

James Lockwood of Michigan Territory, who chronicled his experiences as a local judicial officer on the frontier, observed that many of his cases dealt with disputes related to frontier agriculture. He recalled with precision and a considerable amount of enjoyment one special case involving Joseph Rolette, an old political enemy, and Barrette, a poor French-Canadian farmer:

There was a law at that time [1824] in Michigan preventing stud horses from running at large when over eighteen months of age, under a penalty of ten dollars for each offence, "if willingly or wilfully at large." At this time the water was high in the Mississippi and the old village of Prairie du Chien was an island. One morning shortly after the election, Mr. Rolette with his men brought me two horses of the aforesaid description, and hitched them before my door.[43]

Lockwood then noted that Rolette demanded that Lockwood, as the local JP, take action, but Lockwood refused until a complaint was made. Rolette thereupon chose to single out Barrette for punishment.

On the day of trial, a man by the name of Perkins. . . . , seeing that the suit was brought by an apparently wealthy man to oppress a poor one, volunteered his services to assist in defending him, and on calling the case the defendant demanded a jury. The Legislature of Michigan had some two or three years before this reduced the jury before a Justice of the Peace to six, and the year preceding this trial, they had repealed that law, without any saving clause. Under these circumstances, I decided that the repeal of the law, revived the old one of twelve jurors, and accordingly had a jury of that number summoned and sworn. It so happened that there were some Americans on the jury, and as the trial proceeded, the defendant admitted that his horse was at large, but not "willingly or wilfully," and proved that his horse was old and had been worked down very poor in the spring, and that when he was through with his work and wished to turn him out on the Prairie, to save himself from the penalty of the law, he had taken him to be castrated to the only men on the Prairie that pretended to perform such operations. But he declined doing so, saying that the horse was too poor and weak to live through it, and that he had better turn him out on the Prairie to rest and recruit a few days, as he could do no harm. Under this testimony, the jury brought in a verdict for defendant, stating that Barrette's horse was neither "wilfully nor willingly" at large, contrary to the law.[44]

Eventually, Barrette sued Rolette for trespass (illegally swimming his horse across a slough) and won $5 in damages plus costs.

Whereas some studies on geographical, cost, and case accessibility are available, no historical interpretations have been made ascertaining the adjudication celerity of frontier JPs. Neither contemporary frontier observers nor later historians ever scrutinized how busy justices of the peace were and how speedy trials conducted in JP courts were. Therefore, not even guesses concerning this indicator of the quality of frontier justice can be offered. There are sufficient historical studies and references, however, to estimate the frontier residents' level of acceptance of frontier justice. To ascertain this acceptance, court use, appeals of JP decisions, and extralegal activities must be examined.

Although no statistics are as yet available showing the relative use of JP courts throughout the American frontier, general impressions by JPs and historians have been formed. In 1821, Justice of the Peace David Shannon felt that JP courts in Florida had successfully survived the transition from Spanish to American rule and were readily accepted and used by the populace. "Our court," he wrote, "is resorted to both by Spaniards and Americans, in which they all appear to have the most implicit confidence. In short, all parties seem willingly to submit to the silent but efficient operation of the law."[45] Chroust has found that indeed the frontier court seldom adjourned for lack of cases: "Whenever this happened all parties concerned, the judges, the lawyers, and the general populace included, were profoundly disgusted and deeply disappointed."[46] When Wisconsin Territory became a state, the western portion of the territory (Minnesota) was left unorganized. Lawyers in this region were the driving force behind an extralegal convention at Stillwater, the purpose of which was to create JP courts for public use and to select a delegate for "Wisconsin Territory."[47] In all probability, the JP courts were widely used to adjudicate disputes.

Were the JPs' decisions frequently appealed? Apparently, the answer is no. The decisions of Charles Reame, a JP of Indiana and Michigan territories, were seldom appealed. An appeal meant time, travel, and extra costs, three factors which made appeals prohibitive to all parties. Reame's court became the supreme court of his frontier region; his decisions were arbitrary and personally enforced. He was bribed with gifts of whiskey, and he never decided against rich traders. To enforce his courtroom decrees, Reame would display his long, shining hunting knife if litigants showed any signs of disagreement.[48]

Two men once appeared before him [Reame], the one as plaintiff, the other as defendant. The Justice listened patiently to the complaint of the one and the defense of the other; then rising, with dignity, he pronounced his decision. "You are both wrong. You, Boisvert," to the plaintiff, "you bring me one load of hay; and you, Crely," to the defendant, "You bring me one load of wood; and now the matter is settled." It does not appear that any exceptions were taken to this verdict.[49]

When Henry Sibley was a justice of the peace in Iowa Territory, he too was rarely overruled by superior courts. He exercised power in other territories as well. In a warrant issued by Sibley, a man named Phalen was accused of murdering a U.S. Army sergeant named Hayes. Phalen was arrested in Wisconsin Territory and was taken to jail in Prairie du Chien with no questions asked by local authorities.[50]

In addition to making the JP a powerful local decision-maker, the lack of appeals necessitated the ratification of irregular procedures and the absence of elementary concepts of due process. Justices Johnson and Lockwood of Michigan Territory had no records or forms when they were first commissioned JPs in 1818, and their judicial mistakes were made law because of the finality of their decisions.[51] Nicholas Boilvin had considerable power in his courtroom; his decisions became law despite his flaunting of legal processes. On one occasion, his justice was particularly unbalanced:

Col. Boilvin's office was just without the walls of the fort at Prairie du Chien, and it was much the fashion among the officers to lounge in there of a morning, to find sport for an idle hour, and to take a glass of brandy and water with the old gentleman, which he called taking a little *quelque-chose*. A soldier, named Fry, had been accused of stealing and killing a calf belonging to M. Rolette (French fur trader of long standing in Prairie du Chien region), and the constable, a bricklayer of the name Bell, had been dispatched to arrest the culprit and bring him to trial. While the gentlemen were making their customary morning visit to the Justice, a noise was heard in the entry, and a knock at the door.

"Come in," cried the old gentleman, rising and walking to the door.
Bell—"Here, sir, I have brought Fry to you, as you ordered."
Justice—"Fry, you great rascal: What for you kill M. Rolette's calf?"
Fry—"I did not kill M. Rolette's calf."
Justice—(shaking his fist) "You lie, you great rascal: Bell, take him to jail. Come, gentlemen, come, *let us take a leetle quelque-chose.*"[52]

Although we have no quantitative evidence that appeals were seldom taken from JP courts, all other evidence suggests this notion. Justices of the peace were often the courts of last resort. Given that JP courts were frequently in session and that appeals were rare, was the level of acceptance of JP justice lowered because community residents commonly resolved their disputes by extralegal means? In short, were members of the frontier community merely paying lip service to local frontier legal institutions? The answer to both questions is no.

First, frontier denizens had such great need of frontier JPs that they tolerated occasional judicial corruption. For example, while John Dumoulin, a justice of the peace in St. Clair County, Indiana Territory, was a member of the court of common pleas, he sat in on three cases against himself. He lost one of them. In 1803, he was indicted for assault and battery, but he was acquitted. Later that year, a grand jury accused Dumoulin of being "tyrannically, corruptly, and illegally in conduct of his office," and he was sued for malpractice as a JP. He was investigated by a commission headed by Shadrach Bond, a fellow St. Clair County JP, but nothing came of any of the charges. Dumoulin, a man of dubious character, remained a frontier justice of the peace. In fact, no JP was ever removed from office during Indiana's territorial existence.[53]

Similarly, William Carter took liberties with his justice of the peace commission. Carter adjudged his own case once. In *Carter v. John K. Stone*, the jury found for Carter $156.37 in back debts, and then Carter ordered Stone's property attached and auctioned to pay off the debt. Carter also sentenced two soldiers to six months in prison without indictment or jury trial for allegedly committing the crime of larceny. For this act, Carter was reprimanded by the Utah Territory attorney-general. In spite of these "judicial errors,"

Carter was generally respected and regarded as a model frontier JP by his comrades, and he was elected and reelected justice of the peace for over ten years.[54]

On at least one occasion, frontier inhabitants would not tolerate corruption of the local judiciary. In 1837, William W. Brown settled in Bellevue, Jackson County, Iowa Territory, with his wife and ten men. Brown, a tall, ruddy man, practiced law and operated a hotel, and his men cut wood for river steamers that frequented the Mississippi. He soon became a community pillar. He "was so suave of speech, and his wife so ready with her smiles, that the people elected him a justice of the peace." Shortly thereafter, however, counterfeit money appeared and horses disappeared, and when Brown's men were served with arrest warrants, Brown represented them in court successfully. The night of a town ball, to which Brown and his gang had not been invited, the home of one James Mitchell was robbed, and Bellevue residents suspected that Brown's man James Thompson was the robber. When the sheriff tried to arrest Thompson at Brown's hotel, he was physically thwarted, and the enraged townspeople stormed the hotel, chased Thompson, and shot him dead on the street. Troubles continued until April 1840, when town leaders decided to put a stop to Brown and his gang. They marched on Brown's hotel, and in what has been termed the Bellevue War, Brown was killed, his gang captured, and the hotel burned to the ground by angry frontiersmen. William Brown would no longer use the office of justice of the peace to pervert law and order on the Iowa frontier.[55]

William Brown's fate and the Bellevue uprising were an exception rather than the rule. Frontier citizens needed decision-makers, and they were usually willing to overlook local judicial malfunctions. Not only was some corruption tolerated, but also American frontiersmen seldom used extralegal means to settle disputes of any kind. In *The History of Violence in America*, a comprehensive listing and analysis of vigilante movements throughout American history has been compiled, including nearly all major upheavals and all movements that led to usurpation of the law. Over a sixty-six year period in territories created before 1853, only ten groups of vigilantes, one of them a large group, are listed as having taken the law into their own hands. These actions resulted in the killing of a total of three persons.[56] Before 1853, then, Americans on the frontier rarely resorted to extralegal efforts to subvert local frontier legal institutions.

* * * *

The quality of justice produced by justices of the peace on the American frontier prior to 1853 has been examined with reference to four indicators. First, JPs from a limited sample were found to have had some education and relatively easy access to law materials. No determination was made concerning whether attorneys were present in JP courtrooms. Second, accessibility in terms of geography, cost, and case was discussed, but no conclusive generalization can be made as no hard data have as yet been analyzed. Third, adjudication celerity was not measured or described because of the lack of original sources and historiographical comment. Fourth, the level of local acceptance of frontier justice appeared to be high. JP courts were in at least moderate use, few appeals from JP courts were taken, and there was only a minimal amount of extralegal activity on the frontier. Because only two of the four indicators could be examined, no clear statement on the overall quality of JP justice on the American frontier can be made. After more regional studies have been completed, which consider all four indicators in reference to original JP legal documents, distinct notions about the quality of frontier justice will emerge.

Only a scant amount of scholarship has been devoted to justices of the peace, and most of this scholarship has been harshly critical of the office. JPs have been described as legal ignoramuses and as inefficient and incompetent administrators of justice. In his study of the Ohio Valley, 1775-1818, John Barnhart berates the entire territorial judicial system: with the "exception of the defense of frontier districts, government probably failed to adapt itself to the needs of the mass of the people in the judicial division more than in any other branch." Later, he notes that "one of the most persistently unsatisfactory features of territorial government from the beginning of trans-Appalachian expansion had been the courts."[57] Earl Pomeroy's excellent monograph on a later territorial period, 1861-

1890, reaches the same conclusion. Pomeroy states that "the judicial system was one of the weakest parts of the territorial institution."[58]

An exception to these negative assessments is the evaluation by William N. Davis, Jr., which praises JPs as having accomplished the greatest and most significant legal work on the frontier. Davis chides his fellow historians for ignoring the large numbers of local justices who were not notorious. He theorizes that "the demeanor of the western court [JP] generally, whether unlettered or cultivated, as indeed everywhere else, was one of simple dignity and relative restraint."[59]

Until more specific JP studies of a regional nature have been completed, generalizations about American frontier justices of the peace cannot be precise or conclusive. In-depth examinations of JPs—what they could do, their powers and duties, and their selection and costs; who they were; and what they accomplished, in effect, the quality of their justice—are needed. All of these topics are considered in the remainder of this book in the form of a case study of one frontier region, Washington Territory, 1853-1889.

part II

THE JUSTICES OF THE PEACE OF WASHINGTON TERRITORY

The next three parts of this work present a history of the justices of the peace on the Pacific Northwest frontier which investigates the local judges themselves, their powers and duties, and their functioning courts. This portion, Part II, introduces a personal portrait of the justices, identifying their individual characteristics and the legal restraints their own society placed on them.

In Chapter 2, prosopographical techniques were used on a very limited sample of justices of the peace to determine whether certain historical stereotypes about JPs were true or open to reinterpretation. This same approach is now applied to a large sample of justices of the peace in Washington Territory in order to produce a collective profile showing their relative social, economic, and political status within a frontier society.

After determining who the justices of the peace were, Part II turns to a statutorial discussion of how one could become a JP in Washington Territory. Local justices assumed their offices from a complex series of appointment and election forms, and once in office they were subject to several restraints, the most notable affecting their potential participation as members of the bar.

3

Who Were the Justices of the Peace?

In 1853, the northern half of Oregon Territory became Washington Territory. Nearly four thousand whites had already become residents of the land surrounded by the Pacific Ocean on the west, the forty-ninth parallel on the north, the summit of the Rockies on the east, and the forty-sixth parallel and the Columbia River on the south.[1] In 1853, most of the settlers in Washington Territory resided west of the Cascades in Clark and Lewis counties, with the region between the Rockies and the Cascades uninhabited by whites except for the ferryman at the Spokane River crossing.[2]

Six years after the organization of Washington Territory, its boundaries were increased to include those portions of land in Oregon Territory which were not included in the new state of Oregon. In 1863, Congress reduced the size of Washington Territory to the basic dimensions that formed the state of Washington in 1889.[3] But before attaining territorial status, Americans north of the Columbia River lived under the control of three distinct groups: the British, the Methodists, and the Oregon provisional government.

The English were the first to introduce legal institutions in the form of justices of the peace to the new communities on the Northwest frontier. When the Hudson's Bay Company occupied the Columbia District as early as the 1820s, its officers received and exercised justice of the peace commissions and powers over their employees, other British subjects, and resident Indians. Later, in 1838, the Methodist church in Oregon appointed a justice of the peace for Americans living north of the Columbia, and JPs authorized under the auspices of the Oregon provisional government (1843-1848) had jurisdiction over Americans residing in Washington.

Not until 1848 were American territorial justices of the peace officially extended to Washington through the Oregon Territory Organic Act, and they were reaffirmed in Washington Territory's creation. Thus, justices of the peace arrived in the Northwest with the first British and American settlers and continued to function after the land north of the Columbia River became part of the American territorial system.[4]

A Prosopography for JPs on the Northwest Frontier

Washington Territory remained an official U.S. territory for thirty-six years, from 1853 to 1889. During this period, many justices of the peace were appointed or elected to office, functioning as legitimate judicial officials and issuing scores of legal opinions.

But who were these justices of the peace? What was their place in frontier society? Did they establish leadership in new settlements, or were they merely "the dispatchers" of a frontier community's desire for order? To answer these basic questions about an unheralded, and yet important, officer of the law, a prosopography or collective biography is necessary. Such an approach provides a more personal view of a large group of individuals.

Merely identifying the names of the persons who presided over the lower courts was no easy task. Neither the territorial officials nor the justices themselves made lists of local justices, and few JP election results were recorded. However, by searching the local newspapers, diaries, and histories and by culling legislative, court, county, and census records, individual justices of the peace and their skeletal biographies surfaced.

A total of 197 justices of the peace who served in Washington Territory from 1853 to 1889 have been identified; these include all territorial JPs for whom some basic biographical information was uncovered.[5] In addition, seventy-six other persons held justice of the peace positions, but little or no other evidence specifically detailing their lives has been found.[6]

In order to construct a group profile, the data collected on the justices of the peace identified have been organized around the questions posed in Table 4. Answers to these questions determine certain of the social, political, and economic attributes of JPs.

Table 4

General Biographical Interrogatories Applied to Justices of the Peace of Washington Territory, 1853-1889

1. Where was the subject born?
2. What was the subject's life span?
3. When did the subject migrate to Washington Territory?
4. When was the subject first commissioned a justice of the peace?
5. Was the subject involved in politics?
6. Did the subject hold local political office(s) other than justice of the peace?
7. Did the subject hold an elective political office?
8. Did the subject practice other occupations in addition to being a frontier JP? If so, what occupations?
9. Did the subject own land?
10. What were the subject's estimated real and personal property values?

Sagacious, Social Leaders

The application of questions 1-4 in Table 4 to the data collected on Washington JPs reveals that the justices were seldom born in the Northwest. They usually represented second- or third-generation American families rooted in the eastern United States. Of 159 JPs whose place of birth was recorded, 39 percent were born in the East, 23 percent in the Midwest, and 19 percent in the South. A high percentage of justices, 18 percent, were foreign born, and only 1 percent lived all of their lives in Washington Territory.[7]

Once the future local justices arrived in Washington Territory, they did not instantly become JPs. Before assuming the office, they spent an average of 8.6 years in the territory. Time spans varied. For example, Boliver B. Bishop came west to the California gold fields in 1849. After an unsuccessful mining career, he moved to the north bank of the Columbia near The Dalles in 1850 where he engaged in salmon fishing. Here the people chose him as a justice of the peace for Oregon Territory. Perhaps because of his past judicial experience, when the Washington territorial legislature met to create Skamania County in 1854, Bishop was appointed the county's first JP.[8] Henry Sterns obtained his first commission even quicker than Bishop did. Sterns, born in Illinois, decided to move west at the age of thirty-two, finally settling in Washington Territory in 1853 at Cowlitz Landing. In 1854, he was selected as one of Lewis County's first local justices.[9]

Unlike Sterns and Bishop, both Thomas Cranney and Silas Maxon lived in Washington thirty-one years before their communities awarded them a judicial position. Cranney, born in 1830, came to Whidbey Island at the age of twenty-six where he set up a general store and gradually moved into the lumber business. He proved to be popular in Island County, being elected county clerk, treasurer, auditor, and representative to the Washington territorial legislature before winning his justice of the peace post. Maxon also pursued lumbering and political careers. He moved to Washington Territory from Kentucky in 1847 where he set up a sawmill and made saddles and harnesses. Maxon achieved some political prominence in Clark County as one of its first treasurers before he was elected JP in 1878.[10]

As justices of the peace tended to be established residents of Washington Territory, they were in their late middle age at the time of their first commission. Of 164 JPs studied, the average age upon entering local judicial office was 40.5 years. Most justices fell in a thirty-five to forty-five year span and their ages ranged from eighteen to eighty-six years. These statistics are significant when compared to life expectancy rates in nonfrontier areas of the United States and the United States as a whole. From 1850 to 1890, life expectancy for Massachusetts males varied from 38.3 to 42.5 years. In the first nationwide computation of life expectancy, that computed for 1900, males in the United States could expect to live 47.3 years.[11] Hence, the JPs of Washington Territory were in the prime of their lives.

Thomas Hastie was appointed a justice of the peace for Island County at the age of eighteen when his employer, Isaac Ebey, the Coveland Precinct JP, was murdered by Indians. Hastie worked on Ebey's farm while he farmed his own donation claim. The territory's youngest justice was never elected to his position.[12] At the other extreme was W. H. Martin, also a farmer, who was elected justice of the peace in Lancaster Precinct, Clark County, at the age of eighty-six. Martin had become a successful agriculturalist in

Washington Territory after moving to the Northwest from Virginia.[13]

More representative of the relative age groups of Washington's JPs was William Renton who was born in Nova Scotia in 1818. Renton became a sea captain, and after several years at sea, he settled in the Puget Sound region where he built a mill at Port Blakely and founded the Renton Coal Company. An active leader in Kitsap County, Captain Renton was made a justice of the peace at the age of thirty-nine.[14]

Thus, the JPs of Washington Territory were not young upstarts anxious to make a beginning as recent arrivals to the new land. Instead, after migrating to the territory, they established themselves as permanent residents before assuming local judicial offices, and they became the major community decision-makers only after they had accumulated the years of experience necessary to advise, channel, and create the social directions for new settlements. In essence, the justices of the peace of Washington Territory socially epitomized a group of stable, sagacious veterans of the American frontier.

Political Pundits

The justices of the peace in Washington Territory provided territorial residents with political as well as social leadership. The very nature of the justice court position dictated political comment. *The Owyhee Avalanche,* published in eastern Washington Territory in what later became Idaho Territory, alerted the electorate when it noted, "We respectfully call attention to the announcement of S. C. Horsley as candidate for Justice of the Peace for Silver City Precinct. Mr. H. has filled the position several years elsewhere and bears the reputation of being capable. Parties wishing to know which political mill he blows for, will have to inquire of him for we don't know."[15] Candidate Horsley eventually had to bow out because he was unable to obtain the endorsement of either the Union-Republican party, which made no choice, or the Democrats who backed established Silver City lawyer, James Lynam.[16]

The territory's JPs often participated in the political process beyond merely holding local elective office. Eighty-eight percent (174 of 197) were found to be active politically, 40 percent (79 of 197) held political positions in addition to presiding over their popularly chosen judiciaries, and almost one-third or 31 percent (62 of

197) sat in elective offices other than JP posts. The justices of the peace of frontier Washington formed a foundation for the territory's grassroots political order.

The political involvement of the JPs varied from peripheral interest to total immersion. Napoleon Davis confined his only political activity to a single election in 1872 for justice of the peace of Pollock Precinct, Clark County, and, aside from his JP election, Jerome Ely of Oak Harbor Precinct, Island County, ventured into politics only once, to obtain a political appointment as postmaster.[17] Others were more heavily entangled. John Y. Ostrander, JP in Columbia County, served as registrar at the Olympia land office and as U.S. customs commissioner at Juneau, Alaska, before his election to the bench.[18] And Richard Covington, an original Vancouver settler, entered politics through social influence. When Ulysses S. Grant was stationed at Ft. Vancouver, Washington Territory in 1853, Covington was invited to entertain Grant. Covington, an artist, pianist, violinist, and magistrate, became a close friend of the future president, and subsequently, the local politicos rewarded him with an appointment as county superintendent of schools.[19]

Justices of the peace also played more major local political roles. When Washingtonians chafed under the control of Oregon interests, they called a convention at Monticello in 1852 near the mouth of the Cowlitz River. Forty-four persons gathered and signed a memorial to Congress demanding territorial status; four JPs, Nathaniel Stone, William Plumb, David Maynard, and Sidney Ford, were among them.[20] Another especially active political member of his community was J. E. Willis, justice of the peace in Chehalis. He wrote the charter whereby Chehalis applied to the Washington territorial legislature for city status, and he eventually came to hold the "lucrative position of postmaster."[21]

Once Washington Territory began functioning as a political unit, justices of the peace actively sought and achieved the highest elective offices available—membership in the territorial legislature. W. Byron Daniels, lawyer, editor of the *Vancouver Independent*, surveyor, and JP, served in the House of Representatives from 1876 to 1878 and attained considerable influence in the territory's Republican party.[22] J. R. Bates of Colville Valley also ran successfully for election to the House. As a Democrat and a native of Tennessee, Bates actively opposed a loyalty resolution passed by the Washington territorial legislature after the Confederate firing on Fort Sumter. Although his move was politically unpopular, the Spokane County JP still managed to obtain legislative authorization to build a bridge across the Spokane River connecting Walla Walla to the Colville Road several years after the Civil War.[23]

At the county and precinct level, local justices were particularly prominent. Henry S. Burlingame of Clark County was elected justice of the peace, probate judge, councilman, county treasurer, and county commissioner. As a county commissioner, he completed two terms, 1859-1863. He was joined by fellow JPs George Hart and Solomon Strong. Hart sat as a Clark County commissioner for ten years (1857-1867), and Strong held a commissioner's office for twelve years (1855-1867).[24] No JP surpassed Elias Whitman for political leadership within the community. Whitman served as Walla Walla's first mayor, and he was elected to that position on four more occasions.[25]

The election of local justices frequently caused considerable interest. Shortly after a major eastern portion of Washington Territory was separated and reorganized into Montana Territory by Congress, elections were held. In the contest for JP in Virginia City, the *Montana Democrat* editorialized as follows:

GRATIFYING — We believe the Democrats are more delighted over the defeat of Mayor [J. M.] Castner for Justice of the Peace [by W. M. Stafford] than over the defeat of any other candidate of the opposition, although there were no nominations made by the Democratic convention of candidates for Justices.[26]

The creation of Idaho Territory provoked considerably more controversy with regard to the political nature of the JP. Prior to 1863, among those serving the Lewiston and Boise areas as justices of the peace were Thomas M. Pomeroy of Elk City, Nez Perce County; W. B. Yantis of Shoshone County; and J. L. McGownd of Bannock and J. K. Johnson of Centerville in Boise County. After the organization of Idaho Territory, the first elections were called, and these men won their respective justice of the peace positions.

However, when the new governor, William Wallace, arrived, he voided the elections and appointed his own justices of the peace, all Republicans, to the local judiciaries. Idahoans, particularly those living in Boise County, were infuriated. At meetings held in Bannock, Placerville, and Centerville, some fifteen hundred to two thousand persons passed a resolution condemning Wallace's actions. To calm the citizenry, Wallace ordered new elections in Boise County for JPs and other local officials.[27]

The justices of the peace of Washington Territory helped shape and control frontier politics. Their office, by its own elective nature, demanded some political attention, but they participated far beyond simply paying infrequent political dues. Like Samuel Coombs and George Lyon, justices of King County, many JPs were experienced politicians before they came to the Northwest. Coombs held membership in Maine's House of Representatives, and after he journeyed to Washington Territory, he was chosen King County's first auditor and Seattle's first committing magistrate. Coombs later was appointed warden of McNeil Island Penitentiary.[28] Similarly, Lyon settled in Washington after an active political life in Nevada where he guided the Republican party as its state chairman. His political activism did not end when he moved to Seattle in 1886. As part owner and editor of the *Seattle Times* and as a justice of the peace, Lyon participated in local, territorial, and later state politics.[29] When he died, an obituary describing Lyon's political demeanor and influence to a large extent depicted the level of political involvement of Washington Territory's JPs. He was said to be "firm in his convictions and almost aggressive in pursuing what he thought to be right. . . . At one time he could have had almost any state office he desired."[30] Lyon, together with the rest of Washington's JPs, constituted a formidable portion of the territory's political leadership.

Economic Potentates

In addition to local political leadership, the justices displayed sophisticated financial abilities. The territory's JPs tended to be successful farmers who had title to their land. By applying questions 8, 9, and 10 in Table 4 to Washington's local justices, the JPs emerged as active frontier entrepreneurs. Farming and supply-oriented business overwhelmingly proved attractive to most local justices before, during, and after their commissions.[31] Not surprisingly, justices of the peace usually owned land (ninety of one hundred did), their average real property was estimated at $3,148, and their average personal property was evaluated at $1,652. Accordingly, the JPs represented a significant portion of the local communities' economic elite.

The typical justice of the peace from the economic standpoint was John Campbell, a bucolic squire from Clark County. As a JP, he also farmed his own land valued at $3,200, and his belongings were worth approximately $1,000.[32] Not as fortunate were J. E. Baker and Lloyd Brooke. Baker of Olympia farmed his father's land while he held local judicial office, and he owned no major material goods. Brooke, however, owned a considerable acreage of valuable land early in his judicial career. He claimed the original land site of the city of Walla Walla. During the Indian-white confrontations of the 1850s, he abandoned his claims, and when he failed to return within four years after the wars, he lost title to his lands.[33]

Several of the justices were considered excellent farmers and ranchers by their peers. John Wilson Beck of Yakima County used irrigation ditches on the first fruit orchards planted in the Yakima Valley,[34] and Judge J. E. Freese of Semishmoo raised some of the best apples in Whatcom County.[35] W. P. Murphy became known as one of the largest and most successful cattle raisers of Klickitat County.[36] And Nathan Eaton, Thurston County JP, built a mill on his farm that produced quality lumber. According to the *Washington Standard*, "For years, that mill [Eaton's] has turned out some of the finest specimens of oak plank and other lumber that has ever left this Territory."[37]

Other justices operated successful mercantile businesses. Lewis Day of Wallula represented the Oregon Steam Navigation Company with considerable acumen, and Joseph Brant owned and operated an $18,000 hotel and carriage manufacturing enterprise.[38] While a justice of the peace in Vancouver, he expanded into the livery business. Brant advertised his new economic undertaking in the *Vancouver Register*.

LIVERY
Sale and Exchange
Stables
Corner of 6th and A Streets
Horses, Carriages and Wagons Let by the
hour, day and week at moderate rates

Prices greatly reduced. If people don't
believe it, come and try me on.

Jos. Brant[39]

Like Joseph Brant, William T. Sayward, justice of the peace in
Port Ludlow, Jefferson County, was energetic in his economic
enterprises. He first came west to California and entered the banking business. After the Sacramento fire of 1852, when lumber
prices in California rose from $12 per thousand to $150 per thousand
board feet, the "smart Yankee from Maine" gave up banking for
the lumbering business. Upon his arrival in the Northwest, Sayward
found that investing in a large-scale lumber operation would require
substantial capital. As a result of a "business conversation" with
Simeon Reed, the two cornered the entire flour market of the
Northwest, thereby providing the Jefferson County JP with his
necessary moneys. Sayward then went into the lumbering business
during which time he became a justice of the peace. Later, he sold
his mill and, together with fourteen other investors, formed the
Puget Sound Steam Navigation Company. Unfortunately, the
company folded without ever contributing to "the benefit of navigation."[40]

Like Sayward, G. H. Gerrish, trader and justice of the peace of
Port Townsend, was an aggressive businessman, but he earned a
reputation for being impetuous and untrustworthy in his business
dealings. For example, in June 1853, General A. V. Kautz camped
near Gerrish's house and he asked the JP if his party should go on
to Dungeness. Gerrish advised Kautz that Dungeness had no white
inhabitants and no water, and that the Indians of that region were
away fishing. Kautz took Gerrish's counsel, but the general later
realized he had been deceived. As he wrote in his diary, "Garish
[Gerrish] had a store, and he probably thought that he could get
some trade out of us."[41] Kautz also noted Gerrish's fabricated

stories to his officers about other traders selling alcohol to Indians. In 1864, legal action was taken by a local merchant against Gerrish in district court where he was forced to pay a promissory note. Despite his numerous economic activities, Gerrish never realized his full economic capacities; his tactics simply alienated potential financial associates.[42]

The justices of the peace of Washington Territory were in a higher economic level than the average frontier settler. Their propensity to own land, to engage in diverse economic enterprises, and to hold substantial amounts of real and personal property installed them as economic potentates on the frontier.

* * * *

Washington Territory justices of the peace had established social status in their communities; they parleyed their leadership talents into active local political participation; and they amassed moderate holdings of property. They were not the poor, common men of the frontier, but rather the social, political, and economic elites of new communities who gained control over their frontier environment through local legal institutions.

Selection and Eligibility
of Local Justices

The institution of justice of the peace was formally extended to Washington Territory by the Washington Territory Organic Act of 1853. It was further elaborated in the laws adopted by the Washington territorial legislature from its first session in 1854 to its last in 1889. The Organic Act and these statutes authorized various selection processes, eligibility limitations, and other grants of power for JPs. The legal foundations for Washington Territory justices of the peace evolved directly from federal and territorial law.

The Washington Territory Organic Act became law in March 1853. The judicial system outlined in the act provided "that the judicial power of said Territory [Washington] shall be vested in a supreme court, district courts, probate courts, and in justices of the peace."[1] The territorial supreme court, composed of three men appointed by the president, sat collectively as the supreme court of Washington Territory and individually as district courts. The probate courts and justice of the peace courts were termed lower courts, and cases originating in the lower courts could be appealed to district courts and then to the Washington Territory supreme court.[2] To provide a smooth judicial transition, the Organic Act specifically authorized all JPs serving in that part of Oregon Territory, which was to be Washington Territory, to continue performing their duties until the Washington territorial legislature determined a selection process for new justices.[3]

The Appointive Process

How could a person become a justice of the peace in Washington Territory? One of the first acts of the Washington territorial legislature meeting in early 1854 provided a process for choosing the territory's JPs, by appointment and by election, thereby discontinuing the courts held by justices of the peace north of 46° latitude and the Columbia River that had been authorized under the Washington Territory Organic Act. The legislature stipulated that the legislators appoint justices of the peace with the creation of a county. These appointments were to last until the county held its first elections.

During Washington's territorial period, its legislature approved forty-nine county government bills which established four separate means of receiving justice of the peace appointments. The first type of appointment utilized by the legislature was the *direct appointment.* In the first legislative session, sixteen counties were created, and thirty-five justices of the peace were named. From 1854 to 1867, thirty-six separate county governmental laws specified fifty-six persons as JPs.[4]

The direct appointment process had some drawbacks. The legislature could not aways find enough "qualified" persons to be justices of the peace. County officials in Whatcom, Island, Spokane, Chehalis, Shoshone, and Snohomish counties were chosen, but no JPs were appointed.[5] In addition, the legislature was not familiar with its appointees. In 1861, ——— Parker was appointed justice of the peace for Idaho County, and in 1863 one of three appointed JPs for Boise County was listed as ——— Baird. Probably the least information was known about the justice of the peace appointed for Nez Perce County; to this position, the legislature selected ——— ——— at the same time Sanford Owens was made sheriff.[6]

The difficulty of identifying sufficient numbers of persons to serve in county offices forced appointed JPs to accept several positions. In 1854, Solomon Stilwell was appointed justice of the peace *and* probate judge for Wahkiacum County. That same year, two acts were passed appointing officers for Jefferson County. In each law, four justices were selected, and in each law, J. P. Keller was designated justice of the peace and county commissioner. In the second act, J. K. Thorndike was appointed Jefferson County treasurer and justice of the peace.[7] The merry-go-round effect illustrated by comparing these two Jefferson County enactments suggests that the legislature did not match persons to their respective appointive offices. Instead, the solons were desperate for "bodies" to place in local government, and they took whoever was available. Lloyd Brooke, moreover, must take the honor for having the most appointive positions bestowed by the Washington territorial legislature. In 1854, Brooke assumed the position of justice of the peace of Skamania County. During the same legislative session, he was appointed probate judge and justice of the peace with jurisdiction over all of Walla Walla County. Then, in the following year, Brooke was named auditor, probate judge, and treasurer of Walla Walla County as reconstituted. Thus, within two years, the territorial legislature had commissioned Brooke to six county posts, including two JP courts.[8]

A second type of appointment was the *indirect appointment*, which proved deficient as a usual JP selection process. In 1873, San Juan County was created. Rather than appoint specific county residents to county offices, Charles McCoy, Samuel Trueworthy, and Joseph A. Merrill were named county commissioners, and they were empowered to hold a special term of court to appoint all other county officials required by law.[9] No other county commissioners were ever given this power to appoint justices of the peace when the county was created, but this unusual procedure may have been necessary because of questions raised over the ownership of San Juan County during the 1850s and 1860s by Great Britain and the United States. All boards of county commissioners were given a limited amount of indirect appointment power. Whenever a vacancy occurred in the office of JP, the county commissioners appointed replacements on a temporary basis.[10]

Two other forms of JP appointments were directly related to the common practice of county-making. Many of the counties formed later in the territorial period were created by splitting an established county into two or three counties. When this procedure was used, the legislature determined who were to be named justices of the peace in the new county. When Whitman County was created out of Walla Walla County in 1871, Whitman and Walla Walla counties were united for all judicial purposes; a Walla Walla County JP held an *adjunctive appointment* in Whitman County. This same procedure was used in dealing with justices of the peace in Yakima and Stevens counties. A similar JP appointment device, used only in the 1880s, was the *residual appointment*. Just as all Oregon Territory

JPs who held court in the newly created Washington Territory were legally designated Washington Territory justices of the peace, all Whatcom County JPs who held court in newly created Skagit County in 1883 were legally installed Skagit County justices of the peace. Such appointments were also made in Franklin, Lincoln, Kittitas, Adams, Douglas, Asotin, and Okanogan counties.[11]

The Elective Process

In the first code of laws approved by the territorial legislature as well as in all succeeding codes, the position of justice of the peace was made an elective office once local government was organized. Each election precinct was authorized to select one JP every year, and sometimes more than one justice could be elected if the board of county commissioners so designated.[12] This law seemed to run at odds with the statutes setting a two-year term for a justice of the peace, and it was not until 1888 that this ambiguity was corrected. The Washington territorial legislature passed a law providing for the biennial election in each county precinct (each city was termed an individual precinct) of one justice of the peace, except when the county commissioners authorized two JPs per precinct.[13]

The provision for annual elections may be an indication of the problem of keeping justices of the peace in office. The county auditor was empowered to declare a JP vacancy to exist upon the receipt of a signed statement from *one* legal voter that no one was legally a justice of the peace for his precinct. In such a case, the position was filled by appointment by the county commissioners until an election was held, unless the vacancy was declared less than ninety days before a regular election. Any JP election was validated if ten or more votes were cast.[14] The ease with which one could become a justice of the peace after a vacancy existed suggests that vacancies were endemic to the office.

Like Washington, other territories had loose procedures for filling JP vacancies; the result was that any number of special elections were held. This flexibility had been permitted by Congress in specific statutes codified in 1858 and revised in 1867.[15] By 1880, however, officials in Washington Territory[16] and Washington, D.C., tired of this extravagant display of democracy. The House

Committee on Territories noted that "to require that a vacancy in such an office of an inferior grade [the justice of the peace], must be filled only by election while more important offices are filled by appointment seems an anomaly, and must evidently have been an oversight or mistake made in codifying the Statutes at Large."[17] It was no legislative mistake; nevertheless, the federal government curbed the excessive number of JP elections by a law passed that year. After 1880, when a JP vacancy occurred in any territory, a successor could be appointed or elected in any procedure set up by the territorial legislature, so long as the office was elected at the next regular election as provided by law.[18] However, the processes, both by appointment and by election, for choosing justices of the peace in Washington Territory were so established and without political annoyance that they remained law after the end of the territorial period. At the 1889 Washington Constitutional Convention, delegates refused to change the method of selecting JPs once Washington became a state.[19]

Restrictions on the Office

In order to become a JP, the candidate had to be a qualified voter, which meant that justices of the peace during the territorial period were white, male, and over twenty-one years of age. Upon assuming office, JPs were required to file a $500 bond with at least two sureties. The purpose of the bond was to provide the territory with malpractice insurance and a corruption contingency fund. Aggrieved persons were allowed to sue the territory because of the actions of a justice of the peace, and JPs might "forget" to pay *all* moneys collected to the territory. A JP also had to reside in the county where he would be holding court six months prior to his election. There was no residency requirement for appointive JPs.[20]

Other limits were placed on those who aspired to justice of the peace. No sheriff, coroner, or clerk of a district court could be a JP, but notary publics were allowed commissions. At first, justices were not excluded from sitting on grand and petit juries, but in 1863 they were excluded from serving as jurors in any capacity.[21] Although no legal training was required for the office, certain legislative restrictions were imposed in attempts to control JPs who were lawyers or whose friends were lawyers. In 1812, all territorial judges appointed under the authority of the United States were forbidden to practice law, but this statute did not regulate lower elective courts.[22] In 1854, Washington territorial law prevented justices of the peace from having an office in the same room with a practicing attorney unless the attorney was his law partner, and no law partner of a JP could appear or practice law before any justice of the peace.[23] This attempt to regulate the legal associations of JPs was later amplified in 1863. A law partner of a Washington justice of the peace was barred from practicing law in *any* court in the territory, and after 1879, no JP who was an attorney could appear in his own court, in an appellate court above his court, or in any court directly below his court.[24] This law discouraged some lawyers from becoming or continuing as JPs. For example, when J. E. Willis of Chehalis formed a law partnership with Elwood Evans, a prominent territorial lawyer from Tacoma, Willis felt he had to resign his justiceship in order to enable Evans and himself to practice fully their profession.[25] Clearly, membership in the bar or close association with lawyers was an impediment to becoming a justice of the peace in Washington Territory.

* * * *

Despite legislative restrictions, it was relatively easy to become a justice of the peace in Washington Territory. JPs were normally first appointed and thereafter subject to election. They were required to be white, male, over twenty-one years of age, and residents of the territory for at least six months, and once assuming office, they were subject to certain limitations. These limitations discouraged conflicts of interests within the judicial system by seeking to prevent the combination of attorney and judge in the position of justice of the peace. But the selection and eligibility requirements for the JPs were sufficiently flexible and popular that local justice could function in the new communities on the Washington frontier and remain a viable, unchanged part of the state of Washington's new judiciary.

part III

A JUSTICE OF THE PEACE MANUAL FOR WASHINGTON FRONTIER JUSTICES

A major provision in the Washington Organic Act relating to the territory's justices of the peace stipulated that these local justices were merely to "be limited by law."[1] The act vested the power to shape Washington's local legal institutions in its territorial legislators, and the solons lost little time in carrying out this federal mandate.

One of the legislature's first decisions authorized a commission composed of Edward Lander, then U.S. attorney and later chief justice of the Washington Territory supreme court, Victor Monroe and William Strong, both Washington Territory supreme court justices, to compile a code of laws. The codifiers relied upon Indiana and Ohio statutes (they had practiced law there prior to their migration to Washington Territory) and Oregon Territory statutes which had been copied from Iowa laws.[2] "The commissioners recognized the probable presence of many errors which could require correction at some future time,"[3] but they probably did not foresee the many attempts that would be made to revise their original work. Washington's territorial legislature fully participated in the codification craze which characterized the last half of the nineteenth century in American legal history. The Washington legislature called for numerous commissions on code revisions and adopted five other codes after the 1854 code, all of which brought changes to the justices of the peace. The 1873 code was the last full code revision accepted by the territorial legislature, and as the time for statehood approached, the legislature authorized still another codification commission.

Not everyone in Washington Territory favored the codification movement. In 1869, Governor Alvan Flanders chastised the territorial House for its authorization of so many code revisions. He questioned whether the legislators had examined the codes closely, because if they had, they would have realized that the new codes were often more confusing than the 1854 code. Flanders followed up his criticisms of the territorial legislators with vetoes of bills providing for the compensation of the authors of the 1869 code.[4] Some territorial residents also doubted the efficacy of printing so many codes. While the express purpose of the legislature in creating lucrative commissions for members of the legal profession was to revise statutes, some citizens saw the end product merely as a reprinting of old laws that supplied needed copies for recently established lawyers and public officials. Still others complained that, in spite of constant reprintings and revisions, Washington territorial laws were generally perplexing and disorganized. In 1887, after numerous codifications, the Walla Walla Union *noted:*

The laws of this territory, owing to careless legislation and decisions of the courts, are in such a state of confusion that it is very difficult even for experienced members of the bar to arrive at any definite conclusion in regard to them, much less can a citizen exactly determine the rules that govern his conduct, or the laws that guarantee his rights and privileges. Consultation of our laws by our citizens is rendered still more difficult by the absence of anything that can properly be called an index to the volumes. [5]

Unfortunately, Washington's territorial statutes were formulated in such a manner as to discourage a complete understanding of the law even by those officials directly charged with legal functions.

To deal with the problem of "knowing the law" in many states and territories, manuals were devised for most members of the judicial system, including justices of the peace. Such JP manuals were unquestionably a great help to their possessors, but since they were not regularly updated, changes in jurisdiction or fees or any special area of judicial concern generally went unrecorded.

None of the manuals summarizes the laws of Washington Territory relating to justices of the peace. By examining and then analyzing all of the Washington statutes, however, a complete legal description of the territory's justices of the peace is possible. This section reconstructs a "manual" for Washington's justices of the peace that encompasses the territorial years and describes the intricacies of regular and special JP courts.

The first portion of the manual, Chapter 5, elaborates what justices of the peace could *legally do. Justice court jurisdiction, procedure, powers, duties, and appellate processes are so discussed and arranged that a complete picture of JP related activity before, during, and after a trial is easily recognizable. Chapters 6 and 7 catalogue certain special legal uses made of Washington Territory justices of the peace and the cost of going to JP court.*

5

The Legal Perimeters of Local Justice

Justices of the peace functioned in Washington throughout its territorial period. They had jurisdiction over a variety of civil and criminal disputes; maintained certain established procedures for courtroom operations; exercised various powers; and performed specified duties. All of these actions were regulated by federal and territorial law, and these regulations served to delineate and refine the office of justice of the peace as a working legal institution on the frontier.

The Washington territorial legislature was responsible for outlining what the local justice could legally do. Federal law had authorized the extension of justices of the peace to Washington Territory, and territorial legislators were given the power to shape these local judicial institutions. In some respects, however, the federal government limited this power, particularly in jurisdictional matters that sought to define the boundaries within which the court could operate.

Civil Jurisdiction

Under the Washington Territory Organic Act, justices of the peace were not delegated the "jurisdiction of any case in which the title to land shall in any wise [*sic*] come in question, or where the debt or damages claimed shall exceed one hundred dollars. . . ."[1] All Washington Territory and Oregon Territory courts, including JPs, were to have concurrent jurisdiction over offenses committed on the Columbia River where the river formed a common boundary between the two territories.

The Organic Act also authorized the justices of the peace of Washington Territory to hold two types of general jurisdiction, civil and criminal. Within civil and criminal jurisdiction, the Washington territorial legislature regulated other jurisdictional categories, subject matter and areal; within the subject matter category, two subcategories were legislated: allowable forms of action and monetary limitations.

Regulation of the one subcategory, civil subject matter jurisdiction, was the primary concern of the federal government. Under the Organic Act, the justices had jurisdiction over any civil action where the debt or damages did not exceed $100. Any action concerning a larger amount had to be adjudicated in a district court.[2] This limitation was not popular with Washington Territory residents. People with judicial business might live as far as two hundred miles from a district court, and the $100 limit on JP jurisdiction would compel them to spend much time and money traveling to district court to have their claims heard. In 1865, the Washington territorial legislature memorialized Congress that, under the present jurisdictional limitation, the plaintiff's expenses were so great that the costs "absorb the entire amount of the claim . . . , amount to a prohibition on suitors, and enable dishonest persons to take advantage of them."[3] The legislature urged Congress to amend the Organic Act so as to extend the jurisdictional ceiling from $100 to $250. Congress, which had heard similar pleas from residents in other territories, finally responded by changing the act in 1883.[4] The limit of justice of the peace jurisdiction was increased from $100 to $300 in Idaho, Montana, and Washington territories.[5] This same act had been previously passed for Colorado and Arizona territories, and in 1885 it would be extended to Wyoming Territory.[6]

The Washington Organic Act also forbade a form of subject matter jurisdiction: justices of the peace could not hear cases in which land title was in question.[7] Territorial statutes echoed this provision and provided further guidance. If the question of land title arose during any JP trial, the proceedings were to cease immediately, and the justice was to certify the case for the district court for adjudication.[8]

While congressional interests centered on specific civil subject matter limitations, the Washington territorial legislature defined all other general jurisdictional requirements of justices of the peace. In civil areal jurisdiction, JPs were limited to hearing cases co-extensive with the limits of the county in which they were elected or appointed. Therefore, if a county was divided into three election precincts, it had at least three justices of the peace, and they had jurisdiction over the entire county area, not just their own election precincts.[9]

JP civil subject matter jurisdiction was also regulated by territorial statutes. The legislature restricted justices of the peace to hearing only certain forms of action that did not claim moneys exceeding $100. In cases that involved debts or damages, the justices of the peace could hear actions arising on a contract for recovery of money only; requiring payment of a bond conditioned for payment of money; resulting from an injury to the person or real property, or from a taking or an injury to personal property; enforcing any lien or foreclosing any mortgage on personal property; concerning the fraudulent sale, purchase, or exchange of personal property; and entering judgments for damages after the confession of a defendant.[10]

In cases that contained requests to recover property, JPs could hear actions for replevin, forcible entry, unlawful detainer, and recovery of a mining claim, regardless of property value.[11] A replevin action was brought when a person sought the return of goods unlawfully taken by another. In such an action, a plaintiff could not recover personal property on the weakness of the defendant's title; instead, the plaintiff recovered the property on the strength of his or her title. Thus, in a Washington Territory JP court, a plaintiff in a replevin action had to prove that he or she lawfully owned the property in question; the property was wrongfully retained by the defendant; and the property was not taken for a tax or fine or seized under execution or attachment. Plaintiff also had to make known the alleged cause for property detention and the value of the property, and he or she had to post a bond double the value of the property in order to begin the replevin proceedings. Indeed, the presumption of innocence fully protected the defendant in a JP court replevin action.[12]

An action on forcible entry was held when a person violently took possession of lands and tenements against the will of those entitled to possession, or when a person illegally turned out by force or threat those in possession after an initial peaceful entrance. The plaintiff in such an action had to submit a written complaint to a justice of the peace in the county of the premises in question showing that the defendant had possession of the lands or tenements and that the defendant held possession or entered by force. After the complaint was signed, the JP issued a summons for the sheriff or constable to serve on the defendant requiring a court appearance. The judge also issued a venire at the same time because actions on forcible entry were always held before a jury (six persons or less) trial. The defendant had ten days to appear before the court, and if he or she did not appear or did appear and lost to the plaintiff, the JP then issued a writ of restitution directing the sheriff or constable to cause the plaintiff to be repossessed of the premises.[13]

An action for unlawful detainer was justiciable before a Washington Territory JP when a person wrongfully kept under his control the real or personal property of another person. This type of action was generally useful to landlords to remove tenants who had not paid their rent, or to mortgage holders to repossess property from anyone who failed to keep up mortgage payments. A plaintiff who brought an unlawful detainer action had to prove that the defendant held the land or possessions contrary to the conditions of lease and that the defendant neglected to hand over the property ten days or more past the due date. No charge that violence or force had been used was necessary in order to assert an unlawful detainer action, and a jury trial was optional to the plaintiff or defendant.[14]

Unlawful detainer and forcible entry actions were related. Each dealt with alleged wrongful possession of property, and each allowed an aggrieved person to recover property. The success or failure of a plaintiff to recover property in an unlawful detainer or forcible entry action did not preclude the same plaintiff from going to the same JP court and bringing an action for damages for injury to the same property. The defendant, however, did have one recourse if he or she felt local justice would not serve his or her best interests. The defendant could quickly remove any unlawful detainer or forcible entry action from JP court by raising the issue of title to real property. The mere raising of the issue would force the case directly to the district court.[15]

Justices of the peace in Washington Territory could also hear actions to recover possession of mining claims. A person claiming the right to occupancy and possession of a mining claim withheld by another could complain in writing to a justice of the peace in the county of the claim. In the complaint, the plaintiff had to describe the claim, outline his or her rights to occupy and possess the claim, and allege the defendant wrongfully held the claim. This procedure was similar to that required in unlawful detainer and forcible entry actions; the same remedy to those actions, a writ of restitution, was available to a plaintiff of an action to recover possession of a mining claim.[16]

Although mining activities in Washington Territory had not reached their pinnacle of development in 1854, the law recognized that evidence of local mining customs and regulations established at the district in which the mining claim was located was admissible in justice of the peace courts.[17] This specific statutory reference suggested that the power of Washington Territory JPs to assume jurisdiction over mining claim disputes was further diffused. Three types of law enforcers were found in American mining districts— the alcaldes, councils of miners, and territorial justices of the peace —and of these three, JPs had the least power.[18] In Washington Territory, JPs could exercise jurisdictional options in mining districts if they were accepted by the districts' inhabitants.[19]

The activities of Washington Territory justices of the peace in mining areas were also limited by the lack of mining booms within the territorial jurisdiction. Gold found at Fort Colville in 1855 precipitated a rush to the upper Columbia regions, but the deposits were "small and superficial," causing most would-be miners to leave the Colville region by early 1856.[20] In 1861-1862, mining rushes to Idaho (Orofino, Salmon River, Boise Basin, and Owyhee districts) and Montana (Deer Lodge, Bannock, Alder Gulch, and Last Chance Gulch districts) brought thousands to the outer reaches of Washington Territory.[21] The legislature responded to the increased population by creating five counties (Shoshone, Nez Perce, Idaho, Boise, and Missoula) and by appointing several justices of the peace, but local government under the auspices of Washington territorial officials had little effect on this area.[22] The distance from Montana to Olympia, the large population rush, independent mining associations, the notion that "the machinery of American territorial government in the mining regions worked gradually toward ordered processes of law,"[23] and the creation of Idaho Territory in 1863 and Montana Territory in 1864—all mitigated the power and potential influence of Washington Territory JPs over mining claim adjudications.[24]

The Washington territorial legislature granted wide civil jurisdictional latitudes to justices of the peace, but it also placed jurisdictional limits on JPs. In addition to federal prohibitions concerning cases questioning real property titles and containing debts or damages over $100, Washington JPs were prevented by the legislature from hearing actions for foreclosure of a mortgage or enforcement of a lien on *real* property. This activity was handled by district courts. Washington JP courts were also forbidden to sit on civil suits for false imprisonment, libel, slander, malicious prosecution, criminal conversation, or seduction. These cases were also taken directly to district courts. Moreover, no justice of the peace could listen to arguments in actions against executors or administrators of estates. Washington Territory probate courts had jurisdiction over these civil cases.[25]

Criminal Jurisdiction

Like civil jurisdiction, JP criminal jurisdiction was restricted to the county in which the JP was elected or appointed, and his authority was generally confined by the law to monetary and forms of action subject matter jurisdiction.

As a general rule, justices of the peace heard criminal cases in which a person was charged with the commission of a misdemeanor, a crime punishable by a fine of not more than $100 and/or a term of incarceration of not more than six months. However, this general rule was subject to specific change and exception throughout the territorial period. For instance, in 1854 the first criminal code gave JPs concurrent jurisdiction with district courts in all criminal cases for assaults and batteries, violations of estray laws, obstruction of highways and bridges, neglect of roads, charge of extra tolls at ferries and bridges, public indecency, possession of obscene books and pamphlets for exhibition, and criminal forcible entry and detainer and malicious trespass.

Conviction empowered the JP to fine the defendant up to $30.[26] In 1858, this provision was amended, allowing a fine not exceeding $100, and in 1861, JP criminal jurisdiction was extended to cover petit larceny and public nuisance crimes.[27] In 1875, all previous amendments to the criminal code were accepted, and JPs were given jurisdiction over all criminal cases coming under any city or town ordinance in which conviction would result in a fine not greater than $100, and over petit larceny cases as long as the offense was not punishable by imprisonment.[28]

In addition to the concurrent grant of misdemeanor subject matter jurisdiction to JPs, justices were granted original criminal jurisdiction for specific crimes. From 1854 to 1889, Washington Territory JPs had criminal jurisdiction over cases involving illegal salmon exporters, defective dike builders, graveyard vandals, Indian or Kanaka liquor suppliers, Sunday cockpit operators, JP fee overchargers, firemen evading jury duty, and vagrant fortune-tellers.

After 1856, any person who exported uninspected salmon or salmon that had been inspected and ordered destroyed was subject to an action before a JP and a fine not exceeding $100. One half of the fine was designated to go to the common schools, and the other half was to reward the informer to the action.

No person or corporation could construct or have constructed dikes, canals, or flumes over or across highways without permission from county commissioners. If permission was granted and the constructor built a dike, canal, or flume, he had to keep it in good repair. Failure to live up to this law meant possible prosecution and fine (not exceeding $100) before a Washington Territory justice of the peace.[29]

JPs protected the dead as well as the living. Any person who willfully and maliciously vandalized a graveyard was fined up to $100 by a JP or probate court judge.[30]

The regulation of trading with Indians was also thrust upon JP courts. In 1802, the first permanent Indian Intercourse Act was passed by Congress. Any U.S. citizen wishing to trade with Indians had to obtain a federal permit, and if a trader was caught bartering without it that person was subject to a fine of not over $100 and imprisonment of not longer than six months. Territorial jurisdiction over this act was placed in the "county courts"—justices of the peace.[31] In 1834, the Indian Intercourse Act was revised and amended, authorizing the assessments of fines up to $500 for selling liquor or illegal trade goods to Indians. Imprisonment was omitted, and specific territorial court enforcement was not mentioned in the act.[32] Although regulation of both the liquor trafficker and the commercial trader through the two acts was generally regarded as a failure[33] and "whiskey flowed as freely in the 1830's as it had in 1800,"[34] the Washington territorial legislature in 1855 passed a law whereby anyone selling or giving liquor to Indians within Washington Territory was deemed guilty of a misdemeanor and subject to a fine of not less than $25 or more than $500. A justice of the peace had jurisdiction if he felt the fine should be $100 or less; if he believed the alleged offense necessitated a greater fine, he bound the defendant over to the district court. All fines collected were to be turned over to the county treasury to support the common schools.[35] Three years later, this act was extended to cover Kanakas.[36] In 1857, responding to Indian-white hostilities, the legislature banned all trading and employment with "northern Indians." Any person violating this law could be fined not over $100 and imprisoned not over thirty days. JPs had jurisdiction in all cases, and any fines collected were similarly designated to support the common schools.[37]

Washington's justices of the peace also had the authority to hear cases involving blue laws and other justices' professional behavior. As seventeenth-century Puritans placed the responsibility for upholding community moral standards on their JPs, so Washington Territory society asked its justices to enforce certain rules of morality. JPs were to fine not less than $30 or more than $250 any person found guilty of running a cockpit or racetrack, opening a theater or saloon, or selling spirits or holding court on Sunday. The only judicial business allowed on Sunday was jury deliberations.[38] JPs could also fine other justices of the peace for violations of the fee schedule (up to $1,000) and failure to place the fee schedule in full view of litigants ($20 for every day that the fee schedule was not posted).[39]

Related to JP blue law and self-regulatory jurisdiction was JP criminal jurisdiction over refusals to serve jury duty. In particular, firemen could be exempted from jury duty, but if their claim was false, they had to go before a justice of the peace where they could be fined up to $100 for their evasion of community responsibility.[40]

The last instance of specific criminal jurisdiction for justices of the peace legislated during the territorial period came with "An Act Defining Vagrancy and Providing Remedy Against" in 1875. Under the act, a person committed the crime of vagrancy if he or she was a fortune-teller, a common prostitute, a keeper of a bawdy house, an habitual drunkard or gamester, a wanderer without any visible means of support, a collector of alms for charitable institutions under false pretenses, or a gambler betting in a street or public place. Sheriffs or constables were to arrest any alleged vagrant they saw, and take him or her to a JP for trial. If the defendant confessed or was found guilty of vagrancy, the justice could require a bond for good behavior from the defendant. If the bond was breached or unfulfilled, the vagrant received a jail sentence not exceeding six months.[41] Vagrancy laws have traditionally been open-ended, containing vague catchalls that could be successfully used to control behavior or abused to suppress dissent. The vagrancy law placing jurisdiction in Washington Territory's justices of the peace was no exception.

Criminal jurisdiction for justices of the peace varied according to statute. General rules governing their authority were rare; only in subject matter jurisdiction shared with the territory's district courts was there uniformity. Yet, the criminal jurisdiction of the justices of the peace was not narrowly drawn. Local order could easily be maintained by JPs within the legal boundaries established.

Procedures in Justice Court

Setting jurisdictional limitations for Washington Territory courts, and especially for justices of the peace, was a very important legislative power exercised by Congress and the Washington legislature. Determining civil and criminal authority for JPs influenced the general nature of the office and the community. Oftentimes the outcome of legal cases hinged primarily upon whether a particular court had jurisdiction to hear the case.

Once justice of the peace jurisdiction over a particular dispute was established, persons wishing to use a JP court quickly became cognizant of certain court procedures. The first step in instituting action was for an individual to file a complaint. A trial began in a civil JP court after a complaint had been filed by a potential plaintiff and notice of the complaint had been given to the defendant. Upon complaint to a JP that a criminal offense had been committed, the judge orally examined the complainant and any witnesses under oath. After the examination, the complaint was reduced to writing and a warrant was issued for the defendant's arrest. If the offense was one in which the district court had exclusive jurisdiction, then the JP issued an arrest warrant reciting the substance of the accusations, requiring the arresting officer to deliver the defendant to the next district court, and taking a recognizance (bail) from the defendant.[42]

The second step brought statements by the plaintiff and defendant (termed pleadings) as to the alleged action. In a civil case, pleadings were required before the evidence was presented. Pleadings had to be in writing if the action in court involved the foreclosure of mortgages and the enforcement of liens, forcible entry upon or unlawful detention of lands or tenements, or regaining possession of a mining claim. In all other civil actions, oral pleadings were sufficient. JPs were required to summarize oral pleadings in the court record. No particular form was necessary for either written or oral pleadings, and pleadings could be amended at any time subject to the justice's discretion. Criminal actions had similar requisites.[43] The informal nature of the regulations governing court proceedings indicated the legislature's recognition that the justice of the peace court had to adjust itself to the people in order to be effective and respected.

After pleadings had been read or heard by the judge, the plaintiff and defendant were given an opportunity to decide whether they wanted a jury trial. If either party requested a jury trial, the JP issued a venire, a document ordering the sheriff or constable to submit to the judge a list of qualified jurors and to notify the potential jurors. A jury trial in JP court required six jurors unless the parties to an action agreed to a lesser number.[44] The jurors had to be law-abiding, male, and unrelated to plaintiff or defendant.[45]

Two specific bills enacted by the Washington territorial legislature reflected problems with the jury system in JP courts. In 1862, the legislature moved to meet the problem of financing jury trials.

Plaintiffs were required to pay a $6 fee before a trial began. Once a verdict had been given by a jury, the losing party paid the fee (the plaintiff was reimbursed upon this payment). No fee was charged in criminal cases (where the territory was the plaintiff) and in civil actions of forcible entry and unlawful detainer. Eventually, the jury deposit was repealed by the 1877 legislature.[46]

During that same legislative session of 1877, the solons corrected an abuse of judges against jurors. No justice of the peace could deprive a retired jury of food for more than six hours at any one time. If a JP violated this act, he was deemed guilty of a misdemeanor and fined not less than $25 or more than $500. Justices could no longer legally starve juries into submission.[47]

Powers of JPs

Before and throughout a trial, a justice of the peace had certain delegated powers. Like the original justices of the peace, Washington Territory's JPs were charged with preserving the public peace. To achieve this end, they were given extensive means. If a justice saw a crime being committed, he could verbally order any person to arrest the offender. The arrested person could be detained for one hour without a complaint being filed; if the arrested person had threatened another person or property by speaking "hot and angry words," the arrestee could be summarily imprisoned for a term not exceeding three *months*. If the justice did not want to detain a potential disturber of the peace, he could require a security (a monetary sum) from the disturber by issuing an arrest warrant and holding a hearing. If the arrestee could not afford the set security or refused payment, the justice could sentence him or her to up to one year in jail; in order to appeal such a decision, a defendant had to pay the amount of the security. JPs could also order bail for a defendant, but they could not issue a writ of habeas corpus. Furthermore, if the justice of the peace thought he was privy to a riot, he had the power to seize personally and arrest any *potential* rioter; he could kill any actual rioter without fear of legal reprisal.[48] In short, justices of the peace in Washington Territory had been given extensive powers at the community level. Not only did they have the summary ability to incarcerate individuals who had committed a crime in their presence, but also they could imprison persons who had the potential to commit a crime. Indeed, local judiciaries had the power of "preventive detention" to deal with problems of law enforcement on the Washington Territory frontier.

To insure a fair and orderly trial, JPs could subpoena witnesses, take depositions, issue search warrants, and find persons in contempt of court. A justice of the peace issued subpoenas to compel the attendance of witnesses at his court if the witnesses were within twenty miles of the court. Subpoenas were served by any white person over eighteen years of age. If subpoenaed persons failed to appear in JP court, the judge could attach their property to force an appearance. Witnesses who found it inconvenient to come to court could offer testimony to the JP outside the court session. Such testimony was termed a deposition, and the Washington territorial legislature allowed depositions to be admitted as evidence in JP courts. If someone was hiding evidence or a justice of the peace suspected where evidence could be found, the JP issued a search warrant empowering his agent to enter any premises and obtain the evidence.[49]

The power to grant subpoenas, to take depositions, and to issue search warrants was available to justices of the peace before and during a trial, but the JP's strongest legal tool during a trial was the contempt power. This legal capacity separated the justice of the peace from his community neighbors. A person could be charged with contempt of JP court if he or she exhibited disorderly behavior during a trial, neglected to perform a judicial service, abused the judicial processes, refused to be sworn or answer as a witness, or, as a juror, improperly conversed with a party to the action or received communications from a party without immediate disclosure to the court. Punishment for being cited in contempt of JP court was a fine not exceeding $25 or a jail term not exceeding two days. Persons found in contempt were presumed guilty until they proved themselves innocent.[50]

Remedies in Justice Court

At the end of a judicial proceeding, a justice of the peace could choose from a variety of remedies to impose on the parties to an action. As previously stated, in criminal cases, JPs could fine and/or imprison a person usually up to $100 and/or six months. He could jail a defendant until the fine was paid. In civil cases, once a verdict had been reached, justices attached property or moneys, issued forms of replevin to return property to rightful owners, and ordered restitution of one party to another. In all cases, the execution of a judgment could be stayed by an order from justices of the peace. Such a stay was good for two months if the judgment was more than $25, and for one month if the judgment was $25 or less; all stays required sureties from the parties involved.[51]

A justice of the peace could alter decisions made in his court. He could issue an execution for fees and court costs against a prevailing party after execution on the losing party had been found wanting. Such a power served as a deterrent to unnecessary suits. If a JP did not think a decision made by a jury was fair, or if he felt the crime committed demanded a harsher punishment than he was statutorily capable of giving, he could turn over the case to the district court for a new trial.[52] Although this power was legal in its day, such an act reeks of double jeopardy. The Constitution expressly forbids any person being tried for the same act twice, but this prohibition was not extended to the states and territories until the twentieth century.

Miscellaneous Civil Authority

Thus far, powers vested in Washington Territory's justices of the peace have been discussed with reference to civil and criminal proceedings. JPs also had other delegated authority outside of a trial. Justices could preside over marriages, as could ministers, priests, Quaker meetings, and supreme court and probate judges. These ceremonial powers were restricted geographically to the county of the JP's election and racially to whites not marrying anyone one-fourth or more black or one-half or more Indian. Violation of the territory's miscegenation laws while such laws were in force meant a possible fine of $50 to $500 to a justice of the peace.[53]

JPs also certified bounties for killing wild animals, and appointed and removed guardians. In order to receive money for killing an animal, a person went to a justice of the peace with the scalp of an animal officially declared a nuisance by a county board of commissioners. The JP then issued a certificate payable by the county treasurer and destroyed the scalp. Justices of the peace also appointed guardians to defend the interests of minors and the feeble-minded. They had the power to remove a guardian on broad grounds. If the guardian neglected duties, exhibited fraudulent conduct, left the county, habitually drank, or did not act in the best interest of the ward, he or she lost the appointment.[54]

Judicial Duties

In addition to the wide discretionary powers granted Washington Territory's justices of the peace, they had certain duties to perform that were inherent to the office. Every JP was designated a court of record, and each was required to keep a docket which contained the titles of all actions commenced before him; the objective of the action; the date of a complaint or summons and the order for arrest of a defendant; the date of appearance of plaintiffs and defendants; a brief statement of the plaintiff's complaint and testimony in criminal cases; the demand for a jury trial; all names of jurors and witnesses; the results of the trial and execution of court orders; an appeal, if made; and "such other entries as may be material."[55]

The docket was not the only record required of JPs. Justices also had to submit written transcripts of all criminal trials to prosecuting attorneys. Any justice who committed persons to jail or issued bail was required to submit a copy of his rulings to the district court within ten days. If a justice of the peace neglected this duty, he was not entitled to collect his fees. On the first Monday in January and July, or when he left office, a JP turned over all fines and unclaimed fees to the county treasurer who recorded the source and amount of such moneys.[56] Executing these duties was an important function of the local judiciary, and they consumed a large portion of the official time required of a justice of the peace.

Appeals from Justice Courts

Once a trial was over and all JP powers and duties had been performed, the losing litigant could appeal the decision. Appeals from a justice of the peace court usually went to the territorial district court. Any person could appeal a JP decision in a civil case to district court on the basis of error in judgment or the proceedings. Appellees had twenty days to appeal after the judgment had been rendered, and they had to supply a bond double the amount of costs and judgment. The minimum amount of an appeal bond was $100 with one or more sureties; if a person appealed an action of forcible entry, unlawful detainer, or possession of a mining claim, the bond needed at least two sureties. In addition, in 1881 justices of the peace were given veto power over appeals from their own courts; appeal bonds were made subject to JP approval.[57] Thus, appealing a case from a JP court was a difficult process, particularly for persons with limited assets.

Any defendants convicted in a criminal case before a justice of the peace could appeal to a district court before 1857 and after 1873. Criminal appellees had ten days to appeal to the district court of the same county of conviction, and they had to supply sureties and bonds set by the JP guaranteeing court appearance, court obeyance, and good behavior. The criminal appeal bond corresponded in many ways to bail. In 1857, all criminal appeals were channeled through a special intermediate county court. Although this special court was abolished in 1859, the appellate provision was not altered until 1873, which suggests an oversight by codifiers and a lack of criminal appeals from JP courts.[58]

* * * *

Clearly, the Washington Territory Organic Act, and especially the Washington territorial legislature, created a lower court with considerable jurisdiction, powers, and duties. Justices of the peace in Washington Territory were able to handle any number of local problems. They were granted the means to maintain community order, and some of the powers were in fact broad enough to enable a justice of the peace to influence frontier community behavior. In addition, the difficulty of appealing a justice court ruling made the decisions of the local judiciary even more significant. As the initial portion of this manual for JPs implies, being a justice of the peace meant assuming a legal position of some importance and considerable complexity.

6

Special Courts

Throughout their history, justices of the peace have been given special assignments to handle problems that did not seem to belong in the jurisdiction of other courts. As early as 1351, JPs were specifically charged with enforcing and hearing all cases arising out of a special act, the Statute of Laborers. Assigning JPs special authority was also attempted in Washington Territory. In addition to the civil and criminal jurisdiction available to regular justices of the peace, JPs served in three special court capacities during Washington's territorial period. One court, an experimental judiciary composed of JPs and probate judges, lasted only two years; a second special court, consisting of justices of the peace only, would endure until Washington achieved statehood; and a third court, staffed by local justices and a variety of other persons, evolved into a complex, permanent urban justice system.[1]

Intermediate County Courts

Washington Territory JPs and probate judges sat as an unusual intermediate county court from 1857 to 1859. This court was the territorial legislature's response to the federal government's budgetary cuts in territorial judicial expenses.[2] In August 1856, Congress passed "An Act to Amend the Acts regulating the Fees, Costs, and other Judicial Expenses of the Government in the States, Territories, and District of Columbia, and for other Purposes." Section five of this act stated:

And be it further enacted, That the judges of the supreme court in each of the territories, or a majority of them shall, when assembled at their respective seats of government, fix and appoint the several times and places of holding the several courts in their respective districts, and limit the duration of the terms thereof: Provided, *That the said courts shall not be held at more than three places in any one territory*: And provided, further, that the judge or judges holding such courts shall adjourn the same without delay, at any time before the expiration of such terms whenever in his or their opinion the further continuance thereof is not necessary.[3]

This statute severely curtailed the circuit travel of the upper judiciary, thereby making the use of the courts more difficult and more expensive for territorial residents. In a geographically large territory such as Washington, this judicial restriction forced hardships upon citizens who wished to use the courts, especially those persons residing east of the Cascade Mountains.

To remedy this inequity, the Washington territorial legislature devised a novel judicial system which has had no parallel in American legal history.[4] In 1857, the legislature passed a bill creating an intermediate county court. This court was composed of one probate judge and two justices of the peace chosen by the probate judge, all residing in the same county. If the county only had one JP, he was automatically a member of the special court; but if the one JP and probate judge ever disagreed, the probate judge's opinion prevailed. The county court met if a quorum of one JP and the probate judge was present, and the county auditor served as the court's ex-officio clerk.[5]

The intermediate county court had both civil and criminal original jurisdiction. The court had civil jurisdiction concurrent with the district court in cases that involved no more than $500. JPs could not participate in court voting on a civil case. The court exercised criminal jurisdiction over all defendants charged with a misdemeanor. The court also possessed both civil and criminal appellate jurisdiction, hearing all appeals from justice of the peace courts. Appeals from the intermediate county court went directly to the district court, but only if the case had resulted in a fine of over $100 and a jail sentence of over sixty days.[6] Thus, the appellate provisions for the county court effectively prevented cases that had originated in the justice of the peace court from ever reaching the district or supreme courts of the territory. It also guaranteed a potential conflict of interest for any appeal of a criminal case from a JP court to the intermediate county court. A justice of the peace on the intermediate county court could hear on appeal a case tried before him previously, and the county court's decision was the final adjudication. This situation was similar to the statutory imperfection whereby district court judges collectively forming the territorial supreme court sat over cases appealed from their own district courts.[7]

The intermediate court functioned for only two years. In 1859, the Washington territorial legislature repealed the law providing for the civil and criminal jurisdiction conferred on the special court.[8] One reason for this action was the modification by Congress of its law of 1856. In June 1858, Congress authorized territorial supreme court justices to go on circuit if court business did not involve the federal government and if the territory wanted to pay for the costs of the circuit outside of the three designated district court sites.[9] The Washington legislature quickly took advantage of this provision by ordering the district court to meet at Steilacoom in addition to the designated court sites of Vancouver, Olympia, and Port Townsend.[10] However, the new federal law did not alleviate the problems caused by the act of 1856; the territory did not have enough funds to subsidize extensive district court circuit-riding. In 1858, the territorial legislature memorialized Congress protesting the act of 1856, and in 1862, it urged Congress to allocate Washington Territory two additional district justices in order to overcome the judicial restrictions of the act of 1856.[11]

A more likely reason for the repeal of the intermediate county court in the face of judicial need was politics. On Monday, December 20, 1858, John D. Biles, an upstart, young Democrat Representative from Vancouver, introduced a bill into the territorial House increasing the civil jurisdiction of the intermediate county court.[12] The bill was referred to the House Judiciary Committee chaired by Biles where it was favorably received and reported out of committee to the House. On January 5, 1859, the House passed the Biles bill,[13] and the next day the territorial Council received the bill and referred it to the Council Judiciary Committee chaired by General Hamilton J.G. Maxon, an old, established Democrat also from Vancouver.[14] Three days after receipt of the Biles bill, Maxon announced that the Judiciary Committee recommended indefinite postponement. The Council rejected this recommendation, but upon motion by Maxon, the bill was reassigned to the Committee on Indian Affairs chaired by Maxon's friend and fellow Democrat, James W. Wiley.[15] On January 17, Wiley urged indefinite postponement, and the next day the Council accepted this recommendation, thereby killing the Biles bill.[16]

Representative Biles was upset. He had not anticipated negative Council reaction to a bill designed to help alleviate the growing court congestion and the complaints of territorial residents. He viewed Maxon's act as one inspired by purely political motivations. The day after his bill was killed in the Council, Biles decided to force Maxon's hand by introducing a bill in the House that would *repeal* all civil jurisdiction of the intermediate county court.[17] This bill, House Bill 46, was assigned to Biles' Judiciary Committee where it was changed to repeal all criminal jurisdiction instead of civil jurisdiction in order to affect both JPs and probate judges on the intermediate county court. On January 24, House Bill 46 was approved by the House, 16-10.[18] The next day, the new Biles bill was received by the Council and again it was sent to Maxon's Judiciary Committee. On January 26, Maxon placed the bill before the Council, and he amended the bill to repeal *both* criminal and civil jurisdiction for the county court.[19] The Maxon amended bill passed the Council and was accepted by the House on January 28, 1859. It thereby abolished the special court, and conferred expanded jurisdiction upon Washington Territory JPs.[20]

The real issue behind the abolition of the new court was Isaac I. Stevens. The former territorial governor was serving as delegate to Congress from Washington Territory, having been elected in 1857, and his opponents were rapidly growing in the territory. General Maxon had long been a political crony of Stevens. He had commanded a battalion for Stevens during the Indian wars on Puget Sound, and it was Maxon who told Stevens that Hudson's Bay Company employees were aiding and abetting the Sound tribes.[21] Stevens responded to Maxon's information by ordering all Hudson's Bay Company former agents to Fort Steilacoom, and after their defiance, he declared martial law in the territory. Maxon was Stevens' Democrat anchorman in Clark County and on the territorial Council.

Conversely, Representative Biles was not in the Stevens political camp. Although Biles was a Democrat, Maxon and Stevens excluded him from Clark County Democrat strategy sessions. Biles was a member of a growing faction of anti-Stevens Democrats.[22] Moreover, Biles and Maxon despised each other. At the conclusion of the sixth session of the territorial legislature in 1859, young Biles confronted General Maxon. The *Olympia Pioneer and Democrat* recorded the "main event":

On Monday evening last, a slight altercation took place between the Hon. H. J. G. Maxon, member of the Council from Clark County, and John D. Biles, member of the House from same county, growing out of the lavish use of the word *liar*, applied by the latter towards the former while engaged in conversation. The result was that the lower house discovered its inability to cope with the upper. No other injury resulted to Mr. B. than was sustained by his clothes, which became *sullied* and torn during the conflict. Had it not been for the interference of bystanders the result might possibly have been more serious.[23]

Within this political context, the special JP court was abolished. Even though Washington Territory's judicial problems caused by the act of 1856 had not been resolved, JPs would never again be allowed concurrent jurisdiction with district courts. In 1863, the legislature would restore $500 civil jurisdiction and concurrent criminal jurisdiction to probate courts only,[24] but Washington Territory justices of the peace had to be content with their regular jurisdictional requirements and duties for the remainder of the territorial period.

Contested Elections Court

Another special court composed entirely of justices of the peace lasted from its creation in 1866 until Washington became a state in 1889. This court was the contested elections court. To protect territorial elections from irregularities and fraud, the Washington territorial legislature provided a procedure to challenge the validity of an election. Within twenty days after an election, any qualified voter could file a statement with the district court clerk challenging the legality of the election. Upon receipt of this statement, the clerk issued a commission to convene a special contested elections court consisting of two justices of the peace of the contestant's district. This court retained the powers of JPs and was charged with investigating the complaint and writing a report. Once the report was completed, it was given to the clerk who presented it to a special session of the territorial House which was called by the territorial secretary to sit as judges over the contested election. The role of JPs in this special court was primarily investigative; the justices were not allowed to make decisions, although their report conceivably influenced any vote of the House.[25]

The Urban JP

The two special JP courts formed by the Washington territorial legislature exercised powers and jurisdictions distinct from regular justices of the peace. Judges for an appellate court and for an election inquiry were unusual activities of Washington's JPs. However, the third and most significant special court, the urban justice of the peace court, evolved directly from the regular JP. It developed into a justice court that adopted and expanded regular justice of the peace functions.

Rivalries and confusion over the administration and enforcement of law in urban areas has been a constant theme in American legal history. Such confusion was particularly evident in the history of justices of the peace during their adaptation to urban frontier areas in Washington Territory. As Washington towns and cities developed, their urban dwellers demanded and received the authority to deal with local urban problems from within an urban governmental framework. The Washington territorial legislature granted charters of incorporation to various cities and towns which provided for urban executive branches (mayors), legislative branches (councils), and judicial branches (justices of the peace) of government.

Washington citizens saw a need for this special government, and in particular for special urban JPs. Territorial settlements required special local laws to deal with specific urban problems, such as street maintenance or vagrancy statutes that were not provided by rural county commissioners. Once special ordinances were enacted, local adjudication of the laws was desirable. Many ordinances would fall within the normal jurisdiction of the justice of the peace but some would not. Practicality necessitated a judicial officer for cities and towns that could hear all possible cases involving violations of local ordinances.

Washington territorial statutes initially provided that a justice of the peace could be chosen every year by the people of each election precinct in each organized county.[26] Sometimes two JPs per precinct could be elected if so authorized by the board of county commissioners.[27] However, this arrangement treated rural and urban areas alike, thereby inducing tensions within the system. For example, according to the 1870 U.S. census, Seattle's population was 1,107.[28] It constituted one voting precinct along with the surrounding rural area of King County. One justice of the peace was elected in this precinct, but he could not concentrate only on Seattle's problems. During the 1870s, Seattle tripled in size.[29] In spite of a national depression, Seattle's economy was expanding, and it continued to attract people. The lumber industry was growing, and coal was being mined in rural King County. During this decade, the city experienced a variety of problems, especially criminal activity which was commonplace in a society composed mainly of transient male laborers.[30] During the next decade, Seattle experienced a further rise in population until, by 1890, 42,837 persons were residing in the city.[31] Such a huge population growth in so short a time put a heavy strain on the local judicial system.

Charters of incorporation of Seattle were issued by the Washington territorial legislature in 1865 (repealed in 1867), 1869, 1875, 1877, 1883, and 1886.[32] Each charter contained provisions for a special urban justice of the peace, with exclusive jurisdiction over Seattle ordinances as well as the ordinary jurisdiction of a justice of the peace. By 1886, there was too much business for one urban JP, so the city's new incorporation charter authorized all King County justices to have exclusive jurisdiction over Seattle ordinances.[33] This did not provide a complete answer to the law and order problems of cities like Seattle, but it was a step toward a more efficient and responsive local judiciary.

Like Seattle, several urban areas requested and received incorporation status which included a special urban justice of the peace. In 1888, incorporated cities were officially designated one election precinct by the Washington territorial legislature, and these precincts were entitled to two urban JPs.[34] Throughout the territorial period, twenty-nine cities and towns were incorporated.[35] Of the twenty-nine, several lost their special status during the territorial era. One town merged with an existing county seat, thereby losing its special judicial officer; New Tacoma became Tacoma.[36] In addition, Ainsworth and La Conner were both incorporated and unincorporated during the 1880s, and Lewiston was legislated out of Washington Territory in 1863.[37] Consequently, at the end of the territorial period, twenty-five separate local judicial systems were functioning.

Complexity and diversity characterized the institutional development of urban JPs in Washington Territory. Several different types of urban justices of the peace were created by the legislature; these justices were called a variety of names, were selected by numerous devices, and performed different functions.

The Washington territorial legislature used two general classifications for incorporated urban areas: *town* and *city*. The town classification was used sparingly; Olympia (1859, 1869, 1871, and 1873), Seattle (1865), Tumwater (1869, 1883, and 1886), Port Townsend (1873), and Centralia (1886) were the only incorporated settlements to have a town charter.[38] Of these towns, Olympia (1877), Seattle (1869), and Port Townsend (1881) were eventually reclassified as cities.[39] Town status generally meant that a special judicial official called a *committing magistrate* was created. In the first town charter, the government of the town of Olympia was to be a five-man board of trustees elected to one-year terms. They were to select a justice of the peace in Thurston County to be the committing magistrate. The committing magistrate had the power to hear complaints of violations of town laws and to examine all persons arrested by the town marshal. When acting as committing magistrate, the Olympia judicial official did not have the jurisdiction or fee schedule of a justice of the peace.[40] In 1863, an amendment to the Olympia town charter prohibited the appointment of a committing magistrate by the board of trustees and required the judicial officer to be elected.[41] This revision was further amplified in 1873. Olympians could elect two justices of the peace to be committing magistrates, and these men had to be qualified town voters. The committing magistrates were still forbidden to hold the jurisdiction of a justice of the peace, but they could now charge fees according to JP fee schedules.[42]

The 1859 Olympia judicial system was extended to Seattle, Port Townsend, and Centralia, and a Tumwater charter also was modeled after the Olympia town charter with one important exception.[43] In 1869, Tumwater was incorporated, and the power to legislate local laws was given to a board of trustees. This board of trustees also had the power to appoint a committing magistrate who could hear complaints of violations of town ordinances and could examine all persons arrested by the marshal. However, since no justice of the peace resided in Tumwater, the board of trustees was restricted by law to appoint one of themselves as committing magistrate.[44] Thus, in Tumwater the urban JP took on the functions of legislator and interpreter of all local law. This system was amended in 1883 when Tumwater trustees were forced by law to choose a local justice of the peace as a committing magistrate. Nonetheless, the concept of appointing a member of the governing board of an urban incorporation as a local judicial official would continue in Washington Territory.[45]

There were three means by which the committing magistrate could be selected. First, and most common, the committing magistrate was appointed by the board of trustees from among local justices of the peace. Selection was based upon an indirect democratic exercise. This committing magistrate had two general functions: to hear cases involving violations of ordinances and to examine all persons arrested locally. He could not exercise justice of the peace jurisdiction nor charge justice of the peace court costs. Second, the committing magistrate was elected directly by the people. He had to be a justice of the peace prior to his election, and he had to be a qualified town precinct voter. This committing magistrate had the same functions as the first magistrate, but he could charge justice of the peace fees. Third, the committing magistrate was chosen by the board of trustees from among themselves, and he, too, could not exercise the jurisdictional and monetary powers of a JP.

City charters, like town charters, provided for the office of the committing magistrate in the cases of Olympia (1881), Port Townsend (1860, 1868), New Tacoma (1881), Tacoma (1886), and Cheney (1883).[46] In addition to provisions for committing magistrates, city charters also provided for five other kinds of special urban judicial officials: recorder, judicial officer, police justice, justice of the peace of the city, and blanket JPs.

The *recorder* was a common urban judicial office in the first city charters issued by the Washington territorial legislature, and it may have been borrowed from Oregon Territory incorporation acts. During the short period Washington was part of Oregon Territory (1848-1853), two incorporation charters were issued by the Oregon territorial legislature: to Oregon City (1851) and to Portland (1851). The Oregon City charter authorized the annual election of a city council to be composed of a mayor, a recorder, and five councilmen. This seven-man body had the power to legislate local laws. To adjudicate those laws, a mayor's court was created by the Oregon territorial legislature to be the "conservator of the peace." This judicial official could exercise all the jurisdictions, powers, and fee scheduling of a justice of the peace. The recorder was to keep the minutes of all council meetings, and he was to preside in the mayor's absence over council and court.[47]

The first city charter issued by the Washington territorial legislature, the Steilacoom charter, provided for the recorder's court, but the recorder was not simply a substitute judge in a mayor's court. He was elected to a one-year term. His specific duties were to hear all cases concerning offenses of city ordinances and offenses committed within city limits. He had the same powers and jurisdiction of a justice of the peace. To qualify for office, the recorder had to live in the city ten days after his election, and he could not be absent from the city longer than thirty days. Appeals from his special court were not authorized by the Steilacoom charter, and if a vacancy occurred, the city council could appoint anyone as recorder to serve until a special election was held. This type of recorder's court appeared in the charters of Steilacoom (1854, 1873), Vancouver (1857), and Lewiston (1863).[48]

The original Washington Territory recorder court existed in a modified form in the city charters to Vancouver (1858, 1865, 1868), Seattle (1869), Walla Walla (1873), Goldendale (1879), Waitsburg (1881), La Conner (1883), and Kalama (1871).[49] The recorder court remained an elective office (except for Kalama), but its functions were more clearly outlined. The recorder "shall be *ex-officio* a justice of the peace."[50] Appeals like those from JP courts went to the district court, and if a recorder office was vacant, the council was to designate a local justice of the peace to perform the duties of a recorder until the next election.[51]

The recorder as an ex-officio JP also took on other duties. In Goldendale, the recorder was to be an ex-officio assessor and an ex-officio clerk of the city council as well as an ex-officio justice of the peace.[52] The duties of a recorder were also decreased on occasion. In La Conner, the recorder was prohibited from exercising JP jurisdiction, although he could charge JP fees; in Kalama, the recorder not only was restricted to hearing only those cases involving local ordinance violations, but he also was subject to yearly appointment by the city council (like a committing magistrate).[53]

Thus, the recorder court developed out of a mayor's court. It took a variety of forms, but basically the recorder was a special justice of the peace with expanded jurisdiction. In most recorder courts, the justice was elected directly by the people, and he could hear all cases dealing with local infractions. The recorder was authorized to be an important judicial official in Washington Territory's incorporated cities.

Washington Territory city charters also provided for what was termed a *judicial officer*. This special type of urban justice of the peace was used in only four cities: Seattle (1875), Tacoma (1875), Port Townsend (1881), and Pomeroy (1886). In two of the four, Seattle and Tacoma, other forms of local judicial officials were created before Washington gained statehood.[54]

The judicial officer differed from the recorder and the committing magistrate in several ways. Unlike most recorders, the judicial officer was always an appointive position. In Seattle and Tacoma the council or board of trustees was authorized to appoint a judicial officer for the city; in Port Townsend and Pomeroy, the mayor could appoint a judicial officer, and he would serve with the concurrence of the local legislative governing body.[55] Unlike the committing magistrate, the judicial officer had to be a justice of the peace before appointment, and he retained all JP powers, fees, and jurisdictions. Appeals from the judicial officer's court went to district court.[56]

Thus, the distinction made by the Washington territorial legislature in creating the judicial officer was in the selection process and retention of JP powers. The judicial officer consolidated the normal functions of a justice of the peace in the office of urban JP.

A type of judiciary similar to the judicial officer was found in Seattle in 1886. The amended city charter of Seattle provided for a *police justice* who had exclusive original jurisdiction over all violations of city ordinances. All King County justices of the peace maintaining a residence in Seattle were deemed police justices. Each police justice, in order to hear Seattle cases, had to post a $500 bond to the city treasurer.[57]

The police justice was formulated for use in only two other charters, Seattle (1883) and Spokane Falls (1886); in these charters, his powers were not distributed to a "multitude" of JPs. The earlier Seattle charter provided for the appointment of a police justice from among local justices of the peace. He was to have a limited jurisdiction confined to violations of city ordinances. This form of police justice was similar to the town committing magistrate. The Spokane Falls police justice was selected in a similar fashion, but he maintained both special urban JP and normal JP jurisdictions.[58]

Whereas the judicial officer and police justice functioned in only five cities, the special urban justice of the peace most prominent at the end of the territorial period was the *justice of the peace of the city* (the JPC). Thirteen charters issued during the 1880s provided for the JPC: Colfax (1881), Spokane Falls (1881), Goldendale (1881, 1886), Ellensburgh (1883), Ainsworth (1883), Montesano (1883, 1886), Sprague (1883), Vancouver (1883), Yakima (1883), North Yakima (1886), and Walla Walla (1886).[59]

There were three variations of the JPC. One type was implemented in Colfax, Goldendale, and Spokane Falls. There, the JPC was appointed by the common council, and he had to be a local justice of the peace. He was designated ex-officio assessor, ex-officio clerk of the common council, and ex-officio justice of the peace. This type of justice of the peace of the city was similar to the recorder's court tried by some cities in the early part of the territorial period.[60]

A second type of JPC was provided for Ainsworth, Ellensburgh, Montesano, Sprague, Vancouver, and Yakima. The functions of this officer were restricted to hearing cases concerned with local ordinance violations and normal justice of the peace jurisdiction. In Vancouver, the justice had to supply a $1,000 bond, with two or more sureties approved by the mayor, in order to be appointed by the common council, but in Yakima no bond was required. However, all JPCs of this type had to be justices of the peace before their selection.[61]

The last type of JPC was found in the charters of only Montesano, North Yakima, and Walla Walla. These were the last city charters issued by the Washington territorial legislature. The functions of these judicial officials were similar to those of the JPC of Vancouver (1883), but the selection process differed. The justices of Montesano, North Yakima, and Walla Walla were elected by the people, their only requirement for office being that they had to be a justice of the peace in Washington Territory.[62] The office of justice of the peace of the city, whose selection and function were evolving toward that of the recorder's court, would become the major special urban justice of the peace for most of Washington's cities after statehood.

One last form of special urban justice of the peace was unlike any other previously mentioned. Seven charters did not specify the appointment or election of a particular judicial official. Such cities as Walla Walla (1875), Olympia (1877, 1883), Snohomish (1883), Whatcom (1883), Ellensburgh (1886), and Waitsburg (1886) were authorized to make ordinances whose violation came before any justice of the peace who resided within city limits.[63] The *blanket justice of the peace* provision in certain city charters allowed these cities the flexibility of having local judicial services without undue restriction.

Washington Territory's special urban justices of the peace clearly performed a variety of functions, and the office took several forms, as shown in Table 5. Most of the urban justices were assigned to hear cases involving violations of ordinances and to examine persons arrested by the city or town marshal, in addition to normal JP functions. Some, such as certain recorders and JPCs, were also ex-officio assessors and clerks, while others, such as town committing magistrates, exercised no justice of the peace functions. A gradual uniformity of function was taking place in urban justices of the peace; what began as a separate urban judicial entity eventually became a justice of the peace with certain extra duties to perform.[64]

Table 5

**Functions of Urban Justices of the Peace:
Washington Territory, 1853-1889**

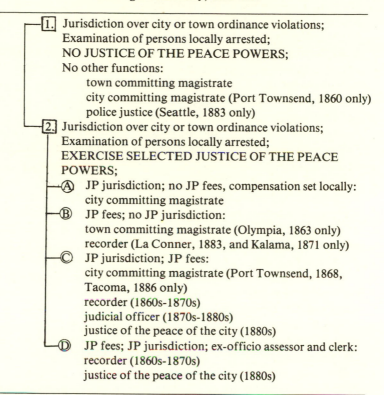

1. Jurisdiction over city or town ordinance violations;
   Examination of persons locally arrested;
   NO JUSTICE OF THE PEACE POWERS;
   No other functions:
       town committing magistrate
       city committing magistrate (Port Townsend, 1860 only)
       police justice (Seattle, 1883 only)

2. Jurisdiction over city or town ordinance violations;
   Examination of persons locally arrested;
   EXERCISE SELECTED JUSTICE OF THE PEACE POWERS;

  Ⓐ JP jurisdiction; no JP fees, compensation set locally:
       city committing magistrate

  Ⓑ JP fees; no JP jurisdiction:
       town committing magistrate (Olympia, 1863 only)
       recorder (La Conner, 1883, and Kalama, 1871 only)

  Ⓒ JP jurisdiction; JP fees:
       city committing magistrate (Port Townsend, 1868,
       Tacoma, 1886 only)
       recorder (1860s-1870s)
       judicial officer (1870s-1880s)
       justice of the peace of the city (1880s)

  Ⓓ JP fees; JP jurisdiction; ex-officio assessor and clerk:
       recorder (1860s-1870s)
       justice of the peace of the city (1880s)

Simplifying the Urban Special Courts

The complexities surrounding urban justices have thus far been narrowed to a discussion of some seven distinguishable local judiciaries. The Washington territorial legislature attempted to simplify and standardize further the incorporation charters of both towns and cities through two acts of general legislation. In 1871, the legislature passed "An Act to Provide for the Incorporation of Towns." This act conferred the status of "town" upon any settlement whose population did not exceed 150 persons. Government for all towns was placed in a five-man board of trustees elected annually by town residents. The board of trustees had the power to make ordinances and to appoint a town recorder as the town's judiciary. The recorder would have jurisdiction over all violations of town ordinances as well as normal justice of the peace jurisdiction; no prior qualifications were necessary in order to become a recorder.[65]

At best, this act was a curious blend of previous town and city charter provisions for committing magistrates and recorders. Committing magistrates were usually required to be justices of the peace, and recorders usually performed functions other than judicial ones, and they were elected.

Only two towns were incorporated under this statute: Olympia (1871, 1873) and Port Townsend (1873).[66] Neither settlement qualified to be incorporated as a town. The 1870 U.S. census put Olympia's population at 1,203 and Port Townsend's at 593.[67] In addition, neither town charter resembled the standardized charter. Port Townsend was governed by a three-man, and not a five-man, board of trustees. The board was authorized to appoint a committing magistrate who could hear only those cases concerning violations of town ordinances, and not all cases under regular JP jurisdiction. Olympia in 1873 was sanctioned by its charter to elect (not appoint) two (not one) committing magistrates. Thus, in practice the attempt to standardize town charters was a failure.[68]

The Washington territorial legislature also tried to make all city charters uniform. In 1877, it approved "An Act to Provide for Incorporation of Cities." Each city could elect a seven-man common council every two years, and a mayor and a JPC annually. The JPC had to be a justice of the peace prior to his election, and he had to supply a bond, the amount to be determined by the council, in order to take office. Jurisdictionally, the justice of the peace of the city retained all normal JP powers, and he heard all cases concerning local ordinance infractions.[69]

Ten city charters were issued under this act: Olympia (1877, 1881), Seattle (1877), Goldendale (1879, 1881), Walla Walla (1879), Dayton (1881), Port Townsend (1881), Spokane Falls (1881), and Waitsburg (1881). Of these ten, only two charters (Seattle and Walla Walla) included verbatim the general provisions established for incorporated cities. Deviations from the act occurred in all other charters.[70]

The Wingard Opinion

It was obvious that the legislature was not following its own laws on incorporation. No town incorporations conformed to the specific language of the 1871 Town Act, and only two out of ten city charters matched the provisions of the 1877 City Act. Were these deviating incorporation charters legal? This question was answered in the Third District Court of Washington Territory in 1881. In a sweeping decision, Judge Samuel C. Wingard, associate justice of the Washington territorial supreme court, voided all city and town charters except those of Seattle and Walla Walla. Judge Wingard held that a general law passed by a legislature superseded a local law; therefore, any local law (i.e., town and city charters) that was inconsistent with general law was invalid. The effect of the Wingard opinion would have been catastrophic: the territory's urban centers would have been left without government and law. The legislature, which was then in session, immediately repealed the town and city general incorporation laws, and in the repeal, all charters previously issued were renewed.[71]

The confusing judicial labyrinth of urban justices of the peace continued to be built. After 1881, thirty-one more incorporation charters were created or revised, and within these charters were all of the previously discussed varieties of urban judiciaries. In fact, the proliferation of urban judicial systems throughout the territorial period was so great that some city and town charters were completely altered during almost every legislative session. Olympia experienced eight different charters, Seattle went through seven changes in urban judicial officials, and Vancouver and Walla Walla each endured six separate incorporations. Such a changing judicial network was likely to confuse not only the residents of individual urban areas, but all components in the legal system as well. The need for special urban justices of the peace in Washington Territory had been satisfied, but the statutes passed by the territorial legislature provided urban residents with a very complex set of local judiciaries.

* * * *

Three special justice courts, then, were created by the Washington territorial legislature—the intermediate county court, the contested elections court, and the urban justice court. All provided judicial services for residents on the Washington frontier that were not furnished by regular justices of the peace. Each judiciary arose to meet a particular problem: the lack of federal moneys to cover judicial expenses, the need to provide a mechanism for deciding contested elections, and the deficiency inherent within a system whereby regular justices tried unsuccessfully to grapple with urban disputes. Justices of the peace, dispatched with a variety of new jurisdictions and unusual powers, were authorized to help alleviate these problems. They in turn developed into separate and distinct special JP courts for Washington Territory.

7

The Cost of Going
to Justice Court

The cost of going to justice of the peace courts on the American frontier affected a variety of people. Plaintiffs and defendants had a natural interest in local court fees as costs determined whether they went to JP court or settled their disputes among themselves. Witnesses and jurors sometimes benefited by local court actions. They were paid by the territory or by parties to the court action for their participation in the legal process. The judge had a direct concern with court costs, for fees charged in the disposition of his office were a major source of income. Thus, court costs were an important consideration in local justice for new settlements.

As fee systems began to be applied to justice courts in the new American communities, JPs and their constituents soon realized that the costs of local court services would not please everyone. Charles Woodmason, Anglican priest and justice of the peace in colonial South Carolina's backcountry, sermonized his disdain for the fee system set up for JPs:

The granting of fees [to] Magistrates was originally well intended, and design'd for Encouragement and Maintenance of sensible Men for, and In, the Administration of Justice. At that Time, few persons were in the Commission. But what was thus plann'd for a Public Benefit, is now most sadly perverted and will hardly admitt of a Remedy, till all Fees are taken away.[1]

Indeed, the problem of adequate compensation for local justices could not be resolved. If the cost of justice was too high, the people felt oppressed, and if the fees set were too low, the people would abuse their legal system. Woodmason continued:

I knew a Magistrate that would take no fee on Administration of a simple Oath, in the Course of Pleading or to any Account for Conscience sake—as he thought the Name of God was thereby profan'd. And yet he afterward was obliged to go on in the beaten Track—as they crowded to him from all Parts, and he thereby brought the whole Weight of Business on himself; and so would it be with any Gentleman who would go about to serve the Country Gratis. Therefore as Matters now stand; the most worthy Magistrates must swim with the stream—Or else use their endeavors with the Legislature, that Gentlemen serve the Public for Honour and not for Profit.[2]

The magistrates in frontier South Carolina and elsewhere turned to legislators for recourse. The legislature set the fee schedules used by JPs, and justices continually petitioned for higher compensation.

Justice Court Fees

In Washington Territory, the legislature set the fees for justices of the peace, witnesses at court, and petit jurors. These fees formed the basic costs of going to justice of the peace court. All fees were regulated by law, and their schedules were the subject of considerable legislative interest. On eleven occasions, the Washington territorial legislature felt it necessary to determine what a justice of the peace could charge.[3]

Before justice of the peace fees were set by the legislature, Washington's JPs depended on fee schedules provided by the Oregon territorial legislature. Upon observation of the justice of the peace fee schedules for Oregon Territory in 1851 and 1853, it becomes apparent that fees were increasing. In all categories, a JP could charge the same price or more in 1853 than in 1851. This trend of rising costs continued with the first Washington Territory fee schedule. The 1854 Washington territorial legislature was not content to accept the fee schedule already in force; instead, it increased the amount chargeable in over one-half of the categories on the justice of the peace fee schedule. The price of a marriage ceremony had gone up 33⅓ percent; charges for a search warrant increased 50 percent; and the cost of rendering a judgment on the basis of a confession or default was up 200 percent from the 1851 fee schedule (see Table 6).[4]

This inflationary trend lasted only ten years. In 1861, perhaps responding to a large migration to the territory which increased the amount of judicial business, the Washington territorial legislature reduced justice of the peace fees in most categories. No increases were written into the law, and only in issuing a summons and in committing a person to jail did fees remain constant. Many fees were returned to 1851 Oregon Territory rates.[5]

In 1862, the legislature drastically altered the 1861 fee schedule. Fees in sixteen of the seventeen categories were increased. For example, the cost of entering a judgment on the basis of a trial went from $0.75 to $1.50; the charge for attending the opening of the polls for an election rose from $3.00 to $6.00; and the fee for issuing a writ of restitution increased from $0.25 to $1.00. The 1862 fee schedule greatly increased the cost of local justice for the territory's citizens (Table 6).[6]

The next six justice of the peace fee schedules enacted by the legislature were special laws which only applied to JPs in certain geographical areas. Three of the six special fee schedules applied only to Walla Walla County.[7] The 1862 Walla Walla fee schedule for JPs was very similar to the 1862 territorial JP fee schedule. All fee categories were the same except for the amount charged for entering a judgment on the basis of a confession or default. In Walla Walla County, this JP activity cost $0.75 per judgment; the rest of Washington Territory's justices of the peace could charge $1.00.[8] Walla Walla County's fee schedule for 1865 was much different from its 1862 counterpart. In every category except attendance at the opening of the polls for an election, rates were substantially increased. In addition, four new categories were now subject to fees. Of particular significance was the minimum floor placed on the amount due for any trial. Walla Walla County JPs received a minimum of $3.00 per trial. This category would be peculiar to Walla Walla County JP fee schedules.[9] The last special justice of the peace fee schedule for Walla Walla County was set in 1868, and it generally returned to 1862 rates or lower. The fee for issuing a summons was reduced from $2.00 to $1.00; the charge for taking an affidavit, from $1.50 to $0.75; and the cost of approving a bond, from $0.50 to $0.25 (Table 6).[10] The inflationary trend of JP fees in Walla Walla County was halted in 1868, as it would be for the entire Washington Territory in 1869.

Table 6

Justice of the Peace Fee Schedules for Oregon Territory (1851, 1853), Washington Territory (1854, 1861, 1862), and Special Counties (1862, 1863, 1865, 1866, 1868)

Fees	1851[a]	1853[a]	1854	1861	1862	1862[b]	1863[c]	1863[d]	1865[b]	1866[e]	1868[b]	1869
(1)	$0.25	$0.40	$0.50	$0.50	$1.00	$1.00	$1.00	$1.00	$2.00	$1.00	$1.00	$0.75
(2)	0.50	0.50	0.75	0.50	1.00	1.00	1.00	1.00	2.00	1.50	1.00	1.00
(3)	0.25	0.30	0.40	0.25	0.25	0.25	0.25	0.25	0.50	0.50	0.25	0.25
(4)	0.10	0.20	0.20	0.10	0.20	0.20	0.25	0.20	0.25	0.30	0.10	0.10
(5)	0.10	0.25	0.25	0.10	0.20	0.20	0.25	0.25	0.30	0.35	0.15	0.15
(6)	0.50	0.50	0.50	0.25	1.00	1.00	1.00	1.00	2.00	1.50	1.00	1.00
(7)	0.50	0.50	0.50	0.25	0.50	0.50	0.50	1.00	1.50	0.75	0.75	0.25
(8)	0.50	0.50	0.75	0.50	1.00	1.00	1.00	1.00	—	1.50	0.75	—
(9)	—	—	—	—	—	—	—	—	0.50	—	0.25	0.50
(10)	—	—	—	—	—	—	—	—	0.25	—	0.15	0.15
(11)	—	—	—	—	—	—	—	—	—	—	—	0.20
(12)	0.50	1.00	1.25	0.75	1.50	1.50	1.50	1.50	2.00	2.25	1.00	0.50
(13)	0.25	0.50	0.75	0.50	1.00	0.75	1.00	0.75	1.25	1.50	0.75	0.50
(14)	0.50	0.50	0.50	0.50	1.00	1.00	1.00	1.00	2.00	—	1.00	0.50
(15)	0.50	0.50	0.75	0.50	1.00	1.00	1.00	1.00	—	1.50	—	—
(16)	0.20	0.50	0.75	0.25	0.50	0.50	0.50	0.50	1.00	0.75	0.50	0.50
(17)	0.50	0.75	0.75	0.50	1.00	1.00	1.00	1.00	2.00	1.50	1.00	1.00
(18)	0.50	0.50	0.50	0.25	1.00	1.00	1.00	1.00	2.00	1.50	1.00	1.00
(19)	—	—	—	—	—	—	—	—	2.00	—	1.00	0.75
(20)	0.75	1.00	1.25	—	—	—	—	—	—	—	—	—
(21)	—	0.25	0.25	0.10	0.20	0.20	0.30	0.20	0.40	0.35	0.25	0.20
(22)	—	—	—	—	—	—	—	—	3.00	—	1.50	—
(23)	3.00	3.00	4.00	—	—	—	—	—	—	10.00	—	5.00
(24)	—	—	0.12	—	—	—	—	—	—	—	—	—
(25)	2.00	3.00	4.00	3.00	6.00	6.00	6.00	5.00	5.00	4.00	3.00	3.00

All dates, unless otherwise marked, apply to all justices of the peace in Washington Territory.

a. Formulated by the Oregon territorial legislature.

b. Applies only to Walla Walla County.

c. Applies only to Boise, Idaho, Nez Perce, and Shoshone counties.

d. Applies only to Whatcom County.

e. Applies only to Stevens, Jefferson, and Kitsap counties; extended in 1867 to Snohomish, Island, Klickitat, Skamania, Whatcom, Lewis, and Clallam counties.

Source: Wash. Terr. Statutes, Sess. 1 (1854): 374; Sess. 8 (1861): 39-40; Sess. 9 (1862): 40-42, 49-50; Sess. 10 (1863): 24-26, 41; Sess. 11 (1865): 73-74; Sess. 13 (1866): 98-99; Sess. 14 (1867): 157; Sess. 15 (1868): 92-93; Sess. 16 (1869): 368;

Ore. Terr. Statutes, Sess. 2 (1851): 150-151; 4 (1853): 23-24.

KEY to Table 6

(1) Issuing a summons
(2) Issuing a criminal warrant
(3) Subpoena of one person
(4) Subpoena of each extra person
(5) Swearing of each witness or juror
(6) Venire for a jury
(7) Taking an affidavit (each)
(8) Issuing a search warrant
(9) Approving a bond
(10) Administering an oath
(11) Taking a deposition per folio (100 words)
(12) Entering judgment on basis of a trial
(13) Entering judgment on basis of a confession or default

(14) Commitment to jail
(15) Issuing an execution
(16) Adjournment or continuance
(17) Issuing a writ of attachment
(18) Issuing a writ of restitution
(19) Issuing a writ of replevin
(20) Copy for an appeal (minimum)
(21) For each folio (100 words) of appeal copy
(22) Minimum general fee per trial
(23) Marriage ceremony
(24) Mileage to and from marriage ceremony per mile
(25) Attending, with clerk of county commissioners, the opening of polls for each election

In 1863, another separate and special fee schedule was created for Boise, Idaho, Nez Perce, and Shoshone counties. There was very little difference between this special fee schedule and the 1862 territorial fee schedule. Increases occurred only in appeal folio costs, swearing of witnesses and jurors, and issuance of subpoenas to more than one person, and these increases were very slight. Why this special law was necessary may be explained in part by the distance of the counties from Olympia. Later that year, all four counties became part of Idaho Territory.[11]

Also in 1863, the Washington territorial legislature passed a special justice of the peace fee schedule that was applicable to Whatcom County only. This special schedule exhibited no rational trend. The county's JP rates for judgments entered on the basis of a confession or default were decreased, and the fee for attending the opening of the polls for an election compared to the 1862 fee schedule. At the same time, Whatcom County justice of the peace fees for taking affidavits and swearing witnesses and jurors were increased. No fee was set for issuing search warrants by a Whatcom County JP (all other territorial justices of the peace could charge $1 per search warrant issued). This omission was probably a legislative oversight.[12]

The last special justice of the peace fee schedule was formulated in 1866 and was applicable to Stevens, Jefferson, and Kitsap counties. In 1867, the same fee schedule was extended to Snohomish, Island, Klickitat, Skamania, Whatcom, Lewis, and Clallam counties. This special fee schedule was highly inflationary. In all but one area (attending the opening of the polls for an election), justices of the peace were authorized to charge the largest amounts at any time during the territorial period. Entering a judgment on the basis of a trial went up to $2.25 from $1.50; performing a marriage ceremony to $10.00 from $4.00; and issuing a search warrant, to $1.50 from $1.00. The 1866 special JP fee schedule represented the apex in local judicial rates chargeable in Washington Territory (Table 6).[13]

In 1869, the last regular justice of the peace fee schedule set by a Washington territorial legislature was drawn. This schedule would be effective during Washington's remaining twenty years of territorial status. Like the 1861 schedule, the 1869 schedule was an attempt to turn back increases in justice of the peace fees. In eighteen fee areas held in common with all previous fee schedules, prices were reduced. Charges for issuing a search warrant or an execution were omitted, and in many areas fees returned to 1861 levels. On its face, the 1869 fee schedule would appear to be a return to cheaper local legal services. However, this generalization is misleading. While justice of the peace fees were reduced from past schedules, four new categories of fees were introduced to general Washington or Oregon territorial JP cost schedules. In addition, these new categories (especially bond approvals and oath administrations) represented common legal occurrences in a functioning legal system. The justices of the peace may have sacrificed in some areas in the 1869 fee schedule, but they had gained financially in other areas (Table 6).[14]

The 1869 justice of the peace fee schedule had another unique feature: the Washington territorial legislature added an enforcement mechanism to the fee schedule. All fee schedules had to be placed in full view of the public; a JP who did not make his schedule public was subject to a $20 fine. Prosecution for such a misdemeanor would take place before any other justice of the peace. Violations of the fee schedule were deemed more serious. JPs were subject to a fine not exceeding $1,000 for overcharges or undercharges. This new legislation indicated the legislators' concern over the conduct of Washington Territory's justices of the peace.[15]

Thus, the fees of the Washington JP were set several times during the territorial period. Of the ten fee schedules, only one (that of 1861) did not reflect an increase in costs. The six special fee schedules represented the highest fees available for Washington's justices of the peace. Congress was attacking laws such as the special fee schedules when, in 1886, it forbade territories to pass local or special laws dealing with the practice of all courts of justice and the jurisdiction and duties of justices of the peace and police magistrates. All present local and special laws remained legal, but future laws would be void. In its three remaining years as a territory, Washington never tested this federal restriction with its special justice of the peace fee schedules.[16]

Witness Costs

Other JP court costs, in addition to the judge's fees, were costs to witnesses and jurors in compensation for their contributions to the legal process. The first witness fee schedule to affect Washington directly was set in 1852 by the Oregon territorial legislature. The losing litigant was instructed to pay a witness $1.00 per day spent in any territorial court session if the court was held in the witness's county of residence. If the court sat outside the witness's home county, the witness would receive $1.50 per day. In addition, a witness was given $0.05 per mile for travel to and from the trial location. This differentiation in fees was an attempt to help compensate a witness for travel expenses. It was of negligible benefit, however, since some counties, such as Clark County which encompassed much of Washington, were too large for the allotted compensation adequately to help defray expenses.[17]

Washington's territorial legislature moved quickly to increase witness fee rates. In 1854, witness fee schedules were expanded in all areas except the charge for each day in a justice of the peace court located in the witness's home voting precinct.[18] In 1861, the legislature again changed witness fees, and, following in the 1861 JP fee schedule tradition, witness fees remained the same or were decreased.[19] Similarly, the following year, witness fees were increased to their highest limits during the territorial period. Mileage to and from court sessions was sizably increased from $0.10 per mile to $0.50 per mile, and the appearance of a witness in a justice of the peace court now cost the plaintiff or defendant $3.00 a day instead of the previous $1.00 a day.[20]

Unlike the numerous special justice of the peace fee schedules formulated by the Washington territorial legislature, only one special witness fee law was ever passed. In 1863, a special witness fee schedule was provided for the courts of Boise, Idaho, Nez Perce, and Shoshone counties. These special witness rates were very similar to the 1862 territorial witness fee schedule.[21]

The last witness fee schedule set by the Washington territorial legislature was added in 1869. In effect, witness fees were standardized and returned to 1861 levels. A witness was now entitled to $2.00 per day for appearance in any court in Washington Territory and $0.10 per mile to and from that court. This schedule would remain the law throughout the remaining twenty years of the Washington territorial era (see Table 7).[22]

Thus, local court costs not only included generally inflated justice of the peace fees for specific activities, but they also would provide for similarly inflated witness fees. Both fee schedules tended to fluctuate at the same time, indicating general legislative concerns, and 1869 marked the last legislative session that would examine justice of the peace and witness fees.

Table 7

Witness Fee Schedules for Oregon Territory (1852),
Washington Territory (1854, 1861, 1862, 1869),
and Special Counties (1862)

Witness Fees	1852[a]	1854	1861	1862	1862[b]	1869
Fee each day in district or probate court	$1.00	$2.00	$2.00	$5.00	$4.00	$2.00
Fee each day in JP court in home county or voting precinct	1.00	1.00	1.00	3.00	3.00 inc. probate	2.00
Fee each day in JP court outside home county or voting precinct	1.50	2.00	1.00	3.00	3.00 inc. probate	2.00
Mileage fee per mile to and from court session	0.05	0.10	0.10	0.50	0.50	0.10

All dates, unless otherwise marked, apply to all witnesses in courts in Washington Territory.

a. Formulated by the Oregon territorial legislature.

b. Applies only to Boise, Idaho, Nez Perce, and Shoshone counties.

Source: Wash. Terr. Statutes, Sess. 1 (1854):375; Sess. 8 (1861):40-41; Sess. 9 (1862):42; Sess. 10 (1863):26; Sess. 16 (1869):368; *Ore. Terr. Statutes*, Sess. 3 (1852):69.

Paying for a Jury

Petit jury fees also have to be taken into consideration in a tabulation of local justice of the peace court costs. In its first session in 1854, the Washington territorial legislature was concerned about jury costs. A petit juror schedule was set, giving each juror $2.00 for every day spent in JP court, plus $0.10 per mile to and from the court location.[23] To help defray the costs of a long jury trial, the legislature also provided for a jury fee of $25.00 to be attached to any judgment against a convicted defendant. In addition, any plaintiff who brought an action against another person had to pay a $6.00 jury fee to the justice of the peace, who charged the amount to the losing party once the verdict was given. In 1862, the special juror fee was dropped for all criminal cases and for all civil actions for forcible entry and unlawful detainer heard before a justice of the peace. The legislature reasoned that charging the territory for a jury in criminal cases seemed counterproductive to the intent of the original juror fee act, and a plaintiff and defendant had no choice in actions for forcible entry and unlawful detainer but to have jury trials. This reasonable exception remained the law for only fifteen years; in 1877, the legislature voided the 1862 statute.[24]

After its initial 1854 juror fee law, the Washington territorial legislature did not change juror fee schedules for seven years. Then within the next seven years, juror fee schedules were altered on four occasions. In 1861, a year when justice of the peace and witness fee schedules were decreased, juror fee schedules were only slightly decreased. The following year all categories were significantly increased. Jurors received $2.00 a day for every day spent in justice of the peace court and $0.20 per mile for travel to and from court. The next two juror fee schedules were special laws applying to certain select geographical areas. These rates continued the rising trend in juror fees, particularly the juror fee schedule of 1863. The 1863 juror fees increased travel reimbursements from $0.20 per mile to and from court to $0.50 per mile, and increased the fee for daily attendance in JP court from $2.00 to $3.00 The special juror fee schedules set by the Washington territorial legislature enabled jurors to collect their fees during the entire territorial period.

Like justice of the peace and witness fee schedules, the last juror fee schedule was enacted in 1869. Similarly, this schedule tended to lower fees, and for jurors, all fees were returned to 1854 levels. This reduction in fees was quite drastic. Justice of the peace court appearances cost $2.00 per day instead of $3.00 per day, and mileage to and from court was now reimbursed at $0.10 per mile instead of $0.50 per mile. The legislature saw costs of juries as prohibitive to fair justice and the territory's treasury. Justice of the peace and witness fees had been reduced in 1869, but such reductions had not been limited to 1854 levels (see Table 8).[25]

Basic local court costs were of some concern to Washington's citizens and legislators. Fluctuations in justice of the peace, witness, and juror rates characterized this concern in the first fifteen years of Washington Territory, from 1853 to 1868. However, from

Table 8

Juror Fee Schedules for Washington Territory
(1854, 1861, 1862, 1869) and Special Counties (1862, 1863)

Juror Fees	1854	1861	1862	1862[a]	1863[b]	1869
Fee each day in district or probate court	$3.00	$2.00	$3.00	$3.00	$4.00	$3.00
Fee each day in inquest	2.00	1.00	2.00	2.00	—	2.00
Fee each day in JP court	2.00	1.00	2.00	3.00	3.00	2.00
Mileage fee per mile to and from court session	0.10	0.10	0.20	0.20	0.50	0.10

All dates, unless otherwise marked, apply to all jurors in Washington Territory.

a. Applies only to Walla Walla County.

b. Applies only to Boise, Idaho, Nez Perce, and Shoshone counties.

Source: Wash. Terr. Statutes, Sess. 1 (1854):373; Sess. 8 (1861):39; Sess. 9 (1862):40, 50; Sess. 10 (1863):26; Sess. 16 (1869):368.

1869 to the end of the territorial period, only one schedule of fees was formulated. The Washington territorial legislature was content with local court costs at a constant level.

Trends in Justice Court Costs

The changes in JP court costs during the Washington territorial era generally mirrored national prices. The territory's justice court fee schedules were first adopted in 1854; the next schedule, passed in 1861, provided for lower fees. After 1861, the legislature increased costs, formulating the highest fee schedule in 1866. Only two more schedules were formed, one in 1868 reducing fees and one in 1869 bringing fees back to 1861 JP court rates.

Similarly, wholesale price indexes fluctuated from 1854 to 1889.[26] Prices in all commodities reached a low point in 1861, but increases followed to a maximum index in 1864. Although price levels dropped in 1868 and 1869, they did not fall to 1861 levels until 1878. These years in question represented a billowing inflation caused by the Civil War and a balancing interregnum period of deflation. Court costs in Washington Territory dropped rapidly and stabilized because its economy was not greatly affected by the deflation and depression related to railroad investments of the immediate postwar era. To a great extent, the changing national price levels corresponded to changing JP court costs.

Justice of the peace court costs, like wholesale price indexes, varied according to case and time. For example, one of the first cases to be heard before a Washington Territory justice of the peace was *Territory of Washington v. Thomas Bozarth*. On the afternoon of December 17, 1860, Judge Nathaniel Hill, at his home on Whidbey Island called his court to order; before him was an action charging Thomas Bozarth with petit larceny. The complainant, Thomas Winn, had accused the defendant of stealing several pairs of Winn's black pantaloons and woolen drawers that were wrapped in a bundle laying on the counter in John Robertson's store. That morning, Winn had asked Hill for a search warrant to find his missing clothing, a subpoena to be served on John Robertson to force him to testify, and a warrant for the arrest of Bozarth. Judge Hill had granted the requests. The defendant opened the proceeding by pleading not guilty. Then Winn, Robertson, Patrick Doyle, and A. J. Bailey were called to testify. Since no one could identify Bozarth as having taken the pants and the pants could not be found, Justice Hill quickly adjudged the defendant not guilty.[27]

The significance of this "panty raid" is that almost everyone directly involved received compensation from the territory for a day's legal work. Judge Hill charged $0.50 for entering the complaint, $0.25 for administering an oath, $0.75 for issuing an arrest warrant, $0.50 for taking an affidavit, $0.75 for issuing a search warrant, and $1.00 for signing four subpoenas even before the trial began. For his part in the trial, Hill received $0.50 for opening court, $1.00 for swearing witnesses, and $1.25 for entering a judgment, making his total JP fee in the Bozarth case $6.50. Winn and Robertson each received $1.50, and Doyle and Bailey each were given $1.00 in witness fees. The constable had to be paid $4.95 for serving the warrants and subpoenas. The *Territory of Washington v. Thomas Bozarth* case cost Washington Territory $16.45.[28]

Another case heard before the courts of Washington Territory was more complicated and time consuming and, therefore, more costly. In the summer of 1866, Captain Howard B. Lovejoy swore out a complaint against Captain William F. Robertson for allegedly possessing and selling obscene pictures. Lovejoy was a well-known pilot on Puget Sound who had settled on Whidbey Island. He was born in Maine in 1805, and after spending most of his early adult life in the Navy, he rounded the Horn in 1849 to look for gold in California. There Lovejoy endured several unsuccessful years at prospecting, and eventually he went into the shipping business, first coming to Whidbey Island in 1853 to take a load of logs to San Francisco. He later founded the Russian-American Trading Company which carried goods to and from Alaska and California, and he engaged in steamboating on the Sound. His eldest son Howard would marry the daughter of Sara Jane Robertson, daughter of the defendant.[29]

The defendant, Captain William Robertson, had much in common with Lovejoy. He was also born on the East Coast, in Virginia in 1809, and his young adult life centered around an Atlantic shipping business headquartered in Baltimore. The Gold Rush brought him around the Horn to California in 1849, but he did not engage in prospecting. Instead, Robertson bought two vessels and went to Puget Sound to start a shipping business. In 1853, his wife and children joined him in locating on Whidbey Island. Captain Robertson fathered three children, Sara Jane, John (a successful builder, contractor, and justice of the peace), and Thomas (known in the community as a troublemaker). Robertson was active politically. In 1859, he was appointed first keeper of the lighthouse at Admiralty Head by President James Buchanan, and in 1862, he became the Island County coroner.[30] Long-standing ill feeling between the claimant and the defendant contributed to Lovejoy's active urging of judicial action. The complaint against Robertson was brought to fruition by the district court which met in Port Townsend after Robertson waived a preliminary hearing before Justice of the Peace John Y. Sewell. After hearing six witnesses, among them Nathaniel Hill, Thomas Bozarth, and Henry Lovejoy, and viewing no obscene materials, the court found the defendant innocent and ordered Justice of the Peace H. E. Morgan of Jefferson County to call a grand jury to investigate the circumstances behind the complaint. Judge Morgan complied with this order and presided over the grand jury investigation. The grand jury concluded that the indictment and prosecution against Captain Robertson were "frivolous and malicious" and that Captain Lovejoy, for involving the legal machinery of the territory in his personal feud, would have to pay all court costs generated in his spiteful actions. By the end of the grand jury pronouncement, court costs had become considerable. Witness fees alone cost over half of the total, in part because of the long-distance traveling to Port Townsend. Captain Lovejoy had to pay $200.65 for his effort to determine community moral standards.[31]

A more typical case was heard and decided by Walla Walla Justice of the Peace J. D. Laman on April 7, 1876. B. M. Washburn sued J. C. Ferguson for $15.75 due him for printing. Both parties hired counsel, and each litigant presented two witnesses at the trial. After Judge Laman heard the testimony and viewed the evidence, he found for the plaintiff. Defendant Ferguson paid $15.75 for printing and $20.20 for court costs (see Table 9).[32]

This legal action cost Ferguson $35.95 in 1876. How much would it have cost him in 1866? In 1856? To answer these questions, justice of the peace witness fees need to be tabulated for these two years. Fifteen JP fee categories were charged; four witnesses were sworn during the trial. In 1876, Walla Walla justice of the peace activities cost $6.20; in 1866, these same services cost $15.00, and in 1856, $6.90. Thus, basic court costs were similar at the beginning and end of the territorial period, but they were much higher during the middle portion.

Table 9

Washburn v. Ferguson: **Justice of the Peace Court Costs,**
1876, 1866, 1856

Fee Categories	1876	1866	1856
Justice of the Peace Fees	$6.20	$15.00	$6.90
Taking a claim (affidavit)	0.25	1.50	0.50
Filing	0.15	—	—
Issuing a summons	0.75	2.00	0.50
Taking an affidavit	0.25	1.50	0.50
Filing	0.15	—	—
Approving a bond	0.50	0.50	—
Filing	0.15	—	—
Issuing a writ of attachment	1.00	2.00	0.75
Taking an answer (affidavit)	0.25	1.50	0.50
Filing	0.15	—	—
Subpoena of one witness	0.35	0.50	0.40
Swearing of five witnesses	0.75	1.50	1.25
Entering judgment on the basis of a trial	0.50	2.00	1.25
Execution	0.50	—	0.75
Restitution	0.50	2.00	0.50
Witness Fees	8.40	14.00	8.40
C. H. Humphrey	2.00	3.00	2.00
Gardner Washburn	2.00	3.00	2.00
W. H. Newell	2.20	4.00	2.20
E. L. Heriff	2.20	4.00	2.20
Constable Costs	5.60	5.60	5.60
Total Justice of the Peace Court Costs	$20.20	$34.60	$20.90

This trend held for witness fees. Assuming that two witnesses traveled two miles each day to and from court and the other witnesses lived within walking distance, total witness costs for a one-day trial in 1876 would be $8.40. These same factors led to a total of $14.00 in 1866 and $8.40 in 1856.

Justice Court Costs Examined and Found Acceptable

At the Constitutional Convention held in Ellensburgh in 1889, the delegates entertained the questions of fees, regular salaries, and abolition of the office of justice of the peace. On July 16, the Judiciary Committee reported to the convention the following provision for the proposed constitution:

The Legislature shall determine the number of justices of the peace to be elected in incorporated cities or towns and in precincts, and shall prescribe by law the powers, duties and jurisdiction of justices of the peace: Provided, ... In incorporated cities and towns having more than five thousand inhabitants the justices of the peace shall receive such salary as may be provided by law, and shall receive no fees for their own use.[33]

Previously, considerable sentiment had been expressed in favor of giving higher state courts better salaries than allowed in the territorial era, and this feeling had been carried down to JPs.[34] The abolition of the fee system except for unsalaried magistrates represented an "important innovation" in Washington's judiciary.[35]

Efforts were made to abolish the justice courts entirely and to reinstitute the fee systems for all JPs, but they failed.[36] Support for justices and salaries remained strong, not because of past abuses, but because, as stated by the *Chehalis Nugget*, "every official in the state from the Governor down to the justice of the peace should be salaried."[37]

Only one newspaper, the *Seattle Post-Intelligencer*, editorialized negatively on past JP financial operations. It referred to the fee system as "one of the worse abuses now existing in the inferior courts,"[38] and once the delegates approved the constitutional provision, it commented:

The palmy days of the justice of the peace in Washington are gone forever. He is to be stripped of all the fees upon which he at present waxes fat, and must be contented with a beggarly salary fixed by law. Indeed, the feeling of the delegates seemed to be such that they would evidently have abolished the office of the justice of the peace if they did not think them absolutely necessary in some cases.[39]

This inflammatory position was not shared by other newspapers in the territory. In fact, of all tabloids examined, only the *Post-Intelligencer* detected abuses in lower court financing. The motivation behind this attack was more likely rooted in the competition which the *Post-Intelligencer* received from the *Seattle Times* and its prominent editor and publisher, George Lyon, who also performed as a respected justice of the peace for King County.

* * * *

The basic costs of going to JP court have been observed by comparing the fee schedules formulated by the Washington territorial legislature and by discussing costs in terms of case and time for several situations. Two generalizations have emerged. First, local court costs fluctuated during Washington's territorial period, especially from 1853 to 1869. They were generally characterized by an increase in all basic fee schedules. The legal foundations of Washington Territory were dependent upon Oregon Territory before Washington legislative action. The Oregon territorial legislature had formulated two justice of the peace fee schedules before 1853 that set an inflationary trend in local court costs. The Washington territorial legislature continued this inflationary trend in JP, witness, and juror fees until 1861 when local court costs were substantially reduced. From 1862 to 1868, the Washington territorial legislature confined most of its fee-setting activity to special schedules which applied only to designated areas. These laws set the highest local court costs during the existence of Washington Territory. Then, in 1869, local court costs were returned to 1861 fee levels, again drastically reducing the cost of going to JP court. The 1869 fee schedules would not be altered for the next twenty years.

It also becomes apparent that territory representatives and justices of the peace were especially affected by the trends in fee schedule settings. It was in the interest of the territory to keep local court costs low. Conversely, it was in the interest of the justices of the peace to keep fee schedules as high as possible while not discouraging potential legal business. The Washington territorial legislature had to consider these two conflicting interests when they set the fee schedules for basic justice court costs. Eventually, after an initial period of high inflationary rates, the legislature formulated costs conducive to the original intent of a JP court—a local court designed to adjudicate local disputes. This court would best function providing its services for plaintiff, defendant, and the territory for a minimal fee. But whenever the scope of the court's activities expanded, the costs correspondingly increased, thereby increasing the fees of the local justice and the legal debts of the territory.

part IV

THE QUALITY OF JUSTICE ON THE NORTHWEST FRONTIER

*Having observed who the justices of the peace in Washington Terri-
tory were and what they could do, let us now turn to an examination of what these JPs in fact did and an evaluation of their judicial
performance. As previously defined, the quality of justice provided
by local judges in Washington Territory can be described through
an assessment of four indicators: the amount of educational training received by officers of the court present in the courtrooms; the
accessibility of the courts to settlers; the adjudication celerity of
functioning courts; and the communities' acceptance level of the
courts and court decisions.[1] Hence, if proceedings before JPs
tended to include persons with some formal education and acquaintance with the law; if JP courts were geographically, financially,
and topically available to many persons; if dispositions of cases
occurred without lengthy delay; and if communities seldom took
their disputes outside JP courts, then Washington Territory justices
of the peace were making fair decisions and were accordingly dis-
pensing a "high" quality of justice.*

In this section, the quality of JP justice in Washington Territory is determined in part through a study of over fourteen hundred cases tried by justices of the peace. The JP court records observed were obtained from the courts of Thomas Cranney, Winfield S. Ebey, Robert Hathaway, Nathaniel Hill, William Robertson, John Y. Sewell, and Richard H. Straub, Coveland Precinct, Island County, 1854-1889; Thomas Donald, John McKnight, and William Uder, Newcastle Precinct, King County, 1885-1889; and Oliver P. Lacy and J. D. Laman, Walla Walla Precinct, Walla Walla County, 1872-1882.[2] Records of justice of the peace courts exist for Pomeroy Precinct, Garfield County, 1883-1889, and Goldendale Precinct, Klickitat County, 1886-1889, but they were not comprehensively examined by this author. No other JP court records for Washington Territory seem to have survived.

Each case has been analyzed in terms of seventeen elements: name of judge, civil or criminal case, type of cause of action, verdict or disposition, method of obtaining a verdict or disposition (trial-determined, pleading, default, dismissal, sending to a grand jury or district court, or granting of a change of venue), attorney or no attorney in court, jury or no jury, number of witnesses, jury costs, JP costs, total court costs, appeal or no appeal, date case began (complaint sworn), date of first court session, date of court decision, and date case closed (satisfaction to rightful party). These elements appeared in most cases, but when they did not, absences were noted. By counting how frequently these elements appeared and by comparing the variety of frequencies to each other, certain trends and historical generalizations emerge. In essence, Part IV forms basic judgments about the quality of justice maintained on the Washington frontier from the examination of some 1,411 cases heard by twelve different justices of the peace functioning throughout the entire Washington territorial period.

8

Justices of the Peace and the ''Law''

The first indicator of the quality of justice provided by Washington Territory justices of the peace involves how much law and education permeated JP court proceedings. Did JPs receive a formal education; did they partake of legal instruction; and did they have access to written materials? How did this education or lack thereof affect the quality of their decisions? Were attorneys present during JP court proceedings, and if attorneys participated in lower court deliberations, what result did their presence produce? Answers to these queries will help provide an accurate description and evaluation of JP court operations.

Judicial Education Levels

To ascertain the educational background of justices of the peace, information on JPs in Washington Territory was collected with specific reference to educational attainment. Owing to the difficulty of identifying sufficient biographical data of frontier residents, some seventy-six persons could be verified only as having been at one time Washington Territory JPs.[1] However, the personal profiles of 197 other justices of the peace that have been assembled contain adequate materials to determine the educational and legal training of JPs in Washington Territory, 1853-1889, and their access to law books.[2]

Nearly one-half (44.6 percent or 88 of 197) of the justices of the peace examined received a formal education beyond fundamental reading and writing skills. All JPs could read and write, whereas from 1850 to 1880 as much as 22.6 percent of the American populace and 11.5 percent of the white population were illiterate.[3] Justices who practiced law before or during their judgeship constituted 11.2 percent (22 of 197) of the sample. This percentage was particularly remarkable in light of legislative enactments restricting JPs and the practice of law. Some justices, such as John Y. Ostrander and George Hill, obtained their legal training prior to their JP service.[4] Others, such as David Maynard and Boliver Bishop, learned enough law on the job to become members of the bar after finishing their terms as justices of the peace. In fact, J. E. Willis of Chehalis frequently advertised in local papers his joint capacities of JP and attorney at law.[5]

Deciding whether a justice had access to law books entailed some historical deductive reasoning. For example, members of the bar were presumed to use law books. Others specifically referred to legal works in diaries, letters and wills. Despite conservative evaluations of biographical data, 54.3 percent of those JPs surveyed (107 of 197) found some law books available for court perusal.

The typical Washington Territory justice of the peace, therefore, brought a relatively high degree of educational and legal qualifications into JP court proceedings. This advanced training becomes evident in a comprehensive examination of justice court records. J. D. Laman, a Walla Walla justice of the peace of some educational attainment but no legal training, kept precise, intelligent notes of his court decisions. For instance, on January 17, 1873, one Lewis P. Barry began a suit against Robert J. Stringer for payment on a promissory note. Judge Laman duly recorded the progress of the case.[6]

Complaint filed January 11th, 1873. Notice issued same day citing defendant to answer January 17th, 1873, at 10 o'clock A.M. Plaintiff files affidavit and bond asking for writ of attachment, the same is approved and filed, and a writ of attachment issued and the papers placed in the hands of J. B. Thompson, constable for service, who returned the complaint served personally on the defendant on the 11th day of January, 1873, in the County of Walla Walla, W.T.

Writ of attachment served by levying upon the following described personal property of the defendant, "to wit," 4 bls. corned Beef, 7 quarters of Beef, and 7 sacks of potatoes, one box stove and a lot of wood sawed. Levy made in the County of Walla Walla, W.T. Writ of attachment duly certified and returned and filed this January 11th, 1873.

January 15th, 1873

Received on the above case from R. J. Stringer by J. D. Cook through J. B. Thompson constable, $34, coin (Atty fees $4.50 coin), total $38.50.

> J. D. Laman
> *Justice of the Peace*

Justice Fees		Constable Fees	
Justice Fees		*Constable Fees*	
2 affidavits	.50	$4.40	
Notice	.75	2.23	
Writ of attachment	1.00	$6.23	
Bond	.50	Justice Fees paid in coin	$4.25
Filing 3 papers	.45	Constable Fees paid in coin	6.00
Filing writ	.50	Paid Brents, Atty. for plain.	23.75
Entering Judg.	.50		$34.00
Satisfaction	.50		
	$4.70		

Received full satisfaction on the above case.
Thos. H. Brents, Attorney for Plaintiff —
> January 16th, 1873

As represented in Laman's proceedings, JP courts were in sound command of the laws. On more rare occasions, justices of the peace lacked the legal foundations necessary for a successful mastery of a case. William Uder, a JP in Newcastle, King County, with little education, had problems deciding how to classify a typical assault and battery case. Judge Uder termed the cause of action a malicious pouring of beer and spoiling of clothes, and he chronicled the ensuing trial.

On this 22, day of May, 1887 Comes Peter Heisenberger before me Wm. Uder a Justace of the Peace in and for New Castle Precinct County of King, and Territory of Washington.

and filed a complaint in My office charging Thomas Mullarkey with having trouwen a quart of Beer over him and spoiled his Cloths he swore out a Warrant, & had Thomas Mullarkey arrested next day.

May the 23, Court Opened at 8 P.M. Prisner being in Court, the following named witnesses were Sworn William George, Ben Morgan, George Loftus, and John Evans and allso prosecuting witnes Peter Heisenberger. Heisenberger stated he had taken George Loftus up from the Ball ground to Collans Salloon to have soom Beer, and Thomas Mullarkey had trown a quart of Beer on him and spoiled his Clothes.

William George testified that Thomas Mullarkey wanted to treat. Heisenberger refused, then Mularkey pushed the table accidently and the Beer fell on Heisenberger and he called Mullarkey a son of a bitch, Mullarky then slapped him in the face.

Ben Morgan testified he was there but was deeply interested in conversation, saw his Clothes wet but dit not see how the Beer got on his Clothes.

George Loftus testafied he seen the Beer fall on Heisenberger but could not tell who throwed it on him.

John Evans thestefied the same as B. Morgan.

Thomas Mullarkey testified he did not throw the Beer on him intentionly it was don accidently so fare as he can remember.

The Courts decision in the case is, it was don accidently, and that the defantant was not guilty. Plaintiff appeals.[7]

Uder's proceedings best illustrate the notion that frontier justice emanated from the "common man," deficient in the law (and in the rudiments of good English) but proficient in practical decision-making. His court represented a minority of functioning JP courts in Washington Territory.

Most JPs probably knew the rudiments of law. They grasped the complexities involved in making important legal decisions, and they understood the technical nature of their profession. When D. Williams sued R. R. Rounds of Walla Walla for $20 in wages, Judge J. D. Laman sat for the case until he heard incontrovertible evidence depriving the plaintiff of his legal standing to sue. Laman thereupon dismissed the case.[8] Charles Hughes was charged in John Y. Sewell's Island County Court with raping Amelia Gildon. Judge Sewell meticulously recorded five pages of detailed testimony stressing the elements necessary for proving that rape had in fact occurred. At the end of the hearing, Hughes was bound over to district court indicted for rape.[9]

Local justices also perceived how to use the extensive powers inherent in their office. Vagrancy and contempt charges have traditionally been employed by courts to control certain individuals. Hence, when Michael Carr was arrested in Walla Walla, he was charged with vagrancy and was quickly brought to trial. At the trial, the court found that Carr "had a land claim in Whitman County, W.T., and that he was nearer a lunatic, than a vagrant"; thus, the defendant was released upon condition he would immediately leave the county.[10] The justice of the peace tried to achieve the desired effect without a conviction. Similarly, when Charles Kraft refused to turn over property to the court for attachment, he was held in contempt, given a two-day jail term, and forced to produce the property.[11]

If a justice wanted to influence community behavior or restrict some activity, he had the legal power to achieve this end. On February 13, 1882, T. T. Burgess, William Bender, and Richard Kelling each paid $30 fines before Justice Vincent Lambert for selling liquor on Sunday in violation of a Walla Walla blue law ordinance. According to the *Washington Standard*, Lambert exhorted the defendants, "The next time I'll make it $50, and after that, $100." The *Standard* wished Lambert would come to Olympia and prevent Sabbath day "business" because the sheriff of Thurston County had stopped blue law enforcement by packing juries with saloon frequenters.[12]

Occasionally, sheriffs also felt the wrath of justices of the peace. For example, R. H. Straub, Island County JP, urged the district court to admonish Sheriff Joseph C. Power who was supposed to arrest Thomas Robertson, but Straub wrote, "Prisoner not found. *Sheriff afraid to make arrest.*"[13] Sheriff Griffin of Walla Walla County may not have been cowardly, but he was careless, at least once. Wrote Judge Laman, "Sheriff Griffin made no return of the complaint and notice, but verbally reported that he had lost the same. Therefore no costs taxed for him."[14]

The JP's judicial activism was not limited to disciplining sheriffs. Justices of the peace aggressively urged compromises on litigants; in one case, Lizzie Cody sued for replevin of two horses, a wagon, and two harnesses, but she finally accepted one thousand board feet of lumber in restitution. JPs sometimes ordered litigants arrested to prevent default judgments; John Smith, defendant in a borrowed money civil suit, was incarcerated by order of the Walla Walla justice court to prevent his flight. And local justices personally investigated disputes to obtain the truth; in a case cited previously,

Judge Nathaniel Hill rigorously pursued the case against Thomas Bozarth until he discovered Bozarth had not committed assault and battery or petit larceny as charged.[15]

Above all, justices were human, and they brought their strengths as well as their failings to the courtroom. Sometimes they recognized their weaknesses by asking a fellow justice to assist them on a case; at other times, they were forced to admit mistakes and reconsider adjudications.[16] Less frequently they brought dishonor to their legal position. In 1883, Joseph B. Lister of Pomeroy was convicted of embezzling justice court funds,[17] and during the 1860s, S. B. Fargo of Walla Walla drank too much to hold court. Fargo, who was termed "a complete rogue," disappeared with considerable moneys belonging to his law partner, Jason Mix.[18] These men were the exceptions, however; most justices of the peace conducted their courts with dignity.

The JP court in Washington Territory, therefore, generally functioned with competence. Judges had a command of their office; they knew their varied powers and they exercised them. For the most part, they had obtained some education beyond ordinary literacy, and they injected a knowledge of the law into court proceedings. The JPs, in conjunction with frontier lawyers, formed a legal cadre capable of performing the complex legal tasks encountered in new communities.

Attorney Participation

Attorneys played a large part in the proceedings before Washington Territory justices of the peace. Many lawyers came to the territory eager to participate in a new judicial system. Most had been educated in the South or Midwest and had passed the bar. The first attorney certified to practice law in Washington Territory, John B. Chapman, regularly defended those accused of misdemeanors before justices of the peace.[19] Lawyers participated in 44 percent of the 1,411 cases observed.[20] This percentage is high considering the limited jurisdiction of JP courts and the ease with which one could take a case to court.

Attorneys were more prominent in criminal than in civil trials. In 1,080 civil cases, 427 or 38.6 percent of the cases involved litigants who had legal advice; in 328 criminal cases, 203 or 61.9 percent of

Table 10

Cross-tabulation of Case Dispositions
by Attorney Participation,
Washington Territory JP Courts, 1854-1889

	Number of Cases
Trial-determined cases with no attorney	166
Trial-determined cases with attorney for plaintiff only	91
Trial-determined cases with attorney for defendant only	27
Trial-determined cases with attorneys for both plaintiff and defendant	182
Default cases with no attorney	305
Default cases with attorney for plaintiff only	123
Default cases with attorney for defendant only	3
Default cases with attorneys for both plaintiff and defendant	5
Dismissal cases with no attorney	270
Dismissal cases with attorney for plaintiff only	63
Dismissal cases with attorney for defendant only	16
Dismissal cases with attorneys for both plaintiff and defendant	17
Pleading cases with no attorney	20
Pleading cases with attorney for plaintiff only	5
Pleading cases with attorney for defendant only	3
Pleading cases with attorneys for both plaintiff and defendant	4
To grand jury or district court cases with no attorney	23
To grand jury or district court cases with attorney for plaintiff only	31
To grand jury or district court cases with attorney for defendant only	3
To grand jury or district court cases with attorneys for both plaintiff and defendant	16

(Table 10 continued)

Change of venue cases with no attorney	2
Change of venue cases with attorney for plaintiff only	4
Change of venue cases with attorney for defendant only	9
Change of venue cases with attorneys for both plaintiff and defendant	13
Total number of cases	1,401
Missing observations	10

the cases had litigants represented by counsel. In part, this high percentage of attorney participation reflected prosecuting attorneys representing the territory in most major criminal activity. Defendants were represented by lawyers in only 28.7 percent of the criminal legal actions considered.

Inasmuch as lawyers were an integral part of a functioning JP court, they necessarily had an effect on court proceedings. Tables 10, 11, and 12 show court trends directly related to attorney participation. In Table 10, the disposition of a case has been cross-tabulated with attorney participation. Of cases determined by trial, only 35.6 percent lacked some form of legal representation; of cases disposed of by a change of venue, only 7.1 percent had no lawyer participation; and of cases sent to a grand jury or district court, only 31.5 percent were without attorneys. These three case dispositions were the most costly legal determinations available and represented the litigants' failure to compromise. Conversely, of cases disposed of by default (the failure of one party to attend court), 70 percent of the default litigants received no legal advice; of cases settled by dismissal (the dispute resolved between litigants), 73.8 percent had no lawyers; and of cases determined by pleading, 62.5 percent lacked attorney participation. These case dispositions were characterized by a spirit of accommodation—the search and discovery of reasonable alternatives acceptable to all parties of a dispute. Thus, attorneys in the lower courts tended to participate in civil trials and criminal prosecutions, but justices of the peace and litigants were more prone to reach agreements without attorneys, thereby avoiding legal sanctions, court interference, and high costs.

When lawyers were present in JP court, they tended to request juries and to call witnesses, two major elements in producing court delays and costs. In Table 11, only sixty cases or 4.3 percent of those cases examined had juries, but in those cases, 91.1 percent had legal representation for at least one party, and usually both parties had lawyers present. In cases without a jury, litigants were without attorneys 58.2 percent of the time. In Table 12, 28.7 percent of all cases recorded had at least one witness testify. In these cases, 77.5 percent had lawyers examining and calling witnesses. Of the 71.3 percent of the cases in which no witnesses were called, 69.3 percent had no attorney in court. In only 4.4 percent of the cases in which no witnesses were called were plaintiff and defendant represented by counsel. Thus, in cases with attorney participation, juries were apt to be impaneled and witnesses were likely to be summoned; therefore, court costs increased substantially.

Table 11

**Cross-tabulation of Cases with or without Juries
by Attorney Participation,
Washington Territory JP Courts, 1854-1889**

	Number of Cases
Jury cases with no attorney	5
Jury cases with attorney for plaintiff only	7
Jury cases with attorney for defendant only	9
Jury cases with attorneys for both plaintiff and defendant	39
Nonjury cases with no attorney	783
Nonjury cases with attorney for plaintiff only	314
Nonjury cases with attorney for defendant only	52
Nonjury cases with attorneys for both plaintiff and defendant	199
Total number of cases	1,408.
Missing observations	3

Table 12

Cross-tabulation of Cases with or without Witnesses by
Attorney Participation,
Washington Territory JP Courts, 1854-1889

	Number of Cases
Cases with witnesses and no attorney	89
Cases with witnesses and attorney for plaintiff only	93
Cases with witnesses and attorney for defendant only	22
Cases with witnesses and attorneys for both plaintiff and defendant	192
Cases without witnesses and no attorney	682
Cases without witnesses and attorney for plaintiff only	221
Cases without witnesses and attorney for defendant only	38
Cases without witnesses and attorneys for both plaintiff and defendant	43
Total number of cases	1,380
Missing observations	31

A careful examination of court records reveals some of the tactics lawyers used in JP courts. In *Husen v. Miller* (1874), the plaintiff L. M. Husen sued defendant A. Miller for recovery of $5 due on two masquerade ball tickets. Judge J. D. Laman of Walla Walla recorded the court action of this case. At 10:00 A.M. on the appointed day for court proceedings to begin, the defendant's attorney, George Isham, filed an answer and a request for a change of venue. Before Judge Laman could rule on the motion for a change of venue, the plaintiff's attorney, N. T. Caton, requested the court's permission to file an amended complaint. This motion was granted against the objections of Isham, who also suggested that the costs for amending a complaint be levied directly against the plaintiff before the court reached a decision on the case. Laman denied this request. After a continuance until 2:00 P.M., both Caton and Isham requested subpoenas for witnesses. A total of seven subpoenas were issued and returned that afternoon by constable Davis. Then the plaintiff's attorney again decided to amend his complaint; Isham objected, and after more debate, Laman accepted the complaint. But when Isham asked to file a reply, Judge Laman decided he had had enough of the masquerade ball ticket case. He announced that he was granting a change of venue. Isham and Caton had haggled an entire day, had accumulated $12.55 in court costs, and had not obtained a decision for their clients.[21]

Attorneys did not always obtain their goals in JP courts. In *John Bryant v. Samuel Kehoe* (1881), Kehoe's attorney J. L. Sharpstein requested a change of venue after two successful previous motions. Judge Laman denied the request.[22] Similarly, in *Patrick Doyle v. Saunders and Company* (1860), Island County Justice Nathaniel Hill allowed Junius T. Turner, defendant's attorney, a small amount of latitude to delay the case until Hill rendered a decision. On December 12, Doyle asked Hill's court to force the defendant to pay him $24.88 due on a bill dated September 5, 1860, and Judge Hill ordered representatives of Saunders and Company to appear in court with the plaintiff on December 17. The usual time lapse customarily given between the date of a civil complaint and the first court appearance was six days, and Turner was quick to point this notion out to Judge Hill. Hill then granted a continuance until December 18 and noted a $0.50 charge for the court's inconvenience. On December 18, the defendant and his attorney came to court with a new excuse for delay, but Judge Hill was more interested in hearing the case. Hill wrote:

Parties appear and defendants ask for a further continuance on account of not having his witnesses present—It appears by evidence of the constable that I. F. Saunders, the principal in the case, was down from his place of residence and employed counsel but did not make application for subpoena for witnesses. The court rules therefore that it was their own fault. The plaintiff being ready with his witnesses—motion overruled—Defendants acknowledge the signature of Saunders & Co. but in answer aver that the money was not to be paid but the payment was to be made in goods—they fail to prove this however. Judgment rendered in favour of plaintiff of

Twenty-four 88/100 dollars together with costs of suit and interest from date 'til paid.[23]

Turner could not prevent an adjudication of this claim, and his efforts resulted in $29.11 in court costs (one witness traveled seventy-five miles, and therefore was reimbursed $9.50 for his appearance).

On other occasions, lawyers were quite skillful in maneuvering legal mechanisms to the benefit of their clients. In *Mark F. Colt v. Frank Bell and L. J. Davis* (1877), the plaintiff had sued for $39.62 in gold coin due him for goods, wares, and merchandise sold and delivered to the defendants. Colt got a writ of attachment from Judge Laman to serve on the defendants in order to secure personal or real property in the event the defendants refused to pay the debt. Bell, one of the defendants, hired two attorneys to represent him, and they succeeded in persuading the plaintiff to drop his attachment. When the time came for the court to meet, the defendants did not appear and Colt won a default judgment. Eventually, L. J. Davis paid the account in full, but because Frank Bell employed good lawyers, he avoided payment of any moneys to the plaintiff.[24]

* * * *

Lawyers took part in many of the cases adjudicated before JP courts. When they appeared in court, they constantly made motions and requests on behalf of their clients. This activity required that presiding JPs have a certain degree of legal sophistication; the justices were generally able to match legal wits with the frontier barristers. Although attorneys often delayed case dispositions, encouraged high court costs, and hindered litigant compromise, their presence in the justice of the peace courtroom assured an elevated level of legal decorum.

Attorney participation, in concert with an educated justice of the peace, made the JP courts of Washington Territory arenas of complex legal forensics. Issues coming before these lower courts were argued and explored; attorneys and justices alike joined in the engaging legal battles. In general, Washington Territory justices of the peace presided over courts that seldom formulated decisions without due regard to law. The significant extent to which JPs were educated and to which attorneys attended justice court complemented and facilitated the JP's ability to make fair decisions.

9

Justice Court Accessibility

The accessibility of justice of the peace courts to the people is of prime importance in any consideration of the quality of frontier justice. Certainly, the previous description of the high level of legal dialogue present within courtrooms in Washington Territory would be of considerably less significance if lower court judicial services were not readily available to most Northwest frontier residents. JP accessibility, in terms not only of geographical distribution, but also affordability and subject matter usage, must be evaluated in order to determine whether citizens could easily approach their justices of the peace to gain their help in settling disputes.

Geographical Accessibility

Justices of the peace were geographically within the purview of most of Washington's residents. Whenever settlers collected, a JP was quickly authorized by the legislature, either by means of county creation or by municipal incorporation. Local justices then began to function. Unlike earlier frontier regions, the Washington frontier apparently had few extralegal JPs, mainly because of the lateness of migration to the Northwest and the speed with which government followed the migration.

Few persons complained about not finding justice of the peace courts in Washington Territory, but many citizens of Washington protested the inaccessibility of district courts. Justices of the peace were more numerous than federal courts, and therefore they were areally closer to the people.[1] A rivalry sprang up among the two courts which resulted in Washington's territorial legislature promulgating laws favoring JP courts at the expense of district courts. When circuit travel for district court judges was reduced, JPs and probate judges were authorized to sit as a special court and were given concurrent jurisdiction with district courts.[2] The legislature also denied plaintiffs compensation for court costs if they brought their case before a district court when they could have sued in a JP court.[3]

The law establishing preferred jurisdiction in JP courts eventually had a far-reaching effect. The Washington Territory supreme court, in *Winfield S. Ebey v. Engle & Hill* (1859), ruled that if the district court pared down a claim originally over $100 to less than $100, the plaintiff could not have been able to foresee this possibility and, therefore, he should not have been forced to bring the case before a justice of the peace. In this case, Engle & Hill sued Ebey, a justice of the peace in Coveland Precinct, for a claim of $280 in district court. The district court found in favor of the plaintiffs, but only in the sum of $15 plus court costs, a total of $49.90. Ebey, well aware of the ramifications of this finding, appealed the case to the territorial supreme court. He argued that Engle & Hill should have brought the case in a JP court, and therefore he was not responsible for any court costs. The supreme court was not convinced and agreed with Engle & Hill, the victorious plaintiffs.[4]

In 1880, however, the supreme court, in *Bagley v. Carpenter*, specifically overruled *Ebey v. Engle & Hill*, holding that final allotments in court proceedings were the test to determine whether the case should have been brought in a justice of the peace court. The court thereby deprived the plaintiff of any moneys to defer court costs.[5] Engle & Hill would have lost $34.90 in 1880 instead of winning $49.90 in 1859. Many persons, including the legislature and even the territorial supreme court, had great confidence in the geographical accessibility of justice of the peace courts.

Cost Accessibility

JP courts in Washington Territory were also within the financial means of many territorial residents. Justices of the peace charged an average of $4.59 per case; witnesses were paid $9.43 per case if they were called; and jurors were given $11.96 per case if they were impaneled.[6] The average total court costs in 1,411 cases examined was $13.13 per case, $11.83 per civil case, and $17.74 per criminal case.

The figure $13.13 should not be viewed as a set mean of JP court costs for litigants. It was inflated by the inclusion of the costs from criminal cases in which fees were often charged to the county or territory. In addition, the median of total court costs was $9.09, which shows that extreme case costs had a limited effect in averaging court costs. But for the purposes of this survey of court cost accessibility, $13.13 will represent the average cost per case, inclusive of certain extreme costs, to bring a complaint to a justice of the peace court in Washington Territory.

In order for the $13.13 figure to have any meaning as it related to people during the 1850s to the 1880s, wholesale price indexes have been examined with reference to wheat, nail, and brick prices.[7] For example, a wheat farmer in the 1850s expected to receive $2 per bushel.[8] To bring a court case, the farmer had to harvest and sell over seven bushels of wheat. In the 1880s, when times were harder, the wheat farmer received $0.96 per bushel for a crop and needed over fourteen bushels to sue a debtor in JP court. A hardware merchant selling nails or bricks who wanted to bring a complaint before a justice court in the 1850s had to sell more than 340 pounds of nails or 2,867 bricks. If the complaint was brought in the 1880s, the merchant would have to sell at least 494 pounds of nails or 1,837 bricks to cover expected court costs.

More specifically, Washington Territory residents who lived in Bickleton, Klickitat County, in 1887, had to forego three pairs of men's riding boots or sixty-six pounds of Rio coffee for one JP decision. A saddle with a double cinch bought two court cases, and three Oxford Bibles paid for one JP court adjudication.[9]

In Island County in 1853, some farmers held substantial amounts of property and sold crops for as much as $800 per year. Farm laborers made as much as $2.50 to $3.00 per day in the winter and about $4.00 per day during the summer. A man with his own hook working at square timber or outing piles for shipping made $6.00 to $7.00 per day minus board.[10] To a laborer, a court case might have meant one-half a week to a week's wages.

Justice of the peace courts in Washington Territory were accessible to many citizens, even those working on a low daily wage basis. In the cases examined, laborers frequently used JP courts and won back wages withheld by employers. Whidbey Island logger William Clark successfully sued his employer Luke Moore for $50 in wages due him for work performed in April, May, June, and July 1863. D. H. Smith of Walla Walla won $8.50 for farm labor performed in 1881, and Marshall Martin, Walla Walla blacksmith, recovered $21 due him for labor performed for James McElhaney.[11] However, persons frequently using JP courts, especially those represented by lawyers with a penchant for juries, had to have some financial resources; they needed to be aware of changing court costs.

In Chapter 7, court cost trends for Washington Territory JP courts were depicted through territorial legislation. Witness and total court costs generally fell in the early 1860s, then rose in the late 1860s, and eventually leveled off during the remainder of the territorial period. Jury costs did not follow this general trend because designated increases and decreases in juror fees were contingent upon mileage to and from court, and juries were chosen because of their close court residence. Even though the legislature changed jury cost formulas, the changes had little real effect on court costs.

Also in Chapter 7, when Washington territorial legislation was analyzed for individual JP court cost trends, four time periods emerged, each having a distinct cost characteristic when compared

Table 13

**Justice of the Peace Costs in JP Courts,
Washington Territory, 1854-1889**

Periods	Number of Cases	Mean Cost	Median Cost	Minimum Case Cost	Maximum Case Cost
1854-1860	9	$4.55	$4.66	$0.25	$9.35
1861	5	2.62	2.60	1.85	3.40
1862-1868	49	6.82	4.53	0.75	23.00
1869-1889	1,311	4.51	4.04	1.00	24.76

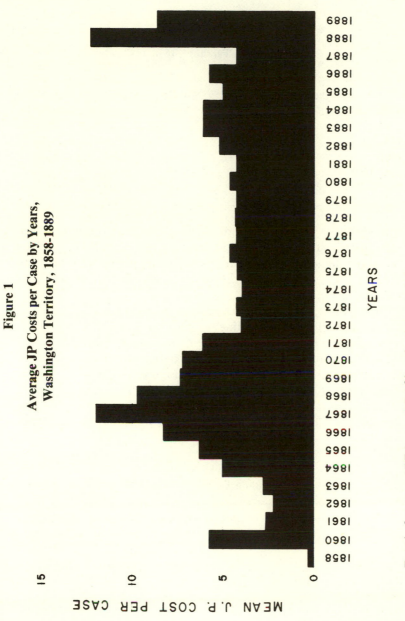

Figure 1

**Average JP Costs per Case by Years,
Washington Territory, 1858-1889**

Total Cases – 1374 or 97.4% of the sample

Mean – $4.59

Table 14

Witness Costs in JP Courts,
Washington Territory, 1854-1889

Periods	Number of Cases	Mean Cost	Median Cost	Minimum Case Cost	Maximum Case Cost
1854-1860	5	$10.56	$10.63	$3.40	$17.80
1861	3	4.43	4.13	0.50	9.60
1862-1868	25	13.27	8.60	1.00	43.20
1869-1889	297	9.13	6.69	1.25	55.10

with the other periods. A gradual rising cost trend occurred from 1854 to 1860; 1861 saw a drastic drop in court costs from previous years; the highest fee levels for the territorial period were set from 1862 to 1868; and fee charges returned to pre-1861 prices from 1869 to 1889.

Data from 1,411 JP court cases have been organized in terms of these four periods to determine whether the legislative cost trends were reflected in the actual practice of the courts. Fees charged by local justices for their court services verified all trends formed by fee schedule statutes (see Table 13 and Figure 1). When the periods were analyzed in terms of homogeneous subsets (where individual JP costs were paired with those that did not differ by more than the shortest significant range), the periods 1854-1860, 1861, and 1869-

Table 15

Juror Costs in JP Courts,
Washington Territory, 1854-1889

Periods	Number of Cases	Mean Cost	Median Cost	Minimum Case Cost	Maximum Case Cost
1854-1860	1	$15.60	$15.60	$15.60	$15.60
1861	0	0	0	0	0
1862-1868	5	11.52	12.10	6.00	15.20
1869-1889	46	11.93	12.50	6.00	27.80

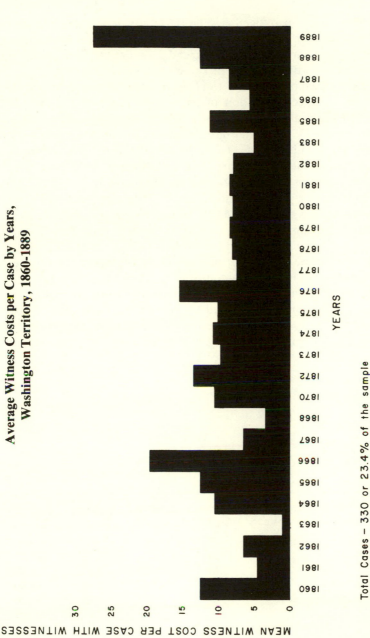

Figure 2

Average Witness Costs per Case by Years,
Washington Territory, 1860-1889

YEARS

MEAN WITNESS COST PER CASE WITH WITNESSES

Total Cases – 330 or 23.4% of the sample

Mean – $9.43

1889 were grouped together. The 1862-1868 period was so different from the other periods that it was grouped alone, further substantiating the court fee schedule trends. A similar verification was realized for witness costs (see Table 14 and Figure 2).

Data based on juror and total court costs did not verify statutory trends. The concentration of cases with juries in the 1869-1889 period made an analysis of juror costs meaningless (see Table 15 and Figure 3). Note that data tabulated for the later two periods have very similar means. Thus, the average juror costs per case did not mirror the inflationary and deflationary juror cost trends. Total court costs, like juror costs, do not precisely match the trends identified (see Table 16 and Figure 4). When grouped in homogeneous subsets, period 1854-1860 was found to resemble period 1862-1868, supposedly the period of highest costs. This deviation occurred because total costs of other variables such as fees charged by constables, sheriffs, attorneys, and newspapers for service on litigants were included in addition to JP, witness, and jury costs, and because an overproportionate number of extreme costs were a part of the sample as indicated by the median. These other variables were subject to more general economic fluctuations than the composition of the Washington territorial legislature.

Table 16

Total Costs in JP Courts,
Washington Territory, 1854-1889

Periods	Number of Cases	Mean Cost	Median Cost	Minimum Case Cost	Maximum Case Cost
1854-1860	7	$27.62	$19.15	$1.75	$84.52
1861	5	5.53	5.39	2.25	14.80
1862-1868	45	25.18	14.78	0.75	82.90
1869-1889	1,307	12.66	9.07	1.45	95.90

Figure 3

Average Juror Costs per Case by Years, Washington Territory, 1860-1889

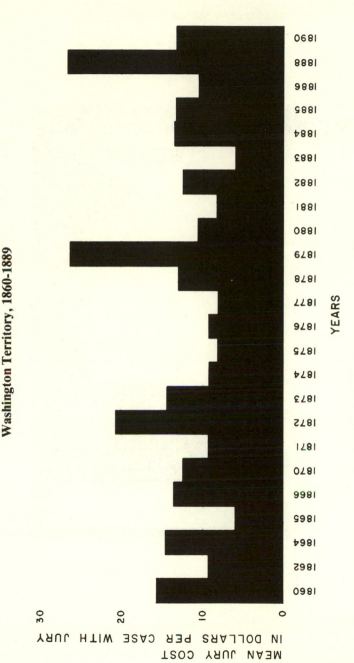

Total Cases – 52 or 3.7% of the sample

Mean – $11.96

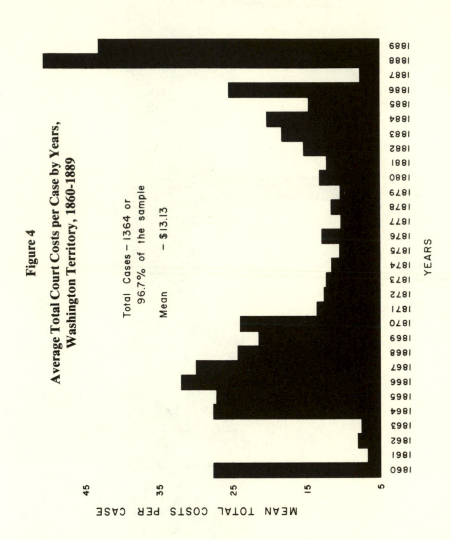

Figure 4

Average Total Court Costs per Case by Years, Washington Territory, 1860-1889

Total Cases – 1364 or
96.7% of the sample

Mean   – $13.13

Perhaps an even more useful analysis of the real costs of going to JP courts can be obtained by comparing total court costs with general wholesale price fluctuations for the years 1860-1889 (see Figure 5). The wholesale price indexes were compiled from prices in the primary markets of the East, South, and Midwest. Although western markets were not used in the compilation, trends in Washington Territory JP court expenses from 1860 to 1871 resembled wholesale price indexes. The year 1861 represented a low point in prices for both graphs; 1862-1868 indicated a pronounced inflationary spiral, with prices beginning to drop by 1865 in wholesale indexes and by 1867 in court costs. However, while wholesale prices continued to plummet after a brief rise in 1872, court costs stabilized. The fall of wholesale prices was a characteristic of the Panic of 1873 and the years of depression thereafter.[12]

Costwise, JP courts in Washington Territory were within the financial means of most residents of the Northwest frontier. At no time throughout the territorial period did court costs run significantly ahead of wholesale price indexes, and the ability to engage these judicial services was not hindered by excessive charges. Residents of Washington Territory found justice courts economically accessible.

Causal Accessibility

While justice of the peace courts were financially and geographically accessible to many citizens in Washington Territory, these courts were also readily available to frontier residents to handle their peculiar problems. Justice of the peace court records have been examined for Washington Territory with reference to type of case. Of 1,411 cases recorded, 1,078 or 76.4 percent were civil cases; 329 or 23.3 percent were criminal cases; and 4 or 0.3 percent were general warrants.[13] For purposes of a manageable discussion, civil and criminal cases have been subdivided into sixteen general causes of action (see Table 17). The number of cases has been tabulated for each of the sixteen groups, and the percentages of each group to the whole have been calculated (see Figure 6). From the pie diagrams, a number of conclusions emerge concerning the typical cases that came before justices of the peace.

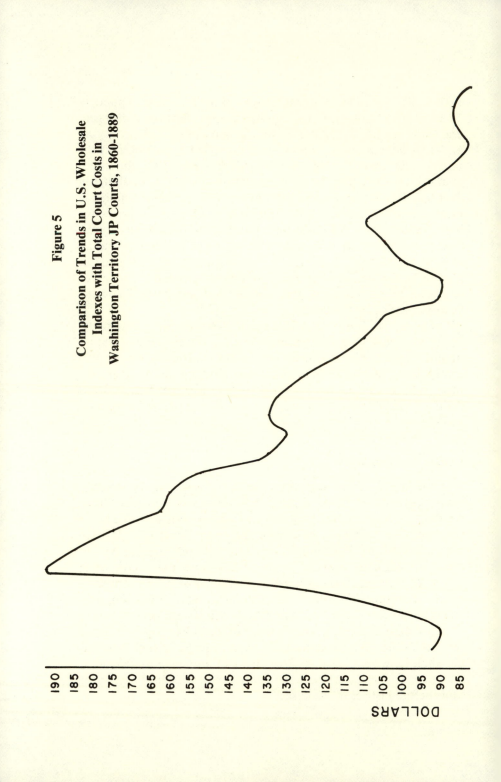

Figure 5

Comparison of Trends in U.S. Wholesale Indexes with Total Court Costs in Washington Territory JP Courts, 1860–1889

190
185
180
175
170
165
160
155
150
145
140
135
130
125
120
115
110
105
100
95
90
85

DOLLARS

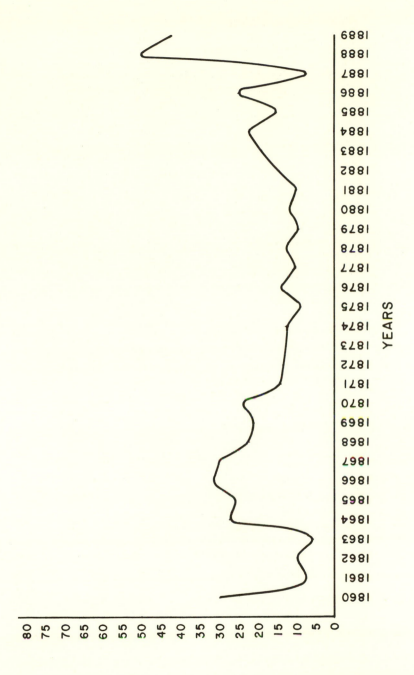

Table 17

**Subdivisions of Civil and Criminal Causes of Action,
Washington Territory JP Courts, 1854-1889**

Civil Cases
1. Debt
    Debt action
    Promissory note
    Promissory note and debt
    Re-execution of a judgment
    Conversion
    Garnishment and debt
    Attachment and debt
    Recovery of a street tax
    Debts to county for road
        maintenance
    Contract
    Re-execution and contempt

2. Mortgage/Lien
    Foreclosure on a mortgage

3. Damages to Persons
    Damages for an assault and
        battery

4. Damages to Property
    Damages for failure to
        deliver a note
    Damages to real property
    Damages caused by hogs
        and keeping estray hogs
    Damages to personal
        property
    Damages and conversion
    Damages and debt
    Damages and forcible entry
        and unlawful detainer
    Damages and replevin

(Table 17 continued)

5. Replevin
    General replevin
    Replevin or the value thereof

6. Forcible Entry/Unlawful
   Detainer
    Unlawful detainer
    Forcible entry and unlawful
        detainer
    Forcible entry, unlawful
        detainer and debt

Criminal Cases
1. Violent Crime to Persons—
   Felony
    Murder
    Rape
    Robbery and assault
    Robbery and assault and
        battery
    Assault and battery with a
        deadly weapon with
        intent to commit a
        bodily injury
    Assault with a deadly weap-
        on with intent to com-
        mit a bodily injury

    Assault with a deadly weap-
        on with intent to
        commit a bodily injury
        and disturbing the peace
    Assault with a deadly weap-
        on with intent to kill

2. Violent Crime to Persons—
   Misdemeanor
    Assault
    Assault and battery
    Assault and battery with a
        deadly weapon

(Table 17 continued)

Assault with intent to rob
Assault with intent to rape
Assault and battery on an
    infant
Assault with a deadly
    weapon
Assault with intent to have
    carnal knowledge
Disturbing the peace by
    striking an officer of
    the law
Assault with intent to
    commit murder
Assault and battery with
    intent to produce a
    miscarriage
Pouring a quart of beer
    over a person thereby
    spoiling his clothes

3. Threats to Commit Violent
   Crime to Persons—
   Misdemeanor
       Threat to commit a criminal
           offense
       Exhibiting a pistol and
           threatening to shoot a
           person
       Threat to kill horses or
           humans
       Threat to commit murder
       Threat to commit an assault

4. Property Crime—Felony
       Grand larceny
       Possession of stolen goods
       Robbery
       Burglary
       Forgery
       Killing cattle

(Table 17 continued)

Stealing horses
Buying and concealing
stolen property
Obtaining property under
false pretenses
Obtaining money and goods
under false pretenses
Breaking and entering

5. Property Crime—
Misdemeanor
Petit larceny
Malicious trespass
Cruelty to animals

6. Morality Crime—Felony
Adultery
Polygamy
Defamation of character
and libel

7. Morality Crime—
Misdemeanor
Gambling
Selling and distributing
obscene literature
Vagrancy
Vagrancy and habitual
drunkenness
Smoking and inhaling opium
Assault by words
Selling liquor and cigars on
Sunday
Selling goods and merchan-
dise on Sunday

8. Maintenance of Judicial
Order Crime—Felony
Perjury

(Table 17 continued)

9. Maintenance of Judicial
   Order Crime—Misdemeanor
   Contempt
   Issuance of a general warrant
   Disturbing the peace

10. State Regulatory Crime—
    Misdemeanor
    Taxes
    Violation of a city ordinance
    Violation of the charter of a
       ferry corporation
    Obstructing a public
       highway
    Creating a nuisance by
       depositing a putrid
       carcass of a dead cow
       by a public road
    Selling merchandise from a
       wagon without a license
    Violation of a game law

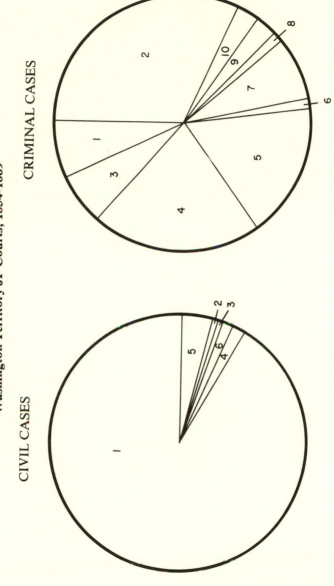

Figure 6

**The Frequency of Subdivisions of Civil and Criminal
JP Cause of Actions to Civil, Criminal, and All Cases,
Washington Territory JP Courts, 1854-1889**

CIVIL CASES

CRIMINAL CASES

(Figure 6 continued)

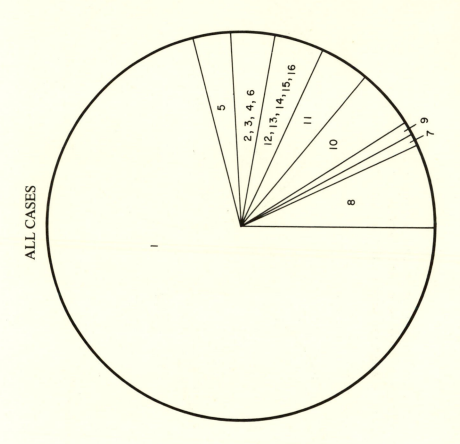

KEY to Figure 6

Percentages of Civil Cause of Actions in Civil Cases
1. Debt   92.86%
2. Mortgage/Lien   0.09
3. Damages to Persons   0.09
4. Damages to Property   1.49
5. Replevin   4.08
6. Forcible Entry/Unlawful Detainer   1.39

Percentages of Criminal Cause of Actions in Criminal Cases
1. Violent Crime to Persons—Felony   6.99%
2. Violent Crime to Persons—Misdemeanor   31.91
3. Threats to Commit Violent Crime to Persons—
     Misdemeanor   6.38
4. Property Crime—Felony   22.19
5. Property Crime—Misdemeanor   17.93
6. Morality Crime—Felony   1.22
7. Morality Crime—Misdemeanor   7.91
8. Maintenance of Judicial Order Crime—Felony   0.30
9. Maintenance of Judicial Order Crime—Misdemeanor 2.43
10. State Regulatory Crime—Misdemeanor   2.74

Percentages of Civil and Criminal Cause of Actions in All Cases
1. Debt   71.14%
2. Mortgage/Lien   0.07
3. Damages to Persons   0.07
4. Damages to Property   1.14
5. Replevin   3.13
6. Forcible Entry/Unlawful Detainer   1.07
7. Violent Crime to Persons—Felony   1.64
8. Violent Crime to Persons—Misdemeanor   7.46
9. Threats to Commit Violent Crime to Persons—
     Misdemeanor   1.49
10. Property Crime—Felony   5.19
11. Property Crime—Misdemeanor   4.19
12. Morality Crime—Felony   0.28
13. Morality Crime—Misdemeanor   1.85
14. Maintenance of Judicial Order Crime—Felony   0.07
15. Maintenance of Judicial Order Crime—Misdemeanor 0.57
16. State Regulatory Crime—Misdemeanor   0.64

The overwhelming majority of cases brought were debt actions. Debt actions usually were begun by a farmer, logger, lumberman, or merchant for products sold or services rendered. Products ranged from alcoholic beverages and foodstuffs to household essentials and clothing. Rare items included a violin, two bobsleds, and several orange plants. Lumber companies and their employees sued each other over wages or debts owed for room and board. Farmers also had disputes over crops and their production. Wheat, barley, oats, hay, straw, vegetables, horses, cattle, sheep, hogs, services of bulls and stallions, harnesses, wheat sacks, reapers, saddles, and patronage—all were frequent subjects of debt suits.

For example, on November 17, 1881, Mssrs. Dagget and Hutchings sued Timothy McCormick to recover $42.00 due them for threshing seven hundred bushels of wheat, oats, and barley at $0.06 per bushel. Both parties were represented by attorneys who hotly contested the suit. Walla Walla justice of the peace J. D. Laman had to render six decisions on motions offered by opposing counsel. In a flurry of cross-examinations and rebuttals of the defendant, McCormick admitted to a conversation with Dagget and Hutchings regarding their threshing work. Judge Laman then quickly closed the case, awarding the plaintiffs their full claim.[14]

Compensation for services performed was another common topic of debt actions. Carpenters, blacksmiths, tailors, painters, shepherds, musicians, cooks, waiters, and gravediggers used justice of the peace courts to recover wages earned. Doctors, veterinarians, teachers, funeral directors, lawyers, and dentists also pursued claims for their services in justice courts.

One dentist who was forced into JP court was H. M. Chamberlin of Island County. He had made and fitted Eliza Jane Terry's mouth for a set of false teeth, but she and her husband Grove refused to pay for the teeth. Chamberlin therefore brought a debt action for $100 against Grove Terry in John Y. Sewell's court. After the initial legal maneuvers, Chamberlin requested a jury. The jury was sworn after Charles Terry, father of the defendant, was successfully challenged from the jury panel. Testimony began with the plaintiff and his dental assistants asserting that Chamberlin had made and fitted Eliza Terry with false teeth. Then the defendant Grove Terry testified: "I told my wife if she wanted the teeth and was satisfied I would fit the bill. My wife said she liked the appearance of the teeth but expressed some dissatisfaction about the fit of them." Realizing that the defendant was trying to portray the plaintiff as an incompetent dentist, Chamberlin then called three witnesses, including Maria Coupe who was the wife of the founder of the county seat of Island County. All three stated their satisfaction with their false teeth fashioned by the plaintiff. The defendants then rebutted by claiming Eliza Terry had accepted the teeth strictly on a trial basis. Finally, both parties rested, the jury deliberated, and a decision was reached. The Terrys had accepted the false teeth made by H. M. Chamberlin, and they had to pay for them and court costs, a total of $179.55. Eliza Terry's new teeth had proven to be a costly legal and dental experience.[15]

Debt actions consisted primarily of cases dealing with goods and services rendered that were characteristic of new developing communities in farming and lumbering regions. Similarly, other civil actions reflected an agricultural and lumber-producing environment. Replevin actions, legal demands for the return of personal property, were usually brought to retake horses wrongfully held. In an 1878 replevin case on a change of venue, Judge Laman personally examined the horse in question and awarded it to the defendant.[16] In actions for forcible entry and unlawful detainer, plaintiffs were usually farmers who were trying to remove farm laborers. Sometimes lumber companies forced loggers out of bunkhouses, and hotel or home owners pushed roomers out of rented rooms. Civil actions, and in particular debt actions (over 71 percent of all cases examined), reflected a growing and expanding frontier economy, thereby providing a high degree of case accessibility in JP courts for residents of Washington Territory.

Criminal cases made up less than a quarter of all cases examined, but their subdivision distributions were more balanced than civil subdivision distributions. Of all criminal cases, the three largest groups of causes of action were violent crime to persons—misdemeanor (31.91 percent), property crime—felony (22.19 percent), and property crime—misdemeanor (17.93 percent). Together, while these groups composed nearly three-fourths of all criminal cases, they made up only 16.84 percent of the entire sample.

Violent crimes to persons classified as misdemeanors were largely composed of assault and batteries. Assault and batteries usually grew out of arguments that became fistfights. Persons were also charged with assaults if they were about to commit a felony. The touching of an individual in an attempt to rape, rob, murder, or abort, if proven, resulted in an assault conviction.

Not knowing what crime to charge a defendant, Judge William Uder ordered Thomas Mularkey tried for pouring beer on Peter Heisenberger and spoiling his clothes, an assault of sorts.[17] Judge Uder sometimes allowed special circumstances to mitigate criminal proceedings. In an assault and battery case heard on January 2, 1888, in Newcastle Precinct, the defendant pleaded guilty, but because the offense had occurred as a result of a New Year's Eve spree, Judge Uder decreed a small fine.[18]

The types of property crimes, misdemeanors, and felonies common in Washington Territory indicated what tangibles were most valued by frontier residents. Killing or stealing cattle and horses was so serious an offense that JPs took specific note of this type of felony rather than classifying them as grand larceny cases. Grand larceny and petit larceny actions appeared most frequently in property crimes; theft of timber, harnesses, and farming equipment were commonplace.

The charge of petit larceny was also used by one judge, Thomas Donald of Newcastle Precinct, to handle an unusual case. In February 1886, a logger was found wandering naked in the woods. He was brought before Judge Donald on a charge of petit larceny. The judge was astute and found the defendant not guilty since he had no possesions. However, Donald was not through with the logger. He tried him for vagrancy, discovered the logger was suffering from delirium tremens, and found him insane.[19]

Newcastle Precinct records, while mentioning loggers, lumbermen, prostitution, and supply merchants, contained no reference to miners. Newcastle was a coal mining region in King County during the 1880s, so whatever problems miners had, they settled them outside of justice courts. Even though JPs were given jurisdiction over mining claim disputes, mining customs had the effect of law. Mining companies and their employees seem to have chosen to ignore the courts and to handle their disagreements within their own specialized community.

Other criminal causes of action of note were morality, judicial order, and state regulatory crimes. When Sarah Conroy called Mary Barrett a whore, Barrett had Conroy charged with assault by words. Judge Thomas Donald made light of the defendant's assertion that she could prove Barrett a prostitute, and he fined her one penny. Conroy refused payment and spent twelve days in the county jail.[20] In February 1886, Thomas Cranney found Ah Tune, Ah Torn and Ah Goon guilty of opium-smoking (Cranney's spellings were no doubt phonetic and inaccurate). They received fifteen- and ten-day jail terms, and Sheriff Joe Power was ordered to destroy the dope and pipe.[21] The Conroy and Ah Tune et al. cases were representative samples of criminal prosecutions on morality charges.

Nathaniel Hill, JP of Island County, deputized Charles Seibert to serve a criminal warrant for contempt on Granville P. Knight. Knight had refused to turn over records helpful to Seibert in an action in which he was being sued by Dr. John Kellogg. Threatened by the contempt citation, Knight appeared in Hill's court to explain how he had given the records to Kellogg; the case was dismissed.[22]

John Bryant, road supervisor, complained to Walla Walla justice J. D. Laman that S. B. Ives had left a dead cow near a public road. Ives was brought to court charged with creating a public nuisance: "the Deft. offered to have the said Cow properly covered up to avoid smell or nuisance and to pay costs if the prosecuting witness would dismiss the case. The Prosecuting witness thereupon asks that the Case be dismissed and such is the order of the Court."[23] Similarly, Jacob J. Straub filed an oath that Ah Loy killed six quail in violation of the game laws of Washington Territory. Ah Loy pleaded not guilty, but he was found guilty by Judge Thomas Cranney and was sentenced to eight days in the Jefferson County jail.[24] Granville Knight, S. B. Ives, and Ah Loy were all parties to JP criminal cases involving laws made and enforced by the judicial or legislative branches of territorial government ostensibly to manage social behavior. Note that in Washington Territory only 1.28 percent of all cases heard by JPs concerned enforcing local or territorial regulatory statutes.

* * * *

Justice of the peace courts heard a variety of civil and criminal cases. The specific causes of action examined exhibit a wide range of legal concerns, but in general they reflect the problems indigenous to citizens of the Northwest frontier, excepting those engaged in mining activity. Consequently, case accessibility, as well as geographical and cost accessibility, of justice of the peace courts to Washington Territory residents was high. JP courts were readily available to resolve the disputes of the Northwest's new communities and institutions.

Perceptions of the Justice Court in Action

Washington Territory JP court proceedings were characterized not only by a high level of justice court usage of the law and relative ease of JP accessibility, but also by speedy disposition of most cases and the frontier residents' acceptance of the lower courts as the final and usual arbiter of community disputes.

Adjudication Celerity

Celerity of adjudication has been tabulated for 1,411 Washington Territory JP cases by measuring the average length of time required for three steps: the first filing of a complaint to the first official hearing of a case; the first court meeting to the announcement of a decision; and the decision announcement to final satisfaction.

From complaint to court action, the average length of time was 9.36 days for all types of cases (1,373 of 1,411 cases or 97.3 percent of the sample). From first court action to a court decision, the average length of time was 0.69 days for all types of cases (1,030 of 1,411 cases or 73 percent of the sample; the higher percentage of missing cases was attributable to the dates for dismissals, changes in venue, and grand jury or district court determinations not being carried past the first and final court appearance). Thus, the average amount of time that a JP took with a case was 10.05 days.

Once the court rendered a decision, the losing party either appealed, complied with the judgment, or refused to cooperate. If adherence to the decision of the court was not forthcoming, a constable or sheriff was sent to collect the amount or property owed. In Washington Territory JP courts, the average length of time from the date of a final decision to the date of final satisfaction was 82.44 days or almost three months. If a potential litigant wanted to bring a suit in justice of the peace court, the suit in essence would be likely to take over 9 days if it ended in a dismissal, a change of venue, or a grand jury/district court determination; or it would last approximately 92.5 days if a final judgment was based upon a trial determination, a pleading, or a default.[1]

This analysis was further broken down by a cross-tabulation of time to case type, civil or criminal. Civil cases were found to take much longer in all phases than criminal cases. From complaint to first day in court, civil cases lasted 10.77 days compared to 4.53 days in criminal cases. From first court appearance to a court decision, civil cases took 0.78 days whereas criminal cases took 0.39 days. The largest difference occurred between court decision and final satisfaction. Civil cases averaged 107.91 days while criminal cases averaged only 12.99. Consequently, the mean length of time for a civil justice case was 119.46 days compared to only 17.91 days for a criminal case.

Two factors caused this difference between civil and criminal cases. First, civil actions customarily allowed defendants six days of preparation between the date a complaint was sworn and the first day of JP court. No such due process protection surrounded criminal defendants of the nineteenth century. Once a criminal complaint was signed and a justice of the peace had sworn out an arrest warrant, criminal defendants were hunted down by constables or sheriffs and brought before the court. When the defendant appeared before a JP and the trial began, the defendant was forced to plead guilty or not guilty, and prosecution witnesses came forth promptly to testify. Second, in criminal cases many more defendants were found guilty than not guilty. The convicted defendant either paid a fine and court costs or went to jail, or both. If the defendant could not afford the fine and court costs, the county or territory paid for the legal proceedings. Conversely, in civil cases, when a defendant could not pay the judgment or court costs, salaries were garnished and properties were attached—two legal processes that required much more time.[2]

Whereas a litigant or attorney who expected to participate in a case before a justice of the peace court could have foreseen the time gap between a completed civil action and a completed criminal action, neither adjudication required a significantly long period of days. That an average case decision only took approximately ten days and a final satisfaction required less than three months constituted evidence of an efficient and speedy justice court system.

In part because processing civil and criminal cases went rapidly, justice of the peace dockets were not very crowded, and so JPs could give their undivided attention to the facts of a case. Of the twelve judges observed, only one, J. D. Laman of Walla Walla, appeared to have a slightly crowded docket.[3] The only justice in a bustling frontier urban community averaged over ninety-six cases per month. Occasionally, Laman was forced to postpone cases. When Joseph Freeman sued Joseph Nibbler for a $51 loan plus interest, Laman wrote: "the Court being engaged in a trial of another cause, this case is on motion of the Court continued until tomorrow February 19, 1874 at 11 o'clock A.M." On February 19, 1874, Judge Laman heard *Freeman v. Nibbler* and found for the plaintiff.[4]

As suggested above, Judge Laman was the exception among the judges whose records were tabulated. Only three other judges heard an average of over three cases per month. Nathaniel Hill usually received about three cases per month. In his diary he recorded his activities for February 1854. On February 10, he wrote: "We have started our plough—we hope to put in some eight or ten acres of Wheat—."[5] Later that day, he held court at his home. Hill convened no other court sessions that February but he did manage to finish sowing his wheat by March 2.

Hill's court was more representative of the usual amount of business handled by JPs than Laman's court. If all judges and all cases are considered, Washington Territory justices of the peace heard 9.79 cases per month. When Laman's court is removed from the sample, the average number of cases received per month drops to 1.89. Whichever case amount is considered, clearly justice court dockets were not crowded and adjudications were not delayed.

Thus, Washington's justices of the peace were handling a reasonable amount of legal business efficiently and speedily. Once causes of action were brought to the attention of JPs, the cases were heard without delay, and judges were not hurried into instant determinations because of other pressing legal business. The quality of JP justice in Washington Territory was enhanced by the high degree of adjudication celerity and proficiency achieved.

Justice Court Acceptance by the Frontier Community

A last indicator to be scrutinized in the determination of the quality of justice disseminated by Washington Territory's JPs is the general community approval of JP decisions. Justice of the peace court usage, appeal rates of JP decisions, and extralegal actions in Washington Territory will indicate whether local justice was accepted.

Court usage in the three geographical areas observed varied according to population. In Coveland Precinct, as population increased, court activity decreased. By the 1880s, JP courts heard one case per year per every 111 people in Island County, Coveland Precinct. In Newcastle Precinct, by the 1880s, JP courts received one case per year per every 135 people. In Walla Walla Precinct, as population stabilized, court activity increased. By the 1880s, JP courts sat for one case per year per every 25 people in Walla Walla Precinct, Walla Walla County. Therefore, in at least one urban frontier region, justice courts were frequently employed, and in two rural areas, residents moderately resorted to JP courts. For the entire sample, justices of the peace adjudicated one case per year per every 31 people; this finding testifies to substantial usage of JP courts by citizens of Washington Territory.[6]

As previously stated, JP courts were used mostly by individual merchants, farmers, farm laborers, lumbermen, loggers, and persons offering professional services. Corporations in the timber business also came to justice courts. In 1880, Puget Mill Company successfully sued E. E. Hickman for payment of a promissory note plus interest before Island County justice of the peace Robert Hathaway.[7] In 1888, Pacific Boom Company complained to Judge Thomas Cranney that the Puget Mill Company owed it $125 in back debts. Puget Mill fought the case through three days of court proceedings, eight witnesses, and two juries (one of them hung), only to lose $66.25 of the claim to Pacific Boom and $86.75 in court costs.[8]

JP courts were used primarily by white males against other white males. Women were denied direct access to justice courts by law and by social custom during much of the territorial period. However, in 1873, Catherine Root successfully sued for recovery of $56.25 from the sale of a horse, and Margaret Johnson was forced to pay $60.00 gold coin on a delinquent promissory note.[9] Chinese and native Americans seldom came before local justices, but when they were involved in JP court proceedings, they usually appeared as defendants. Sing Lee and Sam Sing had their scow attached and sold by order of Judge Robert Hathaway to pay a $76.25 debt.[10] Bob, a male Indian, and Dectotza, an Indian woman, were charged with murder before Judge John Y. Sewell; Bob fled Island County, but Dectotza appeared in court where she was exonerated.[11] And Squiqui, a Skagit chief, was accused of stealing eleven blankets, one sheet, one pillow case, one dozen milk pans, a quantity of tin plates, cups and saucers, two crosscut hand saws, eight yards of linen toweling, and one piece of sheeting. Justice William Robertson issued a search warrant to recover the stolen goods, but none could be found and Squiqui was acquitted.[12] In general, justice court usage reflected the dominant majority society on the Washington frontier.

Court usage also revealed seasonal types of frontier economic activity. In Figure 7, justice of the peace court usage has been graphed by month to show periods of high and low court activity. The greatest period of JP court adjudications was during the winter months of December and January; the lightest period was during the spring and early summer months of April, May, and June. Not surprisingly, wheat farmers, cattle raisers, and loggers worked hardest when JP courts heard their fewest number of cases; conversely, local justices had their highest caseload when wheat farmers, cattle raisers, and loggers tended to be idle. That JP court usage reflected certain economic and social characteristics of frontier life in Washington Territory explains in part the popular employment of the courts by the territory's majority residents.

Justice Courts as Courts of Last Resort

Once a case came before a justice of the peace in Washington Territory, chances of appeal were minimal. Of 1,411 cases observed, only fifty-four or 3.8 percent reached the district court. Upon closer examination, forty-nine of the fifty-four cases appealed were civil cases. This represented 4.5 percent of *all* civil cases heard; five criminal cases appealed constituted 1.5 percent of *all* criminal cases adjudicated. While odds favored civil appeals to criminal appeals, distinctions based upon case class were negligible when compared to the small total amount of all cases taken from justice courts to district courts.

Above the district courts sat the Washington Territory supreme court. During the Washington territorial period, from 1853 to 1889, the supreme court processed 654 cases on appeal. Of those cases, only ten cases or 1.5 percent originated in justice of the peace courts; three of these cases were criminal appeals and seven were civil appeals.[13]

One of the ten cases, *Harland v. Territory of Washington* (1887), became a landmark case. The plaintiff Jeff J. Harland had been arrested for bunko gambling and was brought before a Tacoma justice court. The JP ruled there was sufficient evidence for an investigation and sent the case to a grand jury for possible indictment. The grand jury, which numbered five women among its members, brought forth an indictment, and the district court found Harland guilty as charged. Harland appealed his conviction to the Washington Territory supreme court on the basis that a title defect in the state law granting women the right to sit on grand juries, and incidentally the right to vote, made his indictment and conviction void. In a two-to-one decision, the supreme court found the disputed statute void on a legal technicality.[14] The Harland case exonerated Harland and temporarily denied women the franchise. The other nine cases brought to the upper court from justice courts concerned minor abuses in lower court procedures.

Since few cases begun and decided before a justice of the peace traveled beyond his jurisdiction, and even fewer advanced to the territorial supreme court, JPs in Washington Territory presided over courts of last resort. Litigants who made use of justice courts realized that JPs embodied the judicial power of the community *and* the federal government; appeals to higher territorial courts were geographically and financially prohibitive. In short, justices of the peace monopolized legal decision-making for the new settlements.

Figure 7

**Justice of the Peace Court Case Volume per Month,
Washington Territory, 1854-1889**

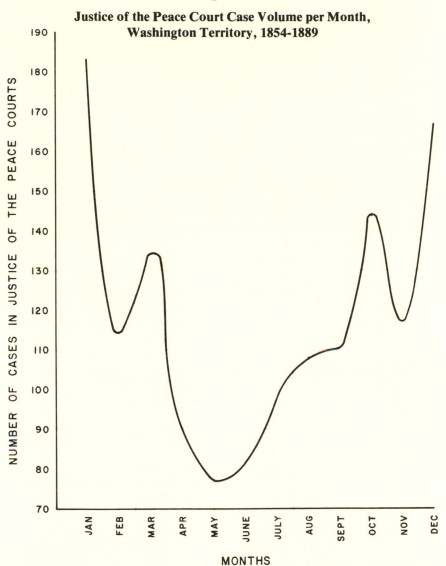

Missing Observations = 2 of 1411 or .14%

Extralegal Actions in Washington Territory

Terminal adjudications gave JPs great influence over developing communities, but that influence would have been lessened if Washington Territory residents had turned to extralegal activity whose purpose was to enforce the law without court action. In Washington Territory, few extralegal movements skirted the law.

Richard Maxwell Brown in *The History of Violence in America* identifies five vigilante movements in Washington Territory[15]— specifically in Pierce County, Clallam County (New Dungeness), Walla Walla County (Walla Walla), King County (Seattle) and Yakima County (Union Gap). One other movement has been identified, a second vigilante action in Pierce County (Steilacoom).[16] The major mob activity of the territorial era, the 1885-1886 anti-Chinese riots of western Washington, is excluded because whites desired the removal of the Chinese rather than changes in an ineffective legal system.

Of the six vigilante groups identified, only two were large movements. One of these occurred in Walla Walla during the 1860s. The *Walla Walla Union* recorded the origins of the local vigilante committee. At a ball given in a tavern, a man named Coghshill was killed by Bill Bunton, "a notorious bad character." Bunton was tried and acquitted, which aroused the ire of Walla Wallans. Fearing for his life, Bunton fled to Montana where he was finally caught and hung. After Bunton's demise, another murderer who escaped to Salt Lake City was shot, and two cattle rustlers and a stage robber were killed. The last four killings could never be traced directly to the vigilante committee.[17]

One of the smaller outbreaks of vigilante activity occurred at Steilacoom in 1870. Charley McDaniel, local outlaw and killer of a man in British Columbia, advised B. Gibson, a recent arrival from Idaho, where he had killed several people, to settle around Steilacoom. With McDaniel's help and encouragement, Gibson squatted and built a house on Charley Wren's land. Wren took Gibson before justice of the peace E. R. Rogers, who ordered Gibson to vacate the claim. At first, the Idaho squatter appeared to obey Judge Rogers' order, but Gibson reentered his claim despite the law and an alarmed neighborhood. Wren again swore out a complaint before Rogers, who issued a call for another trial.

The night before the trial, the two rowdies decided to fix the outcome. They visited settlers around Wren's homestead and threatened them with physical violence if they testified on Wren's behalf. Instead of intimidating Wren's neighbors, Gibson and McDaniel succeeded in uniting them. The next day about forty persons, almost all of whom were former Hudson's Bay Company employees, met at dawn to present a coordinated front at Judge Rogers' court. On their way to Steilacoom, they encountered Gibson and McDaniel about two miles out of town. Gibson was shot and wounded, and McDaniel fled into Steilacoom. The "vigilance committee" placed Gibson in a wagon to take him to Steilacoom, but just outside the town, Gibson grabbed a pistol and shot two farmers, wounding them slightly. He was then killed. Meanwhile, McDaniel entered Westbrook's Saloon, disarmed himself, and offered to talk peacefully. The mob arrived, and someone shouted, "Shoot the son of a bitch!" McDaniel ran and was shot in the head. Later, a priest collected the bodies, performed last rites, and buried them. As quickly as the Steilacoom vigilance committee began, it disbanded.[18]

In over forty-five years of territorial status, only six vigilante movements were organized and only ten persons died as a result of mob action. Few Americans in Washington Territory attempted to avoid law enforcement and the use of local legal institutions. Instead, they decided disputes inside local courts and preferred an established legal presence in the form of justices of the peace. Although JP decisions were technically subject to challenge, very few decisions ever went to the district court or the territorial supreme court on appeal. In effect, JP courts in the territory enjoyed the popular support and enthusiastic backing of most citizens.

Rural-Urban Justice Court Comparisons

Community acceptance of justice court decisions, the adjudication celerity of JP courts, the accessibility of justices of the peace to the populace, and the legal expertise present in JP courtrooms have been examined with reference to a large sample of original documents primarily from JP courts in Walla Walla, Coveland, and Newcastle precincts. As previously observed, the courts in these three precincts functioned separately, and they presided over two distinct population classes. Walla Walla, one of the older settlements in Washington Territory, achieved some stability by the 1860s; it served as a supply depot first for Idaho mines and later for wheat and cattle farmers. Coveland also attracted settlers early in the occupation of Washington Territory, but it never developed into a substantial population center. It remained a rural outpost for retired seamen and active farmers and loggers. Newcastle grew up during the 1880s, thriving largely because of coal mining. By the end of the territorial period, Newcastle had not surpassed Coveland in population. Thus, a dichotomy existed in the samples, an urban-rural dichotomy that must be analyzed before conclusions are made as to the quality of justice in Washington Territory.

By breaking down the sample on the basis of population variables, certain similarities and differences in urban and rural JP court operations can be observed. For example, attorneys attended all JP courts as frequently in urban as in rural areas. In rural and urban areas, respectively, 40.4 percent and 44.7 percent of the cases before justice courts included at least one attorney representing a client or the territory. Lawyers actively participated in JP court proceedings regardless of court location.

Clear differences appear in the frequency of case types, court costs, case dispositions, and verdicts. In rural areas, of 210 cases observed, 51.9 percent were civil and 49.1 percent were criminal; whereas in urban areas, of 1,200 cases sampled, 80.9 percent were civil and only 19.1 percent were criminal. Within the urban criminal sample, only sixteen or 7 percent of the cases dealt with city ordinance violations.

The imbalance between civil and criminal case dispositions in urban and rural areas affected court costs. Since criminal cases cost more than civil cases, the mean total court cost per case was higher in rural than in urban regions. A case brought in a rural area JP court averaged $21.46, while a case heard before an urban JP court averaged $11.82. Similarly, since pleading and grand jury case dispositions usually came from criminal cases, those dispositions appeared more often in rural than in urban courts. Trial-determined cases also occurred more frequently in rural than in urban areas, and defaults and changes of venue predominated more often in urban than in rural courts. These characteristics show that early Washington urban residents were less stable and more mobile than rural inhabitants. Urban plaintiffs won more default judgments and changed venue more often because defendants and their property were hard to reach.[19]

Since defendants often defaulted in urban areas, urban court verdicts tended toward plaintiffs. Of urban cases with verdicts, 91.3 percent went to the plaintiff, an individual litigant or Washington Territory. Of rural cases with verdicts, 74.6 percent went to the plaintiff.

Although urban courts tended to hear many more civil cases than criminal cases while rural courts heard the same amount of each type, celerity of adjudication differed only slightly. A case in an urban JP court averaged approximately ten days from complaint to court decision; in a rural court, a case was likely to run almost nine days. These statistics held, even though urban courts were much busier than rural courts. During the 1880s, urban JPs heard one case per year per every twenty-five persons; rural justices sat for one case per year per every 121 persons. Final satisfaction in urban courts, however, usually took ninety-six additional days versus an average of almost twenty-two extra days in rural courts. Satisfaction for urban civil cases took 117.57 days per case, compared to 37.26 days for rural civil cases; this is another indication of the mobility of urban litigants who delayed final restitution. Therefore, cases brought in urban JP courts lasted longer than those taken to rural courts.

Of major significance in this urban-rural comparison are two factors. First, default judgments were far more common in urban than in rural courts, and final satisfaction of a case took longer in urban than in rural courts. Rural litigants stayed and paid for their local legal decisions; urban parties avoided and delayed adherence to the law. In effect, urban courts served as legal repositories for cases involving litigants from the urban community who were less stable and more mobile than established rural inhabitants.

Second, and most important, urban JPs heard many more cases than rural justices, but the adjudication celerity from complaint to court decision in both urban and rural courts remained relatively constant. Consequently, justice court dockets, on both urban and rural frontiers, had not reached a point of overcrowding. Urban JP courts could have received more cases without affecting the quality of justice they dispensed, and nothing uncovered in this study suggests that Washingtonians made any effort to avoid using either one in favor of the other.

Justice Courts and Washington Statehood

Further evidence of the Washington citizenry's confidence in their justices of the peace occurred at the termination of Washington Territory. When the representatives of the proposed new state met in Ellensburgh in 1889 to draft a constitution, the judiciary article was foremost on their minds. The first section of Article IV as reported from the judicial committee read, "The judicial power of the state shall be vested in a supreme court, superior courts, justices of the peace, and such inferior courts as the legislature may provide."[20] The justice courts were to be guaranteed constitutionally, which had not been the case in the original organic act of Washington Territory.

Debate centered around a motion made by the delegate from Spokane Falls, J. Z. Moore, who moved to strike the words following "justices of the peace." He opposed the creation of probate courts and feared the legislature would create them. John M. Reed of Oakesdale, E. H. Sullivan of Colfax, and D. J. Crowley of Walla Walla objected, Crowley expressing the belief that such a motion might prevent the establishment of police courts. The reservation would have proven unfounded inasmuch as police courts had been derived from justice courts, but Moore became sufficiently swayed by the argument and withdrew his motion.[21]

The judicial article contained other sections directly related to JPs. Section 4 prevented the supreme court from hearing on appeal civil cases involving moneys or property worth $200 or less; Section 6 allowed the superior courts to review all JP decisions, but they could not exercise original jurisdiction over cases unless the value in question amounted to over $100; and Section 10 provided that the "legislature shall determine the number of justices of the peace to be elected in incorporated cities or towns and in precincts, and shall prescribe by law the powers, duties and jurisdiction of justices of the peace."[22] A further proviso allowed JPs to be police court justices and made JPs in incorporated cities and towns of over five thousand inhabitants salaried rather than subject to a fee system.[23]

Other portions of the article elicited considerable debate, particularly salaries for supreme court justices, but the JP sections proved uncontroversial.[24] Over twenty years after the convention, Theodore Stiles, delegate from Tacoma, wrote that the judicial article was perhaps the best drafted portion of the constitution. He noted that "there was less complaint in Washington than in any other state over crowded court calendars and delays in the administration of justice."[25] The entire article was approved by a vote of sixty-seven to six. In essence, the justice court system of the territorial era had been transplanted intact for statehood. Citizens of Washington approved of their justices of the peace and the quality of their justice.

* * * *

The justices of the peace of Washington Territory dispensed a quality of justice generally characterized by reason, accessibility, celerity, and community acceptance. All four indicators used in evaluating the proceedings of JP courts suggest that decisions were fair and consistent. By employing a variety of analyses to large quantities of original documentation and to over fourteen hundred justice court cases in order to consider the operations of JP courts, several generalizations seem possible. Justice courts tended to be staffed by educated personnel and to be frequented by attorneys. People who wanted to use justice courts usually were not inconvenienced by geography, cost, or case type. Adjudications were speedy in justice courts, and court dockets were not crowded. New developing communities, both rural and urban, commonly turned to and accepted the decisions made by local justices. In short, justice of the peace courts on the Washington frontier constituted as fair a judicial system as could be expected for new settlements, and they functioned as well as, if not better than, most established nineteenth-century Anglo-American legal institutions.

Afterword

A RECONSIDERATION
OF THE VIOLENT FRONTIER: THE
LEGAL PERSPECTIVE

Legal historians have long been preoccupied with defining law and its concomitant, order. Depending upon degrees of emphasis, law has been held to be the command of the sovereign, the unconscious embodiment of the people's will, a reflection of society's ideas of rightness,[1] the rules made and enforced by the rich to the disadvantage of the poor and middle classes, and "the prime form of organized power and compulsion in society."[2] In new communities on the American frontier where people were dividing the abundant resources of a virgin land, law was all of these things, and its enforcement and application were entrusted to the justice of the peace. Probably the most significant legal work affecting these new settlers was accomplished within the community.[3] Justices of the peace helped design and weave together the social, economic, and political fabric of the emerging commonwealth.

From the first settlement, Americans recognized the need for an orderly society, and JPs were entrusted with "keeping the peace." Before federal and state governments could exercise formal control over the American inhabitants of adjacent regions, local justices were usually present. Henry Mahon served Alabamans as their justice of the peace for several years until he could be legally installed.[4] Iowans, without American jurisdiction or laws, set up their own court systems in the 1830s.[5] Rump and provisional governments, such as those in Tennessee and Oregon, also provided for JPs.[6] As soon as an area was formally accepted as a territory by the United States, the justice of the peace system was officially extended to its citizens. JPs were given a permanent and very important position in the transplanted American legal hierarchy, and, until recent times, this position was never seriously altered. In reality, the fur trader, miner, cattle raiser, farmer, and merchant marched over the American landscape *with* the justice of the peace. The JP was usually one of their own kind, and he represented a perceived need for an orderly community.

This regional study indicates the need for a new examination of the history of American frontier legal institutions. Old notions concerning local judicial officers must be reassessed. JPs have traditionally been described as new, young, restive residents of newly forming societies; in fact, they were a stable, established, contented group. Justices of the peace have been represented as a number of individuals embracing all economic classes; in fact, JPs were relatively well-to-do property owners who relied upon a variety of economic activities for sustenance. Local judiciaries have been pictured as military heroes chosen primarily because of their abilities to decimate Indian peoples; in fact, justices of the peace usually obtained their offices through active participation in politics.

Similarly, the quality of justice dispensed by JPs must be reevaluated. Justices have been regarded in many quarters as uneducated, illiterate personages with no legal training and no access to written law; in fact, local judges were sometimes learned in the law and often rendered opinions based on written legal sources. JP courts have been characterized as dealing primarily with criminals and crimes of violence; in fact, most litigation consisted of civil actions or nonviolent criminal actions. And the supposedly poor quality of JP decisions has been represented as in part accounting for vigilante or extralegal activities; in fact, few vigilante movements were common in areas of new American settlement, and inadequate JP justice was rarely the cause of those extralegal activities that did occur.

Challenging the generalizations about the legal institution most important to new American communities leads to a reconsideration of a common description of American settlements—that the American frontier was violent. In order to reconsider this description, one qualification must be made. While multiracial relationships were often characterized by violence, the interactions of white, black, red, yellow, and brown peoples were relatively infrequent. In a large sense, frontier racial conflicts were the manifestations of a cultural clash of sovereign peoples. Once white residents had established their dominance by the use of force, they sought to impose their particular culture, including legal systems, upon themselves and others. Nonwhite cultural resistance remained and intercultural violence continued, but an American community emerged and American legal institutions adjudicated some intercultural disputes.

Determining the relative turbulence of this new colonization is, then, by definition an intracultural exercise. One might rationally conclude that the Navahos of New Mexico, the Chinese of Portland, the blacks of Nicodemus, and the whites of the Puyallup River Valley internally were peaceful peoples, and their cultures maintained stability in part because of the representative nature of and the high quality of justice dispersed by communal decision-makers.

Frederick Jackson Turner, in "The Significance of the Frontier in American History," provided an intellectual basis for the conception of the American frontier as violent. Turner observed that "the frontier is the outer edge of the wave—the meeting point between savagery and civilization." [7] To Turner, a region deficient in laws and law enforcement influenced American society by forcing upon settlers antisocial behavior and thereby producing in them an antipathy to control. [8]

Walter Prescott Webb elaborated upon Turner's thesis. Webb stated that "the Westerner was a persistant lawbreaker." [9] According to Webb, new settlers were prone to criminal behavior first because of unstable social conditions inherent in the new land (in other words, Turner's vague buffer zone separating the world of "civilized" and "uncivilized" beings); and second, because statutes, such as land, water, and fence laws, that were applied to new communities were not made for frontier situations. These laws could not be obeyed.

. . . the West was a lawless place. It was turbulent in the early days because there was no law. It was lawless in the later period because the laws were unsuited to the needs and conditions. Men could not abide by them and survive. Not only were absurd laws imposed upon them, but their customs, which might well have received the sanction of law, were too seldom recognized. The blame for a great deal of Western lawlessness rests more with the lawmaker than with the lawbreaker. [10]

Webb's explanation for western lawlessness, presumably including both violent and nonviolent behavior, led to a further causal assumption: that the American frontier was violent because law was static. This legal inflexibility created a positive mind of criminality in the new inhabitants.

By placing the onus of violence upon the law, historians forced themselves to uncover portions of the actual legal record. They examined the laws promulgated in the new settlements and hastily concluded that the American experience reflected its legal embellishments. This circuitous route—that static laws caused the violent frontier which in turn was mirrored in the laws produced by its tumultuous inhabitants—provided historians with unfounded convictions, which unfortunately resulted in doubtful pronouncements.

Philip D. Jordan cites legalities, such as the law prohibiting the carrying of concealed weapons and statutes sanctioning punishments for those convicted of killing animals or humans, as the basis for his generalization that "powder and ball and blade scarred an advancing frontier, seared low country and high country, and scorched and blistered a land of promise with unbelievable violence, so that murder and mayhem were thought by many to symbolize an age."[11] Fred Harrison also elaborates this idea: "Lawlessness in all its vicious forms was on the frontiers first—and intended to stay. Murderers, robbers, gamblers and adventurers ruled the vast, virgin lands with laws of their own, and ruthless six-guns to enforce them. For many years, no decent person or his possessions were safe in these wild lands."[12]

Having drawn such a bloody portrait of American frontier society, historians have had to explain how cultural stability was eventually achieved. According to Jordan, the rewording of statutes; the remaking of Webb's outmoded laws to fit the land; and the unscrambling of the court systems, a "baffling maze of hocus-pocus"—all of these legal lucidities served to tame the resident of the American frontier by 1890.[13] According to Anton-Hermann Chroust, large increases in population toned down the rambunctious Americans: "In a way, the earliest frontier was simply in a state of chronic riot but with the rapid increase in population the community gradually became more prosperous and orderly."[14] Somehow, the proponents of a violent frontier heritage abruptly brought their brawling, destructive, murderous story of American settlement to a halt.

All of this theorizing about the violence indigenous to American frontier society was done without examining working legal institutions. It is one thing to describe a crime, and it is one thing to cite a statute; but it is quite another to view the legal system in action.

Those who have observed the functioning legal system cannot concur with the violence school of American frontier historians. Francis Philbrick doubts whether the creation of new American communities was inordinately influenced by criminals; he reasons that a shortage of moveable property and an abundance of that one great value, land, prevented disorder. Philbrick explains that there was obviously "much vulgarity and swearing, some duelling, much rowdyism, and more or less truculence,"[15] but crimes of violence to persons were not overriding. The most common court cases involved horse stealing, cattle and hog stealing, and fugitive debtors.[16]

In Washington Territory, crimes of violence were the exception rather than the rule. Of justice of the peace cases examined, violent crime constituted only 8 percent of the caseload and only 56 percent of all criminal causes of action. Judge William Strong, the first Washington Territory supreme court justice, wrote that he rarely heard of thefts and murders while he resided in the territory.[17]

The fact is that Washingtonians sometimes exaggerated their society to others. Strong recounted his experience when he met a new teacher in the territory. Since the instructor appeared to be nervous, Strong decided to increase his anxiety. The judge told the newcomer wild stories of lawlessness, even though he admitted in his diary, "We made that out to be a very dangerous country although it was perfectly peaceable."[18]

James Swan, adventurer and social commentator of Shoalwater Bay, also enjoyed telling a good story. He "documented" some of the first justice of the peace court proceedings in the Northwest. In 1855, three years after Swan's arrival in Chehalis County (now Grays Harbor County), the settlers chose their first JPs and constables. John W. Champ was elected justice of the peace, and Charles W. Denter was designated constable for the Shoalwater Bay region. Champ, known as the "Squire," was "about sixty-five years old, tall, wiry, and muscular, with an iron constitution that had withstood the rough-and-tumble of a long life."[19] He had been one of the first Americans to settle in Washington Territory, migrating from Vermont by way of Wisconsin.[20] The constable, or Big Charley, was a logger from the Penobscot River area who had gone around the Horn on a whaling vessel and had been summarily dumped off into Shoalwater Bay. "Charley preferred his ease and a bottle of whisky to anything else."[21]

The seeds of the first court case were sown when Captain Charles Russell decided to make a business trip to San Francisco. To look after his property and affairs while he sailed to California, he hired a man named Bowman. After Russell departed, Bowman graciously helped himself to a small sum of Russell's money, a fact that quickly reached and irritated most of the settlers. Although no one could technically prosecute Bowman (Russell was in California), the sheriff decided to have some fun by writing a note to the thief threatening him with a lynching unless he left the Bay. The note was taken to Judge Champ to sign. Champ, who could not see well, "having smashed his spectacles on a frolic," signed the document thinking it an arrest warrant; and he ordered Big Charley to arrest the offender.[22]

Constable Denter was apprehensive about his first arrest. Most of all, he feared resistance. Thus, instead of informing Bowman of the charge, Big Charley invited him to come to the "Squire's" shack to sample a new shipment of whiskey, and once the two thirsty men arrived, the first court proceedings in Shoalwater Bay commenced. Swan remembered Bowman asking the "Squire" what crimes had been committed, and the justice, according to storyteller Swan, replied:

"What are you 'cused of?" said Champ, with the greatest contempt for the supposed sham ignorance of the prisoner; "why, you are 'cused of stealing Mr. Russell's money."

"I should like to know who accuses me, and who are the witnesses against me," said Bowman, who now began to think that something serious was to happen.

"See here, Bowman," says the 'squire, "I don't want any witnesses; and as for who accuses you, why, I accuse you, and everybody on the beach accuses you, and you know you are guilty as well as I do: there is no use of wasting time over this matter. I am bound to sentence you, and my sentence is that you leave the Bay in twenty-four hours, or receive fifty lashes if you are here after that time. And now, Charley, do you take charge of the prisoner: treat him well, but if you let him escape we will tie you up in his stead." ———

The next morning a schooner arrived from San Francisco, bringing Russell, who was soon made acquainted with the affair, and Champ ordered a new trial to take place, adding that, if Russell desired, they would tie up the offender and give him a few dozen by way of remembrance. But Russell had no desire to punish the fellow any more; so the boys, having had their fun, as they called it, collected some money, which they gave to Bowman to pay his expenses to Astoria, and started him off, and he was seen no more.[23]

Swan's recollections do not show John Champ to have carefully administered the law. But Swan was quick to note, however, that residents of Chehalis County lived in a peaceable utopia with few lawsuits and "bickerings" except for occasional fistfights, and when major disputes did arise, they took them before established American legal institutions.[24]

The stories of Swan and Strong make for engaging listening and reading, but they do not accurately portray Washington Territory JPs and their justice. To many historians, the real question—is there legal evidence which indicates a societal instability?—must be answered negatively. No matter how few or how many criminals, the vast majority of migrating Americans were law-abiding,[25] and most new societies readily attained order and stability. Thus, as Francis Philbrick has written, "That Turner's frontier was totally unreal is evident."[26]

Still, the stress placed upon the violent aspects in American frontier history permeates American frontier bibliography. Even the latest historian to analyze frontier order, W. Eugene Hollon, while recognizing that Americans were basically nonviolent during their settlement of new lands, dwells upon interracial conflict as a dominant force in frontier society.[27]

In order to give balance to any violent societal conclusions, the history of the frontier legal system must be examined in terms of expectations and actual performance. Surprisingly, this history is nonexistent. Only a few judges have attracted the interests of historians, and these jurists have come to represent a stereotypic function of the law in the new American society. Isaac Charles Parker, a federal judge with jurisdiction over the Indian Country (Oklahoma), 1875-1896, sentenced seventy-nine persons to hang, and his story was used to illustrate "a full account of the lawless conditions on our last and wildest frontier."[28] Justices of the peace generally have been ignored, but one local judge has been immortalized. Judge Roy Bean, a JP in west Texas, supposedly held a rough-and-tumble region together by near autocratic means.[29] But Bean and Parker were not in the mainstream of the transplanted American legal experience, and their actions do not accurately portray the administration of the law.

This regional study and call for renewed scholarship concludes that JPs played an important part in the creation and development of a new American society and that the justices of the peace contributed to the relative stability of that society. Once a history of the spread and operation of American legal institutions has been completed, the concept of a violent American frontier will most certainly be the subject of reexamination and probable reconsideration.

APPENDIX I

The following persons have been positively identified as justices of the peace in Washington Territory. They constituted the base of the sample used to complete a prosopography or collective biography of Washington Territory JPs.

1. Abbey, Charles H., of Eaton Precinct, Clark County
2. Abbott, Webster, of Preston Precinct, Clark County
3. A'Hern, Patrick, of Columbia Precinct, Clark County
4. Ames, Willis F., of Goldendale, Klickitat County
5. Backman, George, of Cathlapoodle Precinct, Clark County
6. Baker, J. E., of Olympia, Thurston County
7. Ball, Amos M., of Lewis River Precinct, Clark County
8. Bartlett, James P., of Lewis River Precinct, Clark County
9. Bartlett, John W., of Lewis River Precinct, Clark County
10. Bartlett, Riley, of Pollock Precinct, Clark County
11. Bates, J. R., of Colville Valley Precinct, Spokane County
12. Beall, S. W., of Kalama Precinct, Clark County
13. Bean, A. J., of Battle Ground Precinct, Clark County
14. Beck, John Wilson, of North Yakima, Yakima County
15. Bedell, Charles P., of Washougal Precinct, Clark County
16. Biles, John D., of Vancouver, Clark County
17. Bishop, Boliver B., of Skamania County
18. Blackwood, H. C., of Fern Prairie Precinct, Clark County
19. Boyer, Zadock, of Lincoln Precinct, Clark County
20. Bozorth, Christopher C., of Lancaster Precinct, Clark County
21. Bradley, Joel W., of Chelachie Precinct, Clark County
22. Brant, Joseph, of Vancouver, Clark County
23. Bratton, William, of Lancaster Precinct, Clark County
24. Brickell, T. L., of Vancouver, Clark County
25. Brooke, Lloyd, of Skamania and Walla Walla counties

26. Brown, George, of Steilacoom, Pierce County
27. Bullard, Mark W., of Chehalis County
28. Burlingame, Henry S., of LaCamas Precinct, Clark County
29. Bybee, James, of Preston Precinct, Clark County
30. Campbell, John, of LaCamas Precinct, Clark County
31. Caples, Henry L., of Lancaster Precinct, Clark County
32. Champ, John W., of Chehalis County
33. Chase, Henry M., of Missoula County
34. Clark, Alvan, of LaCamas Precinct, Clark County
35. Clarke, Edward H., of LaCamas Precinct, Clark County
36. Collins, Aaron M., of Sawamish County
37. Cook, S. S., of Preston Precinct, Clark County
38. Coombs, Samuel F., of Seattle, King County
39. Corless, John, of Preston Precinct, Clark County
40. Covington, Richard, of Vancouver, Clark County
41. Cranney, Thomas, of Coveland Precinct, Island County
42. Crate, W. F., of Preston Precinct, Clark County
43. Cross, William N., of Manor Precinct, Clark County
44. Daniel, Travers, of Port Townsend, Jefferson County
45. Daniels, W. Byron, of Kalama Precinct, Clark County
46. David, A. F., of Preston Precinct, Clark County
47. Davis, Jackson, of Fern Prairie Precinct, Clark County
48. Davis, Napoleon, of Pollock Precinct, Clark County
49. Day, Lewis, of Wallula, Walla Walla County
50. Denison, J. S., of Pomeroy, Garfield County
51. Denny, John, of Vancouver, Clark County
52. Diedtrich, F., of LaCamas Precinct, Clark County
53. Donald, Thomas, of Newcastle Precinct, King County
54. Drew, M. S., of Kitsap County
55. Eaton, Nathan, of Olympia, Thurston County
56. Ebey, Isaac N., of Coveland Precinct, Island County
57. Ebey, Winfield S., of Coveland Precinct, Island County
58. Eldridge, E., of Bellingham, Whatcom County
59. Ely, Jerome, of Oak Harbor Precinct, Island County
60. Ennis, Nicholas, of Lewis River Precinct, Clark County
61. Evans, Millton, of Walla Walla County
62. Fairchild, Charles H., of Lancaster Precinct, Clark County
63. Fales, D. R., of Patterson Precinct, Clark County
64. Fargo, S. B., of Walla Walla, Walla Walla County
65. Farnsworth, Charles H., of Pomeroy, Garfield County
66. Fay, Patrick, of Cathlapoodle Precinct, Clark County

67. Ferrin, Jacob, of Fern Prairie Precinct, Clark County
68. Fisher, Solomon W., of Preston Precinct, Clark County
69. Ford, Sidney S., of Lewis County
70. Frost, Morris H., of Steilacoom, Pierce County
71. Galbreath, James, of Walla Walla, Walla Walla County
72. Gardner, Brezel L., of Washougal Precinct, Clark County
73. Gardner, Daniel W., of Lancaster Precinct, Clark County
74. Garvey, Cornelius T., of Chelachie Precinct, Clark County
75. Gerrish, G. H. of Clallam County
76. Gillihan, Gideon B., of Chelachie Precinct, Clark County
77. Goddard, Charles, of Manor Precinct, Clark County
78. Gregory, A. J., of Walla Walla, Walla Walla County
79. Gridley, Harry H., of Vancouver, Clark County
80. Grow, S. L., of King County
81. Hamilton, Erasmus R., of Cedar Creek Precinct, Clark County
82. Harris, Samuel C., of LaCamas Precinct, Clark County
83. Harris, W. H., of Oak Point Precinct, Cowlitz County
84. Harris, William Henry Clay, of Tacoma, Pierce County
85. Hart, George W., of Washougal Precinct, Clark County
86. Hastie, Thomas, of Coveland Precinct, Island County
87. Hastings, J. C., of Pataha Prairie Precinct, Walla Walla County
88. Hathaway, Marshall R., of Patterson Precinct, Clark County
89. Hathaway, Robert J., of Coveland Precinct, Island County
90. Haycock, William, of Preston Precinct, Clark County
91. Hayden, Gay, of Vancouver, Clark County
92. Hill, George Alfred, of King County
93. Hill, Nathaniel D., of Coveland Precinct, Island County
94. Hitchcock, George, of Pollock Precinct, Clark County
95. Hollingsworth, T., of Cathlapoodle Precinct, Clark County
96. Horton, W. P., of Walla Walla, Walla Walla County
97. Hunder, C. H., of Vancouver, Clark County
98. Hurt, David, of LaCamas Precinct, Clark County
99. Keats, John, of Goldendale, Klickitat County
100. Keller, Josiah P., of Jefferson County
101. Kenyon, David W., of Pollock Precinct, Clark County
102. Kerns, J. A., of Cascades Precinct, Clark County
103. Knapp, J. B., of Patterson Precinct, Clark County
104. Kulper, Heinrich, of Chelachie Precinct, Clark County
105. Lacy, Oliver P., of Walla Walla, Walla Walla County
106. Laman, James D., of Walla Walla, Walla Walla County
107. Lambert, D. H., of Patterson Precinct, Clark County

108. Lambert, Vincent, of North Walla Walla, Walla Walla County
109. Leverich, B. N., of Vancouver, Clark County
110. Lister, Joseph B., of Pomeroy, Garfield County
111. Lockwood, R. T., of Pollock Precinct, Clark County
112. Lyon, George G., of King County
113. Manning, James S., of Cedar Creek Precinct, Clark County
114. Martin, W. H., of Lancaster Precinct, Clark County
115. Massey, Edward L., of Walla Walla, Walla Walla County
116. Maulsby, I. T., of Fern Prairie Precinct, Clark County
117. Maxon, Silas D., of Vancouver, Clark County
118. Maynard, Dr. David Swinson, of Seattle, King County
119. McAndrew, Alexander, of Patterson Precinct, Clark County
120. McBride, Gabriel, of Eaton Precinct, Clark County
121. McCann, Dudley, of Preston Precinct, Clark County
122. McCaw, Samuel, of Steilacoom, Pierce County
123. McFarland, C. H., of Klickitat County
124. McKnight, John H., of Newcastle Precinct, King County
125. Miller, Caleb, of Oak Harbor Precinct, Island County
126. Murdy, J. C., of Klickitat County
127. Murphy, W. P., of Klickitat County
128. Nash, Lucious B., of Walla Walla, Walla Walla County
129. Nelson, John, of Klickitat County
130. Nerton, Robert, of Fourth Plain Precinct, Clark County
131. Newland, William S., of Pomeroy, Garfield County
132. O'Donnell, John H., of Battle Ground Precinct, Clark County
133. Oliver, Eliel, of Pomeroy, Garfield County
134. Ostrander, John Y., of Dayton, Columbia County
135. Ottwell, Thomas P., of Cedar Creek Precinct, Clark County
136. Parker, David C., of Cedar Creek Precinct, Clark County
137. Parker, Hollon, of Idaho County
138. Parrish, George W., of Port Townsend, Jefferson County
139. Pease, Sylvester, of Battle Ground Precinct, Clark County
140. Peasly, S., of Klickitat County
141. Pettygrove, Francis W., of Port Townsend, Jefferson County
142. Pincus, A. P., of Preston Precinct, Clark County
143. Plumb, William W., of Thurston County
144. Pomeroy, Joseph M., of Pomeroy, Garfield County
145. Proebstel, G. W., of LaCamas Precinct, Clark County
146. Proebstel, Jacob, of LaCamas Precinct, Clark County
147. Proebstel, William Wendell, of Fourth Plain Precinct, Clark County

148. Reid, David F., of Chelachie Precinct, Clark County
149. Renton, William, of Kitsap County
150. Riley, D. W., of Pomeroy, Garfield County
151. Robertson, William, of Coveland Precinct, Island County
152. Robinson, Thomas W., of Fern Prairie Precinct, Clark County
153. Rogers, Edwin R., of Steilacoom, Pierce County
154. Rounds, John C., of Pollock Precinct, Clark County
155. Russell, C.H.W., of Chehalis County
156. Russell, D. L., of Manor Precinct, Clark County
157. Russell, S. W., of King County
158. Ryan, Thomas Frank, of Pomeroy, Garfield County
159. Sayward, William Taylor, of Port Ludlow Precinct, Jefferson County
160. Scammon, Isaiah L., of Chehalis County
161. Scheuben, August A., of Vancouver, Clark County
162. Scott, Roswell, of Seattle, King County
163. Sewell, John Y., of Coveland Precinct, Island County
164. Sims, John A., of Walla Walla, Walla Walla County
165. Sitton, Jasper, of Eaton Precinct, Clark County
166. Smith, Eben, of Seattle, King County
167. Smith, John F., of Vancouver, Clark County
168. Spencer, D. M., of Pollock Precinct, Clark County
169. Sterns, Henry M., of Cowlitz Landing Precinct, Lewis County
170. Stone, Charles W., of Lewis River Precinct, Clark County
171. Stone, Nathaniel, of Monticello Precinct, Cowlitz County
172. Storey, Dr. John C., of Pomeroy, Garfield County
173. Straub, Richard H., of Coveland Precinct, Island County
174. Strong, Hiram H., of Washougal Precinct, Clark County
175. Strong, Solomon, of Lewis River Precinct, Clark County
176. Suiste, Julius, of Vancouver, Clark County
177. Swan, James G., of Port Townsend, Jefferson County
178. Tate, John W., of Patterson Precinct, Clark County
179. Taylor, Irvine J., of Preston Precinct, Clark County
180. Taylor, John A., of Walla Walla, Walla Walla County
181. Thing, George M., of Patterson Precinct, Clark County
182. Thorndike, J. R., of Port Ludlow Precinct, Jefferson County
183. Timmen, John H., of Pollock Precinct, Clark County
184. Tinsley, E. C., of LaCamas Precinct, Clark County
185. Tubbs, Michael, of Vancouver, Clark County
186. Tuke, John, of Battle Ground Precinct, Clark County
187. Uder, William, of Newcastle Precinct, King County

188. Van Vleet, Lewis, of Washougal Precinct, Clark County
189. Webster, David K., of Fern Prairie Precinct, Clark County
190. Webster, William, of Jefferson County
191. Whipple, S. R., of Patterson Precinct, Clark County
192. White, Charles F., of Cowlitz Landing Precinct, Lewis County
193. White, Gracia W., of Preston Precinct, Clark County
194. Whitman, Elias B., of Walla Walla, Walla Walla County
195. Williams, H., of Kalama Precinct, Clark County
196. Wilmot, John F., of Pollock Precinct, Clark County
197. Woodard, John, of Skamania County

APPENDIX II

The following persons have been positively identified as justices of the peace in Washington Territory, but minimal biographical information about them has been found.

1. Anderson, G. W., of Boise County
2. Baird, J., of Bannock, Boise County
3. Banon, E. H., of Walla Walla, Walla Walla County
4. Barry, J. W., of Walla Walla, Walla Walla County
5. Beal, Charles, of Ship Harbor Precinct, Whatcom County
6. Belcher, William H., of Eaton Precinct, Clark County
7. Binehart, A. C., of Battle Ground Precinct, Clark County
8. Bizer, Reuben, of Ferndale Precinct, Whatcom County
9. Broshears, Joseph, of Thurston County
10. Bumford, B. B., of Walla Walla County
11. Burke, Ervin, of Preston Precinct, Clark County
12. Cahill, William, of Chelachie Precinct, Clark County
13. Cann, T. H., of Seattle, King County
14. Carle, Wilson, of Michises Precinct, Clark County
15. Chenoweth, Justin, of Cascades Precinct, Clark County
16. Cockrehan, R. E., of Upper Skagit Precinct, Whatcom County
17. Cradlebaugh, J. H., of Vancouver, Clark County
18. Crandall, G. N., of Fidalgo Precinct, Whatcom County
19. Drake, J. D., of Dayton, Columbia County
20. Drennen, T. T., of Fern Prairie Precinct, Clark County
21. Dwelley, J. F., of La Conner Precinct, Whatcom County
22. Freese, J. E., of Semiahmoo Precinct, Whatcom County
23. Freis, Lorenzo, of Chelachie Precinct, Clark County
24. Frush, C. W., of King County
25. Gates, N. H., of Skamania County

26. Glover, James N., of Stevens County
27. Green, Gustav, of Lancaster Precinct, Clark County
28. Greeves, Custavus, of Lancaster Precinct, Clark County
29. Hatch, P. S., of Walla Walla County
30. Haven, C. D., of Washougal Precinct, Clark County
31. Hawkins, S. S., of Fern Prairie Precinct, Clark County
32. Hawley, E., of Lynden Precinct, Whatcom County
33. Heebner, William, of Slaughter County
34. Hendrick, J. M., of Walla Walla County
35. Hilts, D., of LaCamas Precinct, Clark County
36. Irwin, C. C., of Fourth Plain Precinct, Clark County
37. Jones, Hillman F., of Seattle, King County
38. Lay, V. C., of Ainsworth, Franklin County
39. Leonard, H. H., of Fern Prairie Precinct, Clark County
40. Mackey, S. P., of Lincoln Precinct, Clark County
41. Madigan, Jason, of Frenchtown Precinct, Walla Walla County
42. Mahin, John, of Washougal Precinct, Clark County
43. Mangan, T. B., of Guemes Precinct, Whatcom County
44. Mastin, W. H., of Steilacoom, Pierce County
45. Mauzey, William K., of Vancouver, Clark County
46. McConnell, G. T., of West Vancouver, Clark County
47. McGownd, J. L., of Bannock, Boise County
48. Miller, J., of Boise County
49. Mills, A. F., of Columbia Precinct, Clark County
50. Murphy, J. M., of Boise County
51. Page, Henry, of Lancaster Precinct, Clark County
52. Pilkey, Solomon, of Spokane County
53. Pollock, John, of Lancaster Precinct, Clark County
54. Pomeroy, Thomas M., of Elk City, Nez Perce County
55. Rand, Jaspar, of Florence, Idaho County
56. Reinhart, S. D., of Whatcom, Whatcom County
57. Sandstrom, Olaf, of Skagit Precinct, Whatcom County
58. Shaugh, W., of Ferguson County
59. Short, Charles F., of Vancouver, Clark County
60. Small, O., of Lewis County
61. Soderberg, Nels, of Seattle, King County
62. Stallcop, James, of Lincoln Precinct, Clark County
63. Stilwell, Solomon, of Wahkiacum County
64. Stone, E. B., of Idaho County
65. Swan, Dr. ———, of Boise County
66. Swayne, A. R., of Boise County

67. Thomas, D. P., of Samish Precinct, Whatcom County
68. Thompson, W. W., of Alpine Precinct, Skagit County
69. Thurmond, James W., of Idaho County
70. Touissant, A. S., of East Vancouver, Clark County
71. Von Pressentin, C.J.O., of Baker Precinct, Whatcom County
72. Weston, Ezra, of Pacific County
73. Wight, D., of Nooksack Precinct, Whatcom County
74. Willis, J. E., of Chehalis, Lewis County
75. Woodham, G. W., of Cedar Creek Precinct, Clark County
76. Yantis, A., of Boise County

Research has also identified justices of the peace for early Montana Territory and Idaho Territory who may or may not have been JPs in Washington Territory prior to its division.

Montana Territory

1. Bissell, Gaylord G., of Madison County
2. Byram, Don L., of Madison County
3. Castner, J. M., of Madison County
4. Duke, James K., of Madison County
5. Egnell, Albert, of Jefferson County
6. Freeborn, William, of Gallatin County
7. Johnson, J. B., of Jefferson County
8. McCarty, O. F., of Madison County
9. McCullough, Joseph, of Virginia City, Madison County
10. Mimms, J. R., of Jefferson County
11. Richmond, Reuben, of Nevada City, Madison County

Idaho Territory

1. Adams, H. O., of Lewiston, Nez Perce County
2. Chambers, M. T., of Lewiston, Nez Perce County
3. Cockrane, ———, of Elk City, Nez Perce County
4. Haas, ———, of Boise County
5. Holton, D. S., of Boise City, Ada County
6. Johnson, J. K., of Centerville, Boise County
7. Lindsay, R. H., of Boise City, Ada County
8. Lynam, James, of Silver City, Owyhee County
9. Martin, Henry, of Placerville, Boise County

10. McGownd, J. L., of Bannock, Boise County
11. Moeller, George, of Oro Fino, Clearwater County
12. Morton, Charles, of Florence, Idaho County
13. Paddock, A. G., of Elk City, Nez Perce County
14. Pomeroy, Thomas M., of Elk City, Nez Perce County
15. Rice, ———, of Centerville, Boise County
16. Stringham, Thomas, of Placerville, Boise County
17. Wollmer, C. P., of Nez Perce County
18. Walker, Charles, of Bannock, Boise County
19. Yantis, W. B., of Shoshone County

APPENDIX III

A specific list of causes of action, average cost, and number of cases for justice of the peace courts in Washington Territory includes:

Cause of Action	Mean Cost	Number of Cases
Adultery	$ 7.45	2
Assault	21.57	12
Assault and Battery	13.41	75
Assault and Battery on an Infant	31.90	1
Assault and Battery with a Deadly Weapon	25.78	2
Assault and Battery with a Deadly Weapon with Intent to Commit a Bodily Injury	6.63	2
Assault and Battery with Intent to Produce a Miscarriage	54.30	1
Assault by Words	31.51	1
Assault with a Deadly Weapon	11.08	5
Assault with a Deadly Weapon with Intent to Commit a Bodily Injury	6.78	2
Assault with a Deadly Weapon and Intent to Commit a Bodily Injury and Disturbing the Peace	32.90	1
Assault with a Deadly Weapon with Intent to Kill	16.50	3
Assault with Intent to Commit Murder	12.63	4
Assault with Intent to Have Carnal Knowledge	18.00	1
Assault with Intent to Rape	31.80	1
Assault with Intent to Rob	61.30	1
Attachment and Debt	20.86	3

Cause of Action	Mean Cost	Number of Cases
Breaking and Entering	6.05	2
Burglary	22.88	11
Buying and Concealing Stolen Property	22.90	1
Contempt	3.70	4
Contract	11.61	4
Conversion	24.65	1
Creating a Nuisance by Depositing a Putrid Carcass of a Dead Cow by a Public Road	4.05	1
Cruelty to Animals	19.25	1
Damages and Conversion	12.55	1
Damages and Debt	15.56	4
Damages and Forcible Entry and Unlawful Detainer	8.60	1
Damages and Replevin	40.60	1
Damages Caused by Hogs and Keeping Estray Hogs	21.70	2
Damages for an Assault and Battery	32.30	1
Damages for Failure to Deliver a Note	13.90	1
Damages to Personal Property	25.28	4
Damages to Real Property	8.25	2
Debt	11.11	768
Debts to County for Road Maintenance	34.75	1
Defamation of Character and Libel	48.80	1
Disturbing the Peace	11.80	3
Disturbing the Peace by Striking an Officer of the Law	—	1
Exhibiting a Pistol and Threatening to Shoot a Person	16.75	3
Forcible Entry and Unlawful Detainer	35.80	8
Forcible Entry, Unlawful Detainer and Debt	6.05	2
Foreclosure on a Mortgage	13.20	1
Forgery	23.95	1
Gambling	—	1
Garnishment and Debt	13.25	2
Grand Larceny	18.42	30
Issuance of a General Warrant	4.30	1
Killing Cattle	28.55	3
Malicious Trespass	19.48	5

Cause of Action	Mean Cost	Number of Cases
Murder	35.38	11
Obstructing a Public Highway	38.35	1
Obtaining Money and Goods under False Pretenses	14.85	1
Obtaining Property under False Pretenses	14.77	3
Perjury	12.65	1
Petit Larceny	16.73	53
Polygamy	28.00	1
Possession of Stolen Goods	45.00	1
Pouring a Quart of Beer over a Person thereby Spoiling his Clothes	—	1
Promissory Note	10.83	138
Promissory Note and Debt	13.24	73
Rape	53.46	2
Recovery of a Street Tax	14.77	1
Re-execution and Contempt	3.80	1
Replevin	18.17	42
Replevin or the Value Thereof	15.58	2
Robbery	21.17	11
Robbery and Assault	13.05	1
Robbery and Assault and Battery	57.40	1
Selling and Distributing Obscene Literature	39.90	1
Selling Goods and Merchandise on Sunday	12.90	2
Selling Liquor and Cigars on Sunday	9.05	11
Selling Merchandise from a Wagon without a License	9.25	2
Smoking and Inhaling Opium	27.65	2
Stealing Horses	25.02	9
Taxes	—	1
Threat to Commit a Criminal Offense	5.15	1
Threat to Commit an Assault	6.43	2
Threat to Commit Murder	14.98	14
Threat to Kill Horses or Humans	—	1
Unlawful Detainer	7.02	5
Vagrancy	19.15	7
Vagrancy and Habitual Drunkenness	7.20	1
Violation of a City Ordinance	10.35	1
Violation of a Game Law	22.28	2

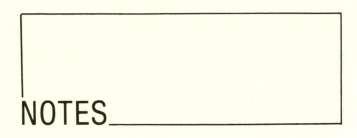

NOTES

Introduction

1. James Willard Hurst, *The Growth of American Law: The Law Makers* (Boston: Little, Brown and Co., 1950), 148; Robert M. Ireland, *The County Courts of Antebellum Kentucky* (Lexington: University of Kentucky Press, 1972), 4; Alice E. Smith, "Courts and Judges in Wisconsin Territory," *Wisconsin Magazine of History* 56 (Spring 1973):185; George Lee Haskins, *Law and Authority in Early Massachusetts* (New York: Macmillan Co., 1960), 35; Dunbar Rowland, *Mississippi: The Heart of the South* (Chicago: S. J. Clarke Publishing Co., 1925), I, 359.

2. Frank Milton, *In Some Authority: The English Magistracy* (London: Pall Mall Press, 1959), 7.

3. Lawrence M. Friedman, *A History of American Law* (New York: Simon and Schuster, 1973), 124.

4. Another useful case study with a more limited treatment of justices of the peace is William English, *The Pioneer Lawyer and Jurist in Missouri* (Columbia: University of Missouri Press, 1947).

Part I

1. U.S., *Statutes at Large* 20:175-179 (1853).

Chapter 1

1. George M. Trevelyan, *History of England* (New York: Longmans, Green and Co., 1928), 164-165; C. Warren Hollister, *The Making of England, 55 B.C. to 1399* (Boston: D. C. Heath and Co., 1966), 140; Charles Austin Beard, "The Office of Justice of the Peace in England in Its Origin and Development," *Studies in History, Economics and Law* (New York: Columbia University Press, 1904), XX, 17-32; Frederic W. Maitland, *The*

Constitutional History of England (Cambridge: University Press, 1926), 206-209; Leo Page, *Justice of the Peace* (London: Faber and Faber, Ltd., 1931), 19-30.

2. George Burton Adams, *Constitutional History of England* (New York: Henry Holt and Co., 1921), 260; Trevelyan, *England*, 165.

3. Beard, "Justice of the Peace in England," 19.

4. Ibid., 20-21.

5. Theodore F.T. Plucknett, *A Concise History of the Common Law* (Boston: Little, Brown and Co., 1956), 167; William S. Holdsworth, *A History of English Law* (London: Methuen and Co., Ltd., 1903), I, 286-287.

6. Maitland, *Constitutional History*, 206-209, 232-233; Plucknett, *History of Common Law*, 167-169; John Percy Eddy, *Justice of the Peace* (London: Cassell and Co., Ltd., 1963), 2; Bertha Haven Putnam, "The Transformation of the Keepers of the Peace into the Justices of the Peace, 1327-1380," *Transactions of the Royal Historical Society* 12 (1929):19-48.

7. Eddy, *Justice*, 1-4.

8. David Herlihy, ed., *Medieval Culture and Society* (New York: Harper and Row, 1968), 358-359.

9. Eddy, *Justice*, 3-9.

10. Ibid., 6.

11. Ibid.

12. Hollister, *Making of England*, 213; Plucknett, *History of Common Law*, 168-169; Eddy, *Justice*, 13; Holdsworth, *History of English Law*, I, 297-298.

13. Ibid.

14. Plucknett, *History of Common Law*, 168-169; Eddy, *Justice*, 11-12; Beard, "Justice of the Peace in England," 70-71.

15. Ibid.; see also Wallace Notestein, *The English People on the Eve of Colonization, 1603-1630* (New York: Harper and Brothers, 1954), 211-227.

16. Notestein, *English People on Eve of Colonization*, 218.

17. Ibid., 227; see also J. H. Gleason, *The Justices of the Peace in England, 1558-1640* (Oxford: Clarendon Press, 1969), 96-122, and C. V. Wedgwood, *The King's Peace, 1637-1641* (New York: Macmillan Co., 1955), 135-170.

18. Louis B. Wright, *The Atlantic Frontier: Colonial American Civilization, 1607-1763* (New York: Alfred A. Knopf, 1947), 52.

19. Ibid., 68; Zechariah Chafee, Jr., "Colonial Courts and the Common Law," *Proceedings of the Massachusetts Historical Society* 68 (1952):132-159.

20. W. Roy Smith, *South Carolina as a Royal Province, 1719-1776* (New York: Macmillan Co., 1903), 141.

21. George Lee Haskins, *Law and Authority in Early Massachusetts* (New York: Macmillan Co., 1960), 35, 105.

22. Leonard Labaree, *Royal Government in America: A Study of the British Colonial System before 1783* (New York: Frederick Ungar Publishing Co., 1930), 373.

23. David Hawke, *The Colonial Experience* (Indianapolis: Bobbs-Merrill Co., 1966), 505-506; Jack M. Sosin, *The Revolutionary Frontier, 1763-1783* (New York: Holt, Rinehart and Winston, 1967), 4.

24. Thomas Perkins Abernethy, *From Frontier to Plantation in Tennessee: A Study in Frontier Democracy* (Chapel Hill: University of North Carolina Press, 1932), 76-78.

25. Ibid., 78.

26. Charlton W. Tebeau, *A History of Florida* (Coral Gables, Fla.: University of Miami Press, 1971), 119-125; Max Farrand, *The Legislation of Congress for the Government of the Organized Territories of the United States, 1789-1895* (Newark, N.J.: William A. Baker, 1896), 20-29; Hubert Howe Bancroft, *History of the Pacific States of North America: Arizona and New Mexico, 1530-1888* (San Francisco: History Co., 1888), XII, 632-638; Howard Lamar, *The Far Southwest, 1846-1912: A Territorial History* (New York: W. W. Norton and Co., 1966), 84-86.

27. Cyrenus Cole, *Iowa Through the Years* (Iowa City: State Historical Society of Iowa, 1940), 103-113; William Salter, *Iowa: The First Free State in the Louisiana Purchase* (Chicago: A. C. McClurg and Co., 1905), 173.

28. The Sundry Inhabitants of Marion County, Alabama Territory, to Governor William W. Bibb, July 4, 1818, in Clarence E. Carter, ed., *The Territorial Papers of the United States: The Territory of Alabama, 1817-1819* (Washington D.C., 1952), XVIII, 365-366.

29. Hubert Howe Bancroft, *History of the Pacific States of North America: Utah, 1540-1886* (San Francisco: History Co., 1888), XXI, 439-450; Dale Morgan, et al., "The State of Deseret," *Utah Historical Quarterly* 8 (April, July, and October 1940):97-173; Lamar, *Far Southwest,* 319-321.

30. Mirth Tufts Kaplan, "Courts, Counselors and Cases: The Judiciary of Oregon's Provisional Government," *Oregon Historical Quarterly* 62 (June 1961):118-157; Hubert Howe Bancroft, *History of the Pacific States of North America: Oregon, 1834-1848* (San Francisco: History Co., 1886), XXIX, 432-433.

31. U.S., *Journals of the Continental Congress, 1774-1789* 32 (1787): 334-343 [Northwest Ordinance]; see also Arthur Bestor, "Constitutionalism and the Settlement of the West: The Attainment of Consensus, 1754-1784," in John Porter Bloom, ed., *The American Territorial System* (Athens: Ohio University Press, 1973), 13-33; Theodore C. Pease, "The Ordinance of 1787," *Mississippi Valley Historical Review* 25 (September 1938): 168; Jack Eblen, *The First and Second United States Empires: Governors and*

Territorial Government, 1784-1912 (Pittsburgh: University of Pittsburgh Press, 1968), 28-48.

32. U.S., *Journals of the Continental Congress, 1774-1789* 32 (1787): 334-343; Francis Philbrick, ed., *The Laws of Illinois Territory, 1809-1818* (Springfield: Illinois State Historical Society, 1950), XXV, Law Ser. V, 136.

33. Pease, "Ordinance," 169.

34. Randolph C. Downes, *Frontier Ohio* (Columbus: Ohio State Archeological and Historical Society, 1935), 148.

35. John D. Barnhart, *Valley of Democracy: The Frontier Versus the Plantation in the Ohio Valley, 1775-1818* (Bloomington: Indiana University Press, 1953), 145.

36. Reginald Horsman, *The Frontier in the Formative Years, 1783-1815* (New York: Holt, Rinehart and Winston, 1970), 87, 102.

37. Philbrick, ed., *Laws of Illinois*, 136; U.S., *Journals of the Continental Congress, 1774-1789* 32 (1787):334-340.

38. U.S., *Journals of the Continental Congress, 1774-1789* 32 (1787): 336-337.

39. Ibid., 337.

40. Francis Newton Thorpe, ed., *The Federal and State Constitutions, Colonial Charters, and Other Organic Laws of the States, Territories, and Colonies Now or Heretofore Forming the United States of America* (Washington, D.C.: U.S. Government Printing Office, 1909), I, 89-92, 261-264; II, 657-662, 964-967, 1111-1118; III, 1364-1373; IV, 1925-1926, 1981-1988, 2025-2027, 2139-2144; V, 2615-2622, 2986-2995; VI, 3413, 3687-3693. See also U.S., *Statutes at Large* 5 (1836):10-16. Eleven other territories within the continental United States were created after the Washington Territory Organic Act (Alaska, Arizona, Colorado, Dakota, Idaho, Indian [Oklahoma], Kansas, Montana, Nebraska, Nevada, and Wyoming), but they had no influence on the statutorial extension of justices of the peace to Washington Territory. See also Farrand, *Organized Territories*, 15, 39.

41. Theodore C. Pease, ed., *The Laws of the Northwest Territory, 1788-1800* (Springfield: Illinois State Historical Society, 1925), XVII, Law Ser. I, 154-160.

42. Ibid., xvii; Downes, *Ohio*, 151-152; John Barnes Dressler, Jr., "The Territorial System and the People: The Emergence of Factionalism in the Northwest Territory," M.A. Thesis, University of Washington (1967), 74-76, 238; George B. Toulmin, "The Political Ideas of Winthrop Sargent, A New England Federalist on the Frontier," *Journal of Mississippi History* 4 (October 1953): 209-214; John R. Wunder, "The Mississippi Territory's First Experience with American Legal Institutions: Sargent's Code, Its Adoption and Abolition, 1798-1803," M.A. Thesis, University of Iowa (1970), 21-23; John R. Wunder, "American Law and Order Comes to Mis-

sissippi Territory: The Making of Sargent's Code," *Journal of Mississippi History* 38 (May 1976):131-155.

43. Pease, ed., *Laws of Northwest Territory*, 37-39, 181-182, 203, 205-206, 215-217, 332, 368-369, 483; Downes, *Ohio*, 149-150. The laws of the Northwest Territory pertaining to justices of the peace were specifically adopted in Indiana, Illinois, Louisiana, Mississippi, and Alabama territories, and were generally copied throughout the territorial system. See also Philbrick, ed., *Laws of Illinois*, xvii; Francis S. Philbrick, ed., *The Laws of Indiana Territory, 1801-1809* (Springfield: Illinois State Historical Society, 1930), XXI, Law Ser. II, cvi; Clarence W. Alvord, *The Illinois Country* (Springfield: Illinois Centennial Commission, 1920), 430.

44. Downes, *Ohio*, 154-155; Philbrick, ed., *Laws of Indiana*, cxlix.

45. Downes, *Ohio*, 154-155.

46. Everett Dick, *The Dixie Frontier: A Social History* (New York: Alfred A. Knopf, 1948), 237-238; Robert M. Ireland, *The County Courts of Antebellum Kentucky* (Lexington: University Press of Kentucky, 1972), 62-104.

47. Pease, ed., *Laws of Northwest Territory*, 154-160; Philbrick, ed., *Laws of Indiana Territory*, cxlvii.

48. Charles Gayarré, *History of Louisiana, the American Domination* (New Orleans: F. F. Hansell and Bros., Ltd., 1903), IV, 21-22.

49. Philbrick, ed., *Laws of Illinois*, xxv; Pease, ed., *Laws of Northwest Territory*, 154-160; *Mississippi Territorial Statutes*, Sargent's Code, Sec. 2 (1799). For application of this system to Orleans and Mississippi territories, see U.S., *Statutes at Large* 2 (1804):283 and 2 (1812):743. All was not as simple to territorial lawmakers; see Philbrick, ed., *Laws of Indiana*, cliv, note 1, for a detailed discussion of the confusing jurisdictions caused by changes in the lower court structures.

50. U.S., *Statutes at Large* 2 (1805):338; Philbrick, ed., *Laws of Illinois*, xl-xli; John R. Wunder, "Constitutional Oversight: *Clarke v. Bazadone* (1803) and the Territorial Supreme Court as the Court of Last Resort," *The Old Northwest* 4 (September 1978):259-284.

51. Philbrick, ed., *Laws of Illinois*, l-li, 6-12, 19-21, 25-26, 136.

52. Ibid.

53. U.S., *Statutes at Large* 3 (1815):237.

54. Philbrick, ed., *Laws of Illinois*, liv; Lonnie J. White, *Politics on the Southwestern Frontier, 1819-1836* (Memphis, Tenn.: Memphis State University Press, 1964), 29-30.

55. Downes, *Ohio*, 157.

56. Ibid., 157-162.

57. Acting-Governor Henry Daingerfield to William B. Shields, William B. Shields to Acting-Governor Henry Daingerfield, Acting-Governor

Henry Daingerfield to the Mississippi Territorial Legislature, December 18, 1811, in Clarence E. Carter, ed., *The Territory of Mississippi, 1809-1817* (Washington, D.C., 1938), VI, 251-252.

58. Ibid.

59. Proclamation by Winthrop Sargent representing the governor of the Territory of the United States Northwest of the River Ohio, June 18, 1793, in Clarence E. Carter, ed., *The Territory Northwest of the River Ohio, 1787-1803* (Washington, D.C., 1938), III, 411.

60. Proclamation of Governor William Clark, January 23, 1816, in Clarence E. Carter, ed., *The Territory of Louisiana-Missouri, 1815-1821* (Washington, D.C., 1951), XV, 192.

61. Alcée Fortier, *A History of Louisiana, the American Domination, 1803-1861* (New York: Manzi, Joyant and Co., 1904), III, 51.

62. Acting-Governor G. K. Walker to John Walker, Chief of the Appalachicolas, September 14, 1835, in Clarence E. Carter, ed., *The Territory of Florida, 1834-1839* (Washington, D.C., 1960), XXV, 286.

63. Alec R. Gilpin, *The Territory of Michigan, 1805-1837* (East Lansing: Michigan State University Press, 1970), 111.

64. Ibid.

65. Bancroft, *Arizona and New Mexico*, XII, 643; Justices of the peace had to be careful not to overextend their position in the frontier community. One of the first laws passed by the New Mexico territorial legislature dealt with the problem of JPs and prostitution. If a justice was convicted of being a pimp, he could expect to be whipped at least thirty lashes publicly and to be carried by a jackass through the streets of his community of residence on a feast day, while the town crier followed and announced the cause of the punishment not less than five times. Lamar, *Far Southwest*, 89.

66. *Utah Territorial Statutes* (1855):123, in William N. Davis, Jr., "Western Justice: The Court at Fort Bridger, Utah Territory," *Utah Historical Quarterly* 23 (April 1955):125; Lamar, *Far Southwest*, 320-322; Bancroft, *Utah*, XXI, 439-456.

Chapter 2

1. For an excellent discussion of the uses of prosopography in history, see J. E. McGuire, "Newton and the Demonic Furies: Some Current Problems and Approaches in History of Science," *History of Science* 11 (March 1973):21-28; Richard L. Hume, "The 'Black and Tan' Constitutional Conventions of 1867-1869 in Ten Former Confederate States: A Study of Their Membership," Ph.D. Dissertation, University of Washington, Seattle, Washington (1969), I and II.

2. Francis S. Philbrick, *The Rise of the West, 1754–1830* (New York: Harper and Row, 1965), 349.

3. Robert M. Ireland, *The County Courts of Antebellum Kentucky* (Lexington: University Press of Kentucky, 1972), 14.

4. James H. Lockwood, "Early Times and Events in Wisconsin," *Collections of the State Historical Society of Wisconsin* (Madison: State Historical Society of Wisconsin, 1855), II, 98-150; Arthur H. DeRosier, Jr., "William Dunbar: A Product of the Eighteenth Century Scottish Renaissance," *Journal of Mississippi History* 28 (August 1966):197; William N. Davis, Jr., "Western Justice: The Court at Fort Bridger, Utah Territory," *Utah Historical Quarterly* 23 (April 1955):99-125; Thomas Perkins Abernethy, *From Frontier to Plantation in Tennessee: A Study in Frontier Democracy* (Chapel Hill: University of North Carolina Press, 1932), 196-197; Eron Rowland, ed., *Life, Letters, and Papers of William Dunbar* (Jackson: Mississippi Historical Society, 1930), 11-12, 106-111; Dunbar Rowland, *Mississippi: The Heart of the South* (Chicago: S. J. Clarke Publishing Co., 1925), I, 354, 363-364, 370, 382-383, 401, 407-408, 476, 479; John Anthony Caruso, *The Great Lakes Frontier* (Indianapolis: Bobbs-Merrill Co., 1961), 190, 194, 202, 235; Randolph C. Downes, *Frontier Ohio* (Columbus: Ohio State Archeological and Historical Society, 1935), 129-130; Theodore C. Blegen, *Minnesota: A History of the State* (Minneapolis: University of Minnesota Press, 1963), 160-162; Charles E. Flandrau, "Lawyers and Courts of Minnesota Prior to and During Its Territorial Period," *Collections of the Minnesota Historical Society* 8 (December 1896):90-95; Cyrenus Cole, *Iowa Through the Years* (Iowa City: State Historical Society of Iowa, 1940), 146-149; Francis S. Philbrick, ed., *The Laws of Indiana Territory, 1801–1809* (Springfield: Illinois State Historical Society, 1930), XXI, Law Ser. II, ccvi-ccix; John Francis Hamtramck Claiborne, *Mississippi: As a Province, Territory, and State* (Jackson: Mississippi Historical Society, 1880), 96, 137, 170, 193, 200-201, 209-212, 224, 244, 258; Moses M. Strong, *History of the Territory of Wisconsin* (Madison: State of Wisconsin, 1885), 97-98; Donald P. Kommers, "The Emergence of Law and Justice in Pre-Territorial Wisconsin," *American Journal of Legal History* 8 (January 1964):25-28; W. A. Provine, "Lardner Clark, Nashville's First Merchant and Foremost Citizen," *Tennessee Historical Magazine* 3 (March 1917):30-46 and 3 (June 1917):115-125; Acting-Governor Winthrop Sargent of the Northwest Territory to William Goforth, William Wells, William McMillan, John S. Gano, and Aaron Cadwell, February 9, 1793, in Clarence E. Carter, ed., *The Territorial Papers of the United States: The Territory Northwest of the River Ohio, 1787–1803* (Washington, D.C., 1934), III, 408-411; Dumas Malone, ed., *Dictionary of*

American Biography (New York: Charles Scribner's Sons, 1935), III, 459-460, VII, 361-362, XVII, 144-145; Peter Lawrence Scanlan, *Prairie du Chien* (Menasha, Wis.: George Banta Publishing Co., 1937), 92, 95, 101-102, 137, 169, 176-180.

These sources were also used for the compilation of data based on other questions from Table 1.

5. Eron Rowland, ed., *William Dunbar*, 12, 100-101; Claiborne, *Mississippi*, 137.

6. Lockwood, "Early Wisconsin," 129.

7. Ibid., 115-116.

8. Dunbar Rowland, *Mississippi*, I, 382; James Willard Hurst, *The Growth of American Law: The Law Makers* (Boston: Little, Brown and Co., 1950), 148.

9. Anton-Hermann Chroust, *The Rise of the Legal Profession in America* (Norman: University of Oklahoma Press, 1965), II, 93.

10. Philbrick, ed., *Laws of Indiana*, ccix.

11. Ireland, *Courts of Kentucky*, 12-14.

12. Provine, "Lardner Clark," 33-35.

13. Lockwood, "Early Wisconsin," 98-104.

14. Ibid., 120-122; Claiborne, *Mississippi*, 96, 244. In 1811, Brisbois and Campbell had a dispute over who owned a heifer worth about $8. They could not find a judge to hear the case, and so they asked a lawyer from Cahokia to arbitrate. Brisbois and Campbell then proceeded to travel by canoe to Cahokia, taking with them witnesses, flour, tea, sugar, hulled corn, deer tallow, and a bundle of beaver skins to pay the lawyer. After the litigants reached the arbitrator and began the proceedings, they decided to settle out of court. No one recorded who eventually obtained possession of the heifer, but the cost of the dispute totaled approximately $3,000, Brisbois and Campbell absorbing $1,500 each. These JPs had sufficient wealth to engage in petty, though expensive, disputes.

15. Blegen, *Minnesota History*, 161-162; Malone, *Biography*, XVII, 144-145; Flandrau, "Courts of Minnesota," 90-91.

16. Davis, "Court at Utah," 100.

17. Everett Dick, *The Dixie Frontier: A Social History* (New York: Alfred A. Knopf, 1948), 336.

18. Chroust, *Legal Profession*, II, 93.

19. Philbrick, ed., *Laws of Indiana*, ccix.

20. Ireland, *Courts of Kentucky*, 14-15.

21. Lockwood, "Early Wisconsin," 116, 126; Theodore C. Blegen, *Readings in Early Minnesota History* (Minneapolis: University of Minnesota Press, 1938), 132-134.

22. Claiborne, *Mississippi*, 96, 131, 134, 174, 225, 241-242, 375; Eron Rowland, ed., *William Dunbar*, 113; Dunbar Rowland, *Mississippi*, I, 354, 363-364.

23. Mary T. Hennessy, "Qualifications of California Court Judges: A Dual System," *Pacific Law Journal* 3 (July 1972):466.

24. Warren E. Burger, "The State of the Federal Judiciary—1971," *American Bar Association Journal* 57 (September 1971):858.

25. U.S. Constitution, Amendment VI.

26. Chroust, *Legal Profession*, II, 93.

27. Philbrick, ed., *Laws of Indiana*, ccix; Dick, *Dixie Frontier*, 229.

28. Claiborne, *Mississippi*, 258.

29. Lockwood, "Early Wisconsin," 126.

30. Provine, "Lardner Clark," 32, 43.

31. Lockwood, "Early Wisconsin," 105; Kommers, "Law in Wisconsin," 26-27.

32. Flandrau, "Courts of Minnesota," 94-95.

33. Militia officers of New Madrid to Governor William Clark of Louisiana Territory, [no date] 1809, in Clarence E. Carter, ed., *The Territory of Louisiana-Missouri, 1806-1814* (Washington, D.C., 1949), XIV, 270.

34. Alice E. Smith, "Courts and Judges in Wisconsin Territory," *Wisconsin Magazine of History* 56 (Spring 1973):185.

35. Presentments of the Grand Jury of Jackson County, Florida Territory, December 1831, in Clarence E. Carter, ed., *The Territory of Florida, 1828-1834* (Washington, D.C., 1959), XXV, 609.

36. David Shannon to Governor Andrew Jackson of Florida Territory, November 24, 1821, in Clarence E. Carter, ed., *The Territory of Florida, 1821-1824* (Washington, D.C., 1956), XXIII, 281-282.

37. Chroust, *Legal Profession*, II, 101.

38. Dick, *Dixie Frontier*, 225-237.

39. Strong, *History of Wisconsin*, 98; Downes, *Ohio*, 129-130.

40. Davis, "Court at Utah," 105-112.

41. Governor William C.C. Claiborne to Richard Claiborne, in Charles Gayarré, *History of Louisiana, The American Domination* (New Orleans: F. F. Hansell and Bros., Ltd., 1903), IV, 193.

42. Eron Rowland, ed., *William Dunbar*, 106-110.

43. Lockwood, "Early Wisconsin," 143-144.

44. Ibid.

45. David Shannon to Governor Andrew Jackson of Florida Territory, November 24, 1821, in Carter, ed., *Territory of Florida, 1821-1824*, XXIII, 281-282.

46. Chroust, *Legal Profession*, II, 103.

47. Henry L. Moss, "Last Days of Wisconsin Territory and Early Days of Minnesota Territory," *Collections of the Minnesota Historical Society* 8 (December 1896):75.

48. Kommers, "Law in Wisconsin," 27-28; Chroust, *Legal Profession*, II, 98.

49. Lockwood, "Early Wisconsin," 107.

50. Flandrau, "Courts of Minnesota," 90-91.

51. Strong, *History of Wisconsin*, 98; Lockwood, "Early Wisconsin," 116.

52. Lockwood, "Early Wisconsin," 126.

53. Philbrick, ed., *Laws of Indiana*, ccvi-ccix.

54. Davis, "Court at Utah," 100-113.

55. Cole, *Iowa*, 146-149.

56. Richard Maxwell Brown, "The American Vigilante Tradition," *The History of Violence in America*, Hugh Davis Graham and Ted Robert Gurr, eds. (New York: New York Times Co., 1969), 218-226.

57. John D. Barnhart, *Valley of Democracy: The Frontier Versus the Plantation in the Ohio Valley, 1775-1818* (Bloomington: Indiana University Press, 1953), 99, 211.

58. Earl S. Pomeroy, *The Territories and the United States, 1861-1890* (Seattle: University of Washington Press, 1947), 61.

59. Davis, "Court at Utah," 99.

Part II
Chapter 3

1. Arthur S. Beardsley, "Bench and Bar of Washington: The First Fifty Years, 1849-1900," MS, University of Washington Law School Library (Seattle, Washington), Ch. 3, 62-66.

2. Ibid., Ch. 2, 49; Arthur S. Beardsley and Donald A. McDonald, "The Courts and Early Bar of Washington Territory," *Washington Law Review and State Bar Journal* 17 (April 1942): 76-77; William Strong, MS, University of Washington Law School Library (Seattle, Washington), 42.

3. U.S., *Congressional Globe*, 37th Cong., 3d Sess. (1863), 1509. See also John R. Wunder, "Tampering with the Northwest Frontier: The Accidental Design of the Washington/Idaho Boundary," *Pacific Northwest Quarterly* 68 (January 1977):1-12.

4. Charles Austin Beard, "The Office of Justice of the Peace in England in Its Origin and Development," *Studies in History, Economics and Law* (New York: Columbia University Press, 1904), XX, 1-184; Mirth Tufts Kaplan, "Courts, Counselors and Cases: The Judiciary of Oregon's Provisional Government," *Oregon Historical Quarterly* 62 (June 1961):117-163.

5. See Appendix I.

6. See Appendix II.

7. The place of birth of justices of the peace of Washington Territory (1853-1889) included 29 foreign-born (Canada 6, England 8, France 1, Germany 5, Ireland 7, and Scotland 2) and 130 in the United States (from the East, 61: Connecticut 1, Maine 10, Massachusetts 5, New Hampshire 4, New Jersey 1, New York 26, Pennsylvania 9, and Vermont 5; from the South, 32: Alabama 1, Kentucky 7, Louisiana 1, Maryland 3, Missouri 5, North Carolina 2, South Carolina 1, Tennessee 6, and Virginia 6; from the Midwest, 37: Illinois 11, Indiana 7, Iowa 2, Michigan 1, and Ohio 16; and from the West, 2: Washington Territory 2).

8. B. F. Alley and J. P. Munro-Fraser, *An Illustrated History of Clarke County, Washington Territory* (Portland: Washington Publishing Co., 1885), 300; Hubert Howe Bancroft, *History of the Pacific States of North America: Washington, Idaho and Montana, 1854-1889* (San Francisco: History Co., 1890), XXXI, 37; H. K. Hines, *An Illustrated History of the State of Oregon* (Chicago: Lewis Publishing Co., 1893), 1258-1259.

9. Bancroft, *Washington, Idaho and Montana*, XXXI, 36; U.S., Bureau of the Census, *Eighth Census of the United States: 1860 Population Census, Washington Territory* (1860).

10. U.S., *Eighth Census: Washington Territory*; Alley and Munro-Fraser, *History of Clarke County*, 260-265, 300, 394-395; Jimmie Jean Cook, *"A particular friend, Penn's Cove,"* A History of the Settlers, Claims and Buildings of Central Whidbey Island (Coupeville, Wash.: Island County Historical Society, 1973), 64-66.

11. U.S., Bureau of the Census, *Historical Statistics of the United States: Colonial Times to 1957* (1960):24.

12. U.S., Bureau of the Census, *Ninth Census of the United States: 1870 Population Census, Washington Territory* (1870); Edmond Meany File, MS, Pacific Northwest Collection, University of Washington Library (Seattle, Washington); Mrs. Richard Burton Hassell, "A Whidbey Island Tragedy," *Washington Historical Magazine* 2 (July 1901):142-145; John M. Izett, "Whidbey Island History," *Washington Historical Magazine* 1 (July 1900):199-200.

13. U.S., *Eighth Census: Washington Territory.*

14. Ibid.; Meany File, MS; Washington Biography Pamphlet File, MS, Pacific Northwest Collection, University of Washington Library (Seattle, Washington).

15. *The Owyhee Avalanche* (Ruby City, Idaho Territory), July 14, 1866.

16. Ibid., August 4, 1866.

17. U.S., Bureau of the Census, *Tenth Census of the United States: 1880 Population Census, Washington Territory* (1880); U.S., *Ninth Census: Washington Territory*; *Washington Standard* (Olympia), February 17, 1882.

18. Thomas W. Prosch, "Dr. D. S. Maynard, the Pioneer Physician of Seattle," address to the King County Medical Society, March 7, 1904, MS, Pacific Northwest Collection, University of Washington Library (Seattle, Washington); *Seattle Post-Intelligencer* (Seattle, Washington), March 2, 1914.

19. Alley and Munro-Fraser, *History of Clarke County*, 303, 324, 340.

20. Edmond S. Meany, *History of the State of Washington* (New York: Macmillan Co., 1941), 156; Bancroft, *Washington, Idaho and Montana*, XXXI, 52-53.

21. *Lewis County Nugget* (Chehalis, Washington Territory), October 13, 20, 1883, and February 9, 1884; *The Nugget* (Chehalis, Washington Territory), January 8, 1886, and September 10, 1886.

22. Alley and Munro-Fraser, *History of Clarke County*, 305-306, 353-354.

23. Bancroft, *Washington, Idaho and Montana*, XXXI, 218, 251.

24. Alley and Munro-Fraser, *History of Clarke County*, 260-261, 300-306, 341.

25. "Fragments of Early History," *Up-To-The-Times* 6 (May 1912): 5060; *Walla Walla Union* (Walla Walla, Washington), August 5, 1896; *Walla Walla Washington Statesman* (Walla Walla, Washington Territory), April 6, 1866.

26. *The Montana Democrat* (Virginia City, Montana Territory), September 6, 1866.

27. *Golden Age* (Lewiston, Washington Territory), January 8 and February 8, 1863; *Boise News* (Bannock City, Idaho Territory), October 6, 1863; *Capital Chronicle* (Boise City, Idaho Territory), August 14, 1869.

28. H. K. Hines, *An Illustrated History of the State of Washington* (Chicago: Lewis Publishing Co., 1893), 513-514.

29. Clarence B. Bagley Scrapbook, MS, Pacific Northwest Collection, University of Washington Library (Seattle, Washington), XVIII, 29.

30. Ibid.

31. Occupations of the justices of the peace residing in Washington Territory, 1853-1889, included 115 farmers, 21 lawyers, 19 merchants (general), 9 miners, 8 teachers, 7 lumbermen, 6 millers, 6 real estate salesmen, 6 teamsters, 5 doctors, 5 livery owners, 5 loggers, 4 carpenters, 4 newspaper editors, 4 seamen, 3 hotel owners, 2 carriage or wagon makers, 2 coopers, 2 druggists, 2 farm laborers, 2 ferry owners, 2 musicians, 2 penitentiary wardens, 2 railroad engineers, and an apiarian, architect, blacksmith, brick molder, fisherman, fishery owner, furniture dealer, gunsmith, Indian agent, painter, policeman, saddle and harness maker, saloon keeper, shoemaker, and tinner. Only two JPs listed their only occupation as justice of the peace.

32. U.S., *Eighth Census: Washington Territory*; Alley and Munro-Fraser, *History of Clarke County*, 260-265.

33. U.S., *Eighth Census: Washington Territory*; Bancroft, *Washington, Idaho and Montana*, XXXI, 77, 139; *Walla Walla Union* (Walla Walla, Washington), June 14, 1934; *Pioneer and Democrat* (Olympia, Washington Territory), April 12, 1861.

34. Frank S. Farquhar, "Historical Sketches of Yakima County," *Washington Historical Magazine* 2 (July 1901):190-194.

35. *Whatcom Reveille* (Whatcom, Washington Territory), June 22, 1883.

36. H. O. Lang, ed., *History of the Willamette Valley* (Portland: Himes and Lang, 1885), 900.

37. *Washington Standard* (Olympia), June 27, 1879.

38. *Walla Walla Washington Statesman* (Walla Walla, Washington Territory), December 22, 1864, and May 25, 1866; U.S., *Eighth Census: Washington Territory*.

39. *The Vancouver Register* (Vancouver, Washington Territory), July 17, 1869.

40. Bagley Scrapbook, MS, I, 13; Bancroft, *Washington, Idaho and Montana*, XXXI, 32, 272.

41. "Extracts from the Diary of General A. V. Kautz," *The Washington Historian* 1 (July 1900):185.

42. Ibid., 181-186, 1 (April 1900):12-15; Bancroft, *Washington, Idaho and Montana*, XXXI, 27; *Washington Standard* (Olympia), March 22, 1864.

Chapter 4

1. U.S., *Statutes at Large* 20 (1853):175.

2. Ibid.

3. Ibid., 178-179.

4. *Washington Territorial Statutes*, Sess. 1 (1854):478-488; Sess. 2 (1855):39; Sess. 4 (1857):52-53; Sess. 5 (1858):51; Sess. 6 (1859):61-62; Sess. 7 (1860):420-421, 436-437, 469-470; Sess. 8 (1860-1861):7-8, 13-14, 19-20, 30-31, 57-58; Sess. 9 (1861):304; Sess. 10 (1863):3-6, 31; Sess. 11 (1865): 47-48; Sess. 14 (1867):168-169; Sess. 17 (1871):134-136; Sess. 18 (1873):461-463; Sess. 23 (1883):87-100; Sess. 25 (1888):70-72.

Justices of the peace in Washington Territory receiving their commissions by direct appointments from 1854 to 1867 included 35 in 1854 (by county: 1 Clark, 3 Skamania, 1 Walla Walla, 2 Cowlitz, 1 Wahkiacum, 1 Pacific, 4 Lewis, 3 Chehalis, 3 Thurston, 1 Sawamish, 3 Pierce, 3 King, 8 Jefferson, 1 Clallam), 1 in 1855 (1 Walla Walla), 3 in 1857 (3 Slaughter), 3 in 1859 (1 Skamania, 1 Walla Walla, 1 Spokane), 3 in 1860 (1 Klickitat, 1 Spokane, 1 Missoula), 6 in 1861 (3 Klickitat, 1 Lewis, 1 Idaho, 1 Nez Perce), 4 in 1863 (3 Boise, 1 Ferguson), and 1 in 1867 (1 Klickitat).

5. *Wash. Terr. Statutes*, Sess. 1 (1854):487-488; Sess. 5 (1858):51; Sess. 7 (1860):469-470; Sess. 8 (1861):13-14, 19-20.

6. Ibid., Sess. 9 (1861):304; Sess. 10 (1863):3-4.

7. Ibid., Sess. 1 (1854):478-487. Two statutes designating county government appointees for Jefferson County were approved by the Washington territorial legislature in 1854. The first statute included the following appointments: Josiah P. Keller as county commissioner and JP; F. W. Pettygrove as county commissioner and probate judge; D. F. Brownfield as county commissioner; A. A. Plummer as auditor; J. K. Thorndike as treasurer; J. B. Brown as assessor; Charles Bradshaw as sheriff; G. W. Barrish as JP; W. T. Sayward as JP; and William Webster as JP. The second statute included the following appointments: Josiah P. Keller as county commissioner and JP; F. W. Pettygrove as JP; A. A. Plummer as auditor; J. K. Thorndike as treasurer and JP; —— Klinger as assessor; W. T. Sayward as sheriff; William Webster as JP; William Dunn as county commissioner; P. W. Pettygrove as county commissioner; and L. B. Hastings as probate judge.

8. *Wash. Terr. Statutes*, Sess. 1 (1854):479-480; Sess. 2 (1855):39.

9. Ibid., Sess. 18 (1873):461-463.

10. Ibid., Sess. 1 (1854):224; Sess. 7 (1860):240; Sess. 10 (1863):338; Sess. 18 (1873):331. See also Dorothy O. Johansen, *Empire of the Columbia* (New York: Harper and Row, 1967), 208-210.

11. *Wash. Terr. Statutes*, Sess. 10 (1863):6; Sess. 11 (1865): 47-48; Sess. 17 (1871):134-136; Sess. 23 (1883):87-100; Sess. 25 (1888):70-72.

12. Ibid., Sess. 1 (1854):222-223; Sess. 7 (1860):239; Sess. 10 (1863):337; Sess. 18 (1873):330.

13. Ibid., Sess. 1 (1854):224; Sess. 7 (1860):240; Sess. 10 (1863):338; Sess. 18 (1873):331; Sess. 25 (1888):120.

14. Ibid., Sess. 20 (1877):208-209.

15. Wilfred J. Airey, "A History of the Constitution and Government of Washington Territory," Ph.D. Dissertation, University of Washington, Seattle, Washington (1945), 274-275.

16. Ibid.

17. U.S., *Congressional Record*, 46th Cong., 2d Sess. (1880), 2244-2245.

18. U.S., *Supplement to Rev. Statutes at Large* 2 (1880):280.

19. Quentin Shipley Smith, *The Journal of the Washington State Constitutional Convention of 1889*, Beverly Paulik Rosenow, ed. (Seattle: Book Publishing Co., 1962), 615-616; Washington, *Constitution* (1889), Art. IV, Sec. 10.

20. *Wash. Terr. Statutes*, Sess. 1 (1854):223; Sess. 7 (1860):239; Sess. 10 (1863):337; Sess. 18 (1873):330-331.

21. Ibid., Sess. 1 (1854):431, 444; Sess. 10 (1863):400.
22. U.S., *Statutes at Large* 2 (1812):788.
23. *Wash. Terr. Statutes*, Sess. 1 (1854):226.
24. Ibid., Sess. 10 (1863):411; Sess. 21 (1879):129-130.
25. *The Nugget* (Chehalis, Washington Territory), January 8, 1886.

Part III

1. U.S., *Statutes at Large* 20 (1853):175.
2. Arthur S. Beardsley, "Compiling the Territorial Codes of Washington," *Pacific Northwest Quarterly* 28 (January 1937):5-6.
3. Ibid., 7.
4. Wash. Terr., *Journal of the House of Representatives, 1868–1869:* 406, 430; Beardsley, "Compiling Codes," 17-18.
5. *Walla Walla Union* (Walla Walla, Washington Territory), December 17, 1887.

Chapter 5

1. U.S., *Statutes at Large* 20 (1853):175-176.
2. Ibid.
3. *Washington Territorial Statutes,* Sess. 11 (1865):162-163.
4. Earl S. Pomeroy, *The Territories and the United States, 1861–1890* (Seattle: University of Washington Press, 1947), 60.
5. U.S., *Statutes at Large* 22 (1883):407.
6. Ibid., 12 (1863):700; 16 (1871):77; 23 (1885):287; Pomeroy, *Territories*, 60.
7. U.S., *Statutes at Large* 6 (1853):175-176.
8. *Wash. Terr. Statutes*, Sess. 1 (1854):235; Sess. 7 (1860):252-253; Sess. 10 (1863):367; Sess. 18 (1873):369.
9. Ibid., Sess. 1 (1854):224-226; Sess. 7 (1860):240, 242; Sess. 10 (1863): 338-339; Sess. 18 (1873):332-333. The repetition of this statute twice within each code is evidence of the failure of codifiers to refine and shorten existing laws.
10. Ibid., Sess. 1 (1854):226-227; Sess. 7 (1860):243; Sess. 10 (1863):340; Sess. 18 (1873):333-334.
11. Ibid., Sess. 1 (1854):242-248; Sess. 7 (1860):260-267; Sess. 10 (1863): 355-370; Sess. 18 (1873):356-373.
12. Ibid., Sess. 1 (1854):242-244; Sess. 7 (1860):260-263; Sess. 10 (1863): 355-368; Sess. 18 (1873):356-359.

13. Ibid., Sess. 1 (1854):244-247; Sess. 7 (1860):263-266; Sess. 10 (1863): 358-361; Sess. 18 (1873):359-363.

14. Ibid., Sess. 1 (1854):247-248; Sess. 7 (1860):266; Sess. 10 (1863):360-361; Sess. 18 (1873):361-363.

15. Ibid., Sess. 1 (1854):247-248; Sess. 7 (1860):265-266; Sess. 10 (1863): 360-361; Sess. 18 (1873):361-363.

16. Ibid., Sess. 1 (1854):248; Sess. 7 (1860):267; Sess. 10 (1863):370; Sess. 18 (1873):372.

17. Ibid., Sess. 1 (1854):248; Sess. 7 (1860):267; Sess. 10 (1863):370; Sess. 18 (1873):373.

18. Charles Howard Shinn, *Mining Camps: A Study in American Frontier Government* (New York: Harper and Row, 1965 [originally published in 1884 by Charles Scribner's Sons]), 176.

19. Ibid., 176-177. The right of the community to interfere in extreme cases always existed, and no justice of the peace was ever successfully forced upon a mining district by some outside power.

20. William J. Trimble, *The Mining Advance into the Inland Empire* (Madison: University of Wisconsin, 1914), 15-29; Rodman W. Paul, *Mining Frontiers of the Far West, 1848-1880* (New York: Holt, Rinehart and Winston, 1963), 37.

21. Trimble, *Mining Advance*, 62-80.

22. *Wash. Terr. Statutes*, Sess. 8 (1860):7-8; Sess. 8 (1861):13-14; Sess. 9 (1861):3-4; Sess. 10 (1863):304.

23. Trimble, *Mining Advance*, 227.

24. Ibid., 62-227; Paul, *Mining Frontiers*, 161-175.

25. *Wash. Terr. Statutes,* Sess. 1 (1854):227; Sess. 7 (1860):243-244; Sess. 10 (1863):340-341; Sess. 18 (1873):334-335.

26. Ibid., Sess. 1 (1854):259-260.

27. Ibid., Sess. 5 (1858):9; Sess. 8 (1861):65.

28. Ibid., Sess. 19 (1875):51-52.

29. Ibid., Sess. 3 (1865):11-12; Sess. 18 (1873):521.

30. Ibid., Sess. 4 (1857):28.

31. U.S., *Statutes at Large* 2 (1802):139-145.

32. Francis Paul Prucha, *American Indian Policy in the Formative Years: The Indian Trade and Intercourse Acts, 1790-1834* (Lincoln: University of Nebraska Press, 1962), 261-269; U.S., *Statutes at Large* 4 (1834): 729-735.

33. Greg Russell Hubbard, "The Indian Under the White Man's Law in Washington Territory, 1853-1889," M.A. Thesis, University of Washington, Seattle, Washington (1972), 6-7.

34. Prucha, *Indian Policy*, 275.

35. *Wash. Terr. Statutes*, Sess. 2 (1855):32-33.
36. Ibid., Sess. 5 (1858):33.
37. Ibid., Sess. 4 (1857):26-27.
38. Ibid., Sess. 13 (1866):86-87.
39. Ibid., Sess. 15 (1869):373.
40. Ibid., Sess. 15 (1868):29-30.
41. Ibid., Sess. 19 (1875):89-91.
42. Ibid., Sess. 1 (1854):106-108, 231. In 1866, this procedure was amended whereby civil actions could be commenced before a JP with only a summons. Ibid., Sess. 13 (1866):100-101.
43. Ibid.
44. Ibid., Sess. 1 (1854):235. Exceptions to this rule were actions for forcible entry which always required a jury trial, and any actions before the special intermediate county court which required a set number of six jurors. Ibid., Sess. 1 (1854):248-250; Sess. 4 (1857):13-16.
45. Ibid., Sess. 1 (1854):235; Sess. 7 (1860):253; Sess. 10 (1863):348; Sess. 18 (1873):347-348.
46. Ibid., Sess. 9 (1862):58.
47. Ibid., Sess. 20 (1877):256.
48. Ibid., Sess. 1 (1854):87, 104-106, 212, 260.
49. Ibid., 233-234.
50. Ibid., Sess. 1 (1854):248-250; Sess. 16 (1869): 167-171.
51. Ibid., Sess. 1 (1854):233, 238, 261.
52. Ibid., 241, 260.
53. Ibid., Sess. 1 (1854):404; Sess. 2 (1855):36.
54. Ibid., Sess. 1 (1854):407-408; Sess. 2 (1855):16-17.
55. Ibid., Sess. 1 (1854):227-228; Sess. 7 (1860):244-245; Sess. 10 (1863): 341-342; Sess. 18 (1873):339.
56. Ibid., Sess. 1 (1854):262; Sess. 4 (1857):4; Sess. 7 (1860):336; Sess. 23 (1883):70.
57. Ibid., Sess. 1 (1854):252; Sess. 7 (1860):269-271; Sess. 10 (1863):363-366; Sess. 18 (1873):367.
58. Ibid., Sess. 1 (1854): 261; Sess. 4 (1857): 4-5; Sess. 6 (1859):5; Sess. 7 (1860):136; Sess. 10 (1863):385; Sess. 18 (1873):392.

Chapter 6

1. *Washington Territorial Statutes,* Sess. 4 (1857):13-17; Sess. 6 (1859):5; Sess. 13 (1866):46-49.
2. Arthur S. Beardsley and Donald A. McDonald, "The Courts and

Early Bar of Washington Territory," *Washington Law Review and State Bar Journal* 17 (April 1942):76.

3. U.S., *Statutes at Large* 11 (1856):49-51 [italics mine].

4. Beardsley and McDonald, "Courts," 77.

5. *Wash. Terr. Statutes*, Sess. 4 (1857):13-17.

6. Ibid.

7. John D.W. Guice, *The Rocky Mountain Bench: The Territorial Supreme Courts of Colorado, Montana, and Wyoming, 1861-1890* (New Haven, Conn.: Yale University Press, 1972), 11-12.

8. *Wash. Terr. Statutes*, Sess. 6 (1859):5.

9. U.S., *Statutes at Large* 11 (1856):366.

10. *Wash. Terr. Statutes*, Sess. 6 (1859): 27.

11. Ibid., Sess. 5 (1858):88; Sess. 9 (1862):143.

12. *Pioneer and Democrat* (Olympia, Washington Territory), December 10, 17, 24, 1858; Wash. Terr., *Journal of the House of Representatives* (1858-1860), 40-41.

13. Wash. Terr., *House Journal* (1858-1860), 73.

14. Wash. Terr., *Journal of the Council* (1859-1861), 62, 64; *Pioneer and Democrat* (Olympia, Washington Territory), December 10, 17, 1858, and January 21, 1859.

15. Wash. Terr., *Council Journal* (1859-1861), 78.

16. Ibid., 116, 120.

17. Wash. Terr., *House Journal* (1858-1860), 61.

18. Ibid., 170, 180, 188.

19. Wash. Terr., *Council Journal* (1859-1861), 184, 189.

20. Ibid., 190; Wash. Terr., *House Journal* (1858-1860), 213.

21. Hazard Stevens, *The Life of General Isaac I. Stevens* (Boston: Houghton, Mifflin and Co., 1901), II, 168-171, 186-187, 242.

22. Edmond S. Meany Pioneer File, MS, Pacific Northwest Collection, University of Washington Library (Seattle, Washington).

23. *Pioneer and Democrat* (Olympia, Washington Territory), February 4, 1859.

24. *Wash. Terr. Statutes*, Sess. 10 (1863):199-200.

25. Ibid., Sess. 13 (1866):46-49. This proceeding, and particularly the use of judicial officers, suggests a civil law basis rather than the common law foundation of American territorial jurisprudence.

26. Ibid., Sess. 1 (1854):222.

27. Ibid., 223.

28. U.S., Bureau of the Census, *Ninth Census of the United States: 1870*, 283-284.

29. U.S., Bureau of the Census, *Tenth Census of the United States: 1880*, 362.

30. Edmond S. Meany, *History of the State of Washington* (New York: Macmillan Co., 1941), 269-279; Murray Morgan, *Skid Road* (New York: Ballantine Books, 1951), 55-153; Earl S. Pomeroy, *The Pacific Slope* (New York: Alfred A. Knopf, 1965), 146-150.

31. U.S., Bureau of the Census, *Eleventh Census of the United Sates: 1890*, 351-353.

32. *Wash. Terr. Statutes*, Sess. 19 (1875):148-149; Sess. 20 (1877): 354; Sess. 23 (1883):177-180; Sess. 24 (1886):250-262.

33. Ibid., Sess. 24 (1886):250-262.

34. Ibid., Sess. 25 (1888):120.

35. Ibid., Sess. 1 (1854):455-458; Sess. 4 (1857):69-73; Sess. 6 (1859):31-34; Sess. 7 (1860):433-436; Sess. 9 (1862):17-24; Sess. 10 (1863):43-46; Sess. 12 (1865); Sess. 16 (1869):481; Sess. 17 (1871):142-152; Sess. 19 (1875):169-170; Sess. 21 (1879):168-169.

Incorporated cities and towns in Washington Territory at their initial incorporation date included Steilacoom (1854), Vancouver (1857), Olympia (1859), Port Townsend (1860), Walla Walla (1862), Lewiston (1863), Seattle (1865), Tumwater (1869), Kalama (1871), Tacoma (1875), Goldendale (1879), Colfax (1881), Dayton (1881), New Tacoma (1881), Spokane Falls (1881), Waitsburg (1881), Ainsworth (1883), Chehalis (1883), Cheney (1883), Ellensburgh (1883), La Conner (1883), Montesano (1883), Snohomish (1883), Sprague (1883), Whatcom (1883), Yakima (1883), Centralia (1886), North Yakima (1886), and Pomeroy (1886).

36. Ibid., Sess. 23 (1883):310-335.

37. Ibid., Sess. 25 (1886):424, 449.

38. Ibid., Sess. 5 (1859):31-34; Sess. 12 (1865); Sess. 16 (1869):426-437, 481; Sess. 17 (1871):115-127; Sess. 18 (1873):514-519, 524-527; Sess. 24 (1886):444-447.

39. Ibid., Sess. 15 (1869):437-455; Sess. 20 (1877):345-347; Sess. 22 (1881):115-130.

40. Ibid., Sess. 5 (1859):31-34.

41. Ibid., Sess. 10 (1863):42.

42. Ibid., Sess. 18 (1873):524-527, 532.

43. Ibid., Sess. 12 (1865); Sess. 16 (1869):481; Sess. 18 (1873):514-519; Sess. 24 (1886):444-447.

44. Ibid., Sess. 16 (1869):481.

45. Ibid., Sess. 23 (1883):135-138.

46. Ibid., Sess. 7 (1860):433-436; Sess. 15 (1868):137; Sess. 22 (1881):55-61, 66-87; Sess. 23 (1883):335-350; Sess. 24 (1886):185-208.

47. *Oregon Territorial Statutes*, Sess. 2 (1851):5-10, 16-22.

48. *Wash. Terr. Statutes*, Sess. 1 (1854):455-456; Sess. 4 (1857):69-73; Sess. 10 (1863):43-46; Sess. 18 (1873):492-494.

49. Ibid., Sess. 5 (1858):49-50; Sess. 11 (1865):151-152; Sess. 14 (1868): 109-136; Sess. 15 (1869): 437-455; Sess. 17 (1871):142-152; Sess. 18 (1873): 502-504; Sess. 21 (1879):188-197; Sess. 22 (1881):138-148; Sess. 23 (1883): 288-295.

50. Ibid., Sess. 18 (1873):502.

51. Ibid., 502-504.

52. Ibid., Sess. 21 (1879):188-197.

53. Ibid., Sess. 17 (1871):142-152; Sess. 23 (1883):288-295.

54. Ibid., Sess. 19 (1875):148-149, 169-170; Sess. 22 (1881):115-130; Sess. 24 (1886):324-350.

55. Ibid.

56. Ibid.

57. Ibid., Sess. 24 (1886):250-262.

58. Ibid., Sess. 23 (1883):177-180; Sess. 24 (1886):300-323.

59. Ibid., Sess. 22 (1881):157-167; Sess. 23 (1883):162-168, 191-197, 207-209, 214-234, 242-270; Sess. 24 (1886):350-393, 438-442, 447-448.

60. Ibid., Sess. 22 (1881):157-167.

61. Ibid., Sess. 23 (1883):162-168, 191-197, 207-209, 214-234, 242-270.

62. Ibid., Sess. 24 (1886):350-395, 438-442.

63. Ibid., Sess. 19 (1875):177; Sess. 20 (1877):345-347; Sess. 23 (1883): 114-121, 143-148, 295-310; Sess. 24 (1886):273-299, 395-418.

64. Ibid., Sess. 1-25 (1854-1889).

65. Ibid., Sess. 17 (1871):51-58.

66. Ibid., Sess. 17 (1871):115-127; Sess. 18 (1873):514-519, 524-532.

67. U.S., Bureau of the Census, *Ninth Census of the United States: 1870*, 283-284.

68. *Wash. Terr. Statutes*, Sess. 18 (1873):514-519, 524-532.

69. Ibid., Sess. 20 (1877):173-175.

70. Ibid., Sess. 20 (1877):345-347, 354; Sess. 21 (1879):168-169, 188-197; Sess. 21 (1881):55-61, 87-102, 115-130, 138-156, 166-167.

71. Ibid., Sess. 21 (1881):22-23; *An Illustrated History of Southeastern Washington* (Spokane, Wash.: Western Historical Publishing Co., 1906), 155-158.

Chapter 7

1. Richard J. Hooker, ed., *The Carolina Backcountry on the Eve of the Revolution: The Journal and Other Writings of Charles Woodmason, Anglican Itinerant* (Chapel Hill: University of North Carolina Press, 1953), 124.

2. Ibid.

3. *Washington Territorial Statutes,* Sess. 1 (1854):374; Sess. 8 (1861): 39-40; Sess. 9 (1862):40-42, 49-50; Sess. 10 (1863):24-26, 41; Sess. 11 (1865): 73-74; Sess. 13 (1866):98-99; Sess. 14 (1867):157; Sess. 15 (1868):92-93; Sess. 16 (1869):368.

4. Ibid., Sess. 1 (1854):374; *Oregon Territorial Statutes,* Sess. 2 (1851): 150-151; Sess. 4 (1853):23-24.

Most of the fee schedule legislation dealing with court costs concerned JP legal rates. In Table 6, reference is made to a variety of fee categories available to local judges. These categories can be divided roughly into four areas: JP activity prior to a trial; JP activity during a trial; JP activity after a trial; and miscellaneous JP activity not related to an adversary proceeding.

5. *Wash. Terr. Statutes,* Sess. 8 (1861):39-40.

6. Ibid., Sess. 9 (1862):40-42.

7. Ibid., Sess. 9 (1862):49-50; Sess. 11 (1865):73-74; Sess. 15 (1868): 92-93.

8. Ibid., Sess. 9 (1862): 49-50.

9. Ibid., Sess. 11 (1865):73-74.

10. Ibid., Sess. 15 (1868):92-93.

11. Ibid., Sess. 9 (1862):40-42; Sess. 10 (1863):24-26; Sess. 11 (1865):73-74; Sess. 15 (1868):92-93.

12. Ibid., Sess. 10 (1863):41.

13. Ibid., Sess. 9 (1862):40-42; Sess. 10 (1863): 24-26, 41; Sess. 13 (1866): 98-99; Sess. 14 (1867):157.

14. Ibid., Sess. 16 (1869):368.

15. Ibid., Sess. 16 (1869):373.

16. U.S., *Supplement to Rev. Stat. at Large* 1 (1880 [second edition]): 503-505.

17. *Ore. Terr. Statutes,* Sess. 3 (1852):69.

18. *Wash. Terr. Statutes,* Sess. 1 (1854):375.

19. Ibid., Sess. 8 (1861):40-41.

20. Ibid., Sess. 9 (1862):42.

21. Ibid., Sess. 10 (1863):26.

22. Ibid., Sess. 16 (1869):368.

23. Ibid., Sess. 1 (1854):373.

24. Ibid., Sess. 1 (1854):244-247, 375-376; Sess. 9 (1862):58; Sess. 10 (1863):348; Sess. 18 (1873):347-348; Sess. 20 (1877):202.

25. Ibid., Sess. 8 (1861):39; Sess. 9 (1862):40, 50; Sess. 10 (1863):26; Sess. 16 (1869):368.

26. U.S., Bureau of the Census, *Historical Statistics of the United States: Colonial Times to 1957* (1960), 115.

Wholesale price indexes for all commodities from 1854 to 1889 included

1854 (108 [wholesale price index]), 1855 (110), 1856 (105), 1857 (111), 1858 (93), 1859 (95), 1860 (93), 1861 (89), 1862 (104), 1863 (133), 1864 (193), 1865 (185), 1866 (174), 1867 (162), 1868 (158), 1869 (151), 1870 (135), 1871 (130), 1872 (136), 1873 (133), 1874 (126), 1875 (118), 1876 (110), 1877 (106), 1878 (91), 1879 (90), 1880 (100), 1881 (103), 1882 (108), 1883 (101), 1884 (93), 1885 (85), 1886 (82), 1887 (85), 1888 (86), 1889 (81).

27. *Territory of Washington v. Bozarth*, Island County, Washington Territory (1860).

28. Ibid.

29. *Territory of Washington v. Robertson*, Island County, Washington Territory (1866); Jimmie Jean Cook, *"A particular friend, Penn's Cove," A History of the Settlers, Claims and Buildings of Central Whidbey Island* (Coupeville, Wash.: Island County Historical Society, 1973), 37-39, 94-95.

30. Cook, *Central Whidbey*, 60-62.

31. *Territory of Washington v. Robertson*, Island County, Washington Territory (1866).

Justice of the peace court fees included JP services of John Y. Sewell of $14.40, witness fees of $19.00, sheriff fees of $8.80, and constable fees of $8.20, for a total of $50.40.

District court fees included clerk services of James Seavey of $11.85, sheriff fees of E. Hathaway of $9.15, bailiff services of E. D. Smith of $5.25 and T. F. Sane of $3.80, prosecuting attorney fees of J. K. Kennedy of $12.50, and six witness fees of $17.60, $11.80, $8.00, $8.40, $10.00, and $12.00, for a total of $110.35.

Justice of the peace court retrial fees included JP services of H. E. Morgan of $12.50, sheriff fees of $8.70, and witness fees of $18.70, for a total of $39.90.

The total court costs of the three proceedings were $200.65.

32. *Washburn v. Ferguson*, Walla Walla County, Washington Territory (1876). See also Table 6.

33. Quentin Shipley Smith, *The Journal of the Washington State Constitutional Convention, 1889*, Beverly Paulik Rosenow, ed. (Seattle, Wash.: Book Publishing Co., 1962), 615-616.

34. Washington, *Proceedings of the Washington Constitutional Convention* (1889):225-228; *Washington Standard* (Olympia, Washington Territory), July 26, 1889; *Walla Walla Union* (Walla Walla, Washington Territory), July 20, 1889.

35. Wilfred J. Airey, "A History of the Constitution and Government of Washington Territory," Ph.D. Dissertation, University of Washington, Seattle, Washington (1945), 467.

36. Smith, *Journal*, 616; *Tacoma Ledger* (Tacoma, Washington Terri-

tory), July 20, 1889; *Puget Sound Weekly Argus* (Port Townsend, Washington Territory), August 1, 1889; *Globe* (Tacoma, Washington Territory), July 25, 1889.

37. *The Nugget* (Chehalis, Washington Territory), July 19, 1889; Smith, *Journal*, 616-617.

38. *Seattle Post-Intelligencer* (Seattle, Washington Territory), July 22, 1889.

39. Ibid., July 23, 1889.

Part IV

1. See Chapter 2 above.

2. Justice Court Records, 1853-1888, MS, Coveland Precinct, Island County, Clerk of the Court, Island County Courthouse, Coupeville, Washington, Vols. I-III; Execution Docket for Island County, 1853-1889, MS, County Auditor's Office, Island County Courthouse, Coupeville, Washington; Island County Commissioners Records, 1853-1887, MS, County Auditor's Office, Island County Courthouse, Coupeville, Washington, Vols. I-III; Justice's Docket, 1889-1911, MS, Coveland Precinct, Island County, County Auditor's Office, Island County Courthouse, Coupeville, Washington; Justice of the Peace Records, 1885-1921, MS, Newcastle Precinct, King County, on microfilm, University of Washington Library, Seattle, Washington; Justice of the Peace Records, 1872-1882, MS, Walla Walla Precinct, Walla Walla County, Clerk of the Court, Walla Walla County Courthouse, Walla Walla, Washington, Vols. I-II.

These records were read closely for the data used throughout Part IV in order to analyze the proceedings of justice of the peace courts. Unless otherwise indicated, the information for the tables in this section was drawn from the above justice court records.

Garfield County records were inaccessible to this author because of local historical society and county courthouse reluctance to allow a full-scale examination of them. Both the Garfield and Klickitat County records represented small samples; a cursory check indicates no deviation from the findings presented in Chapters 8-10.

Chapter 8

1. See Chapter 3 above.

2. See sources included in Appendix I.

3. U.S., Bureau of the Census, *Historical Statistics of the United States: Colonial Times to 1957* (1960), 206, 214.

Year of Census	Percentage of Total Population That Was Illiterate	Percentage of White Population That Was Illiterate
1850	22.6	10.7
1860	19.7	8.9
1870	17.0	9.4
1880	20.0	11.5

Literacy rates in 1850 and 1860 were based upon people twenty years of age or older; literacy rates in 1870 and 1880 were based upon people ten years of age or older.

4. *Seattle Post-Intelligencer* (Seattle, Washington), June 21, 1919; Thomas W. Prosch, "The Pioneer Dead of 1914," *Washington Historical Quarterly* 4 (January 1915):12.

5. H. K. Hines, *An Illustrated History of the State of Oregon* (Chicago: Lewis Publishing Co., 1893), 1258-1259; C. T. Conover, "Just Cogitating: 'J.P.' Marriage First Judicial Act in County," *Seattle Times* (Seattle, Washington), February 12, 1961; *Lewis County Nugget* (Chehalis, Washington Territory), October 13, 1883.

6. *Barry v. Stringer*, Walla Walla County, Washington Territory (1873).

7. *Territory of Washington* (Peter Heisenberger) *v. Mularkey*, King County, Washington Territory (1887).

8. *Williams v. Rounds*, Walla Walla County, Washington Territory (1881).

9. *Territory of Washington v. Hughes*, Island County, Washington Territory (1882).

10. *Territory of Washington v. Carr*, Walla Walla County, Washington Territory (1879).

11. *Glime v. Kraft*, Walla Walla County, Washington Territory (1874).

12. *Washington Standard* (Olympia, Washington Territory), February 17, 1882.

13. *Territory of Washington v. Robertson*, Island County, Washington Territory (1883).

14. *Tierney v. Dutro*, Walla Walla County, Washington Territory (1873).

15. *Cody v. Ewing*, Walla Walla County, Washington Territory (1875); *Rose v. Smith*, Walla Walla County, Washington Territory (1877); *Territory of Washington v. Bozarth*, Island County, Washington Territory (1860).

16. *Territory of Washington v. Gallaher*, Walla Walla County, Wash-

ington Territory (1874); *Territory of Washington v. Kelly and Burnett*, Walla Walla County, Washington Territory (1873); *Whiteaker v. Richardson*, Walla Walla County, Washington Territory (1875).

17. *Territory of Washington v. Lister*, Garfield County, Washington Territory (1883).

18. *Walla Walla Washington Statesman* (Walla Walla, Washington Territory), December 22, 1865; Meany Pioneer File, MS, University of Washington Library, Pacific Northwest Collection, Seattle, Washington.

19. Arthur S. Beardsley, "Bench and Bar of Washington: The First Fifty Years, 1849-1900," MS, University of Washington Law School Library, Seattle, Washington, Ch. 2, 16-18, Ch. 3, 62; Benjamin Kizer, "History of the Spokane Bar and Bench," MS, University of Washington Law School Library, Seattle, Washington, Ch. 1, 1-12.

20. Types of cases by attorney participation in Washington Territory JP courts, 1854-1889, included 663 civil cases with no attorney, 212 civil cases with an attorney for plaintiff only, 44 civil cases with an attorney for defendant only, and 161 civil cases with attorneys for both plaintiff and defendant.

They also included 125 criminal cases with no attorney, 109 criminal cases with an attorney for plaintiff only, 17 criminal cases with an attorney for defendant only, and 77 criminal cases with attorneys for both plaintiff and defendant.

21. *Husen v. Miller*, Walla Walla County, Washington Territory (1874).

22. *Bryant v. Kehoe*, Walla Walla County, Washington Territory (1881).

23. *Doyle v. Saunders & Co.*, Island County, Washington Territory (1860).

24. *Colt v. Bell and Davis*, Walla Walla County, Washington Territory (1877).

Chapter 9

1. Earl S. Pomeroy, *The Territories and the United States, 1861-1890* (Seattle: University of Washington Press, 1947), 58.

2. See Chapter 6.

3. *Washington Territorial Statutes,* Sess. 1 (1854):202.

4. *Winfield S. Ebey v. Engle & Hill*, 1 Allen (Washington Territory) 72-73 (1859).

5. *H. B. Bagley v. Ara Carpenter*, 2 Allen (Washington Territory) 19-22 (1880).

6. The median represents that point beyond which one-half of the sample fell. The median for JP costs was $9.09, for witness costs $6.85, and

for juror costs $12.50. Since these figures do not vary significantly from the mean, it can be assumed that many extreme court costs were absent in these three categories.

7. U.S., Bureau of the Census, *Historical Statistics of the United States: Colonial Times to 1957* (1960), 123-124.

The mean wholesale price of wheat per bushel included $1.57 in the 1850s, $2.00 in the 1860s, $1.49 in the 1870s, and $0.96 in the 1880s. The mean wholesale price of nails per one hundred pounds included $3.87 in the 1850s, $5.23 in the 1860s, $3.72 in the 1870s, and $2.66 in the 1880s. The mean wholesale price for bricks per one thousand bricks included $4.58 in the 1850s, $8.22 in the 1860s, $7.09 in the 1870s, and $7.15 in the 1880s.

8. In a letter from Island County, Washington Territory, in 1853, these same wheat prices were quoted. Wheat never sold for under $2 a bushel, and wheat to be used as seed sold for as high as $6 per bushel. Walter Crockett to Dr. Harvey Black, October 15, 1853, MS, University of Washington Library, Seattle, Washington.

9. Coffee on Whidbey Island in 1853 sold for $0.12 ½ a pound to $0.30 a pound in ibid.; Hazel Addie Jensen, *Across the Years: Pioneer Story of Southern Washington* (N.P.: Private printing, 1951), 68-71.

10. Crockett to Black, October 15, 1853, MS.

11. *Clark v. Moore*, Island County, Washington Territory (1863); *Smith v. Summers*, Walla Walla County, Washington Territory (1881); *Martin v. McElhaney*, Walla Walla County, Washington Territory (1881).

12. U.S., Bureau of the Census, *Historical Statistics*, 115.

13. See Appendix III.

14. *Dagget and Hutchings v. McCormick*, Walla Walla County, Washington Territory (1881).

15. *Chamberlin v. Terry*, Island County, Washington Territory (1866).

16. *Keogh v. Woodworth*, Walla Walla County, Washington Territory (1878).

17. *Territory of Washington* [Heisenberger] *v. Mularkey*, King County, Washington Territory (1887).

18. *Territory of Washington v. Searock*, King County, Washington Territory (1888).

19. *Territory of Washington v. Averill*, King County, Washington Territory (1886).

20. *Territory of Washington v. Conroy*, King County, Washington Territory (1886).

21. *Territory of Washington v. Ah Time, Chinaman*, Island County, Washington Territory (1886); *Territory of Washington v. Ah Tune, Ah Torn, Ah Goon,* Island County, Washington Territory (1886).

22. *Territory of Washington v. Knight,* Island County, Washington Territory (1862).

23. *Territory of Washington v. Ives,* Walla Walla County, Washington Territory (1878).

24. *Territory of Washington v. Ah Loy,* Island County, Washington Territory (1886).

Chapter 10

1. Medians of adjudication celerity do not give a fair representation of distribution because 78 percent of the cases from complaint to the beginning of a trial took less than ten days, 98.5 percent of the cases from trial commencement to decision took less than one day, and 87.3 percent of the cases from decision to satisfaction took less than three months. Median and mean differences are insignificant.

2. In criminal proceedings, 126 of 184 cases examined (68.5 percent) resulted in convictions of defendants. In civil proceedings, 708 of 753 cases examined (94 percent) resulted in findings in favor of plaintiffs.

3. Individual justices of the peace and their caseloads for Washington Territory included Thomas Cranney (Island County) hearing 26 cases or 2.60 per month, Thomas Donald (King County) hearing 14 cases or 1.75 per month, Winfield S. Ebey (Island County) hearing 2 cases or 2.00 per month, Robert Hathaway (Island County) hearing 53 cases or 4.42 per month, Nathaniel Hill (Island County) hearing 32 cases or 2.67 per month, Oliver P. Lacy (Walla Walla County) hearing 39 cases or 9.75 per month, J. D. Laman (Walla Walla County) hearing 1,161 cases or 96.75 per month, John McKnight (King County) hearing 1 case or 1.00 per month, William Robertson (Island County) hearing 10 cases or 2.00 per month, John Y. Sewell (Island County) hearing 61 cases or 5.08 per month, Richard H. Straub (Island County) hearing 6 cases or 1.00 per month, and William Uder (King County) hearing 5 cases or 1.67 per month.

4. *Freeman v. Nibbler,* Walla Walla County, Washington Territory (1874).

5. Nathaniel D. Hill, MS, Island County Historical Society, Coupeville, Washington, 12.

6. U.S., Bureau of the Census, *Eighth Census of the United States: 1860; Ninth Census: 1870; Tenth Census: 1880; Eleventh Census: 1890.*

The population of Coveland Precinct, Island County, was 294 in 1860, 469 in 1870, and 606 in 1880; the mean number of justice court cases per decade per year was 6.33 in the 1860s, 5.90 in the 1870s, and 5.50 in the 1880s. The population of Walla Walla Precinct, Walla Walla County, was 3,699 in 1870 and 3,588 in 1880; the mean number of justice court cases per

decade per year was 105.15 in the 1870s and 146.33 in the 1880s. The population of Newcastle Precinct, King County, was 540 in 1880; the mean
number of justice court cases per decade per year was 4.00 in the 1880s.

7. *Puget Mill Co. v. Hickman*, Island County, Washington Territory
(1880).

8. *Pacific Boom Co. v. Ford, Stearns and Baird*, representatives Puget
Mill Co., Island County, Washington Territory (1888).

9. *Root v. Casten*, Walla Walla County, Washington Territory (1873);
Paine, Paine and Moore v. Johnson, Walla Walla County, Washington
Territory (1873).

10. *Jesup v. Sing Lee and Sam Sing*, Island County, Washington Territory (1876).

11. *Territory of Washington v. Bob, an Indian*, Island County, Washington Territory (1864); *Territory of Washington v. Dectotza, an Indian
Woman*, Island County, Washington Territory (1864).

12. *Johnson v. Squiqui, Chief of the Scatchet* [Skagit] *Tribe of Indians*,
Island County, Washington Territory (1863).

13. *Newberg and Abrams v. J. D. Farmer*, 1 Allen (Washington Territory) 182-185 (1862); *John and Charles Mullen v. Lewis A. Mullen*, 1 Allen
(Washington Territory) 192-194 (1862); *Alfred Washburn v. Lawton Case*,
1 Allen (Washington Territory) 253-255 (1869); *John McKilver v. Danl.
Manchester*, 1 Allen (Washington Territory) 255-257 (1869); *Seattle Coal &
Transportation Co. v. Thomas Lewis*, 1 Allen (Washington Territory) 488
(1875); *S. Baxter & Co. v. Jacob Scoland and T. A. Jensen*, 2 Allen (Washington Territory) 86-91 (1881); *Herman Hadlan v. City of Olympia*, 2
Allen (Washington Territory) 340-345 (1884); *Cyrus J. Cole v. Territory of
Washington*, 3 Struve (Washington Territory) 99-100 (1887); *Jeff. J. Harland
v. Territory of Washington*, 3 Struve (Washington Territory) 131-163
(1887); *Renwick W. Taylor v. L. M. Ringer*, 3 Struve (Washington Territory) 539-543 (1887).

14. *Jeff. J. Harland v. Territory of Washington*, 3 Struve (Washington
Territory) 131-168 (1887).

15. Richard Maxwell Brown, "The American Vigilante Tradition,"
The History of Violence in America, Hugh Davis Graham and Ted Robert
Gurr, eds. (New York: New York Times Co., 1969), 225.

Vigilante movements in Washington Territory from 1853 to 1889 included
a small action in Pierce County in 1856, a small action in New Dungeness,
Clallam County, in 1864, a large action in Walla Walla from 1864 to 1866,
a small action in Steilacoom, Pierce County, in 1870, a large action in
Seattle in 1882, and a small action in Union Gap (Yakima City), Yakima
County, in 1885.

16. *Daily Pacific Tribune* (Olympia, Washington Territory), January 22, 24, 26, 1870.

17. *Walla Walla Union* (Walla Walla, Washington), June 24, 1934.

18. *Daily Pacific Tribune* (Olympia, Washington Territory), January 26, 1870.

19. In case dispositions cross-tabulated with urban and rural justice of the peace courts in Washington Territory, the number of urban cases included 380 trial-determined, 410 default, 318 dismissal, 21 pleading, 43 to grand jury or district court, and 26 change of venue. The number of rural cases included 86 trial-determined, 26 default, 48 dismissal, 11 pleading, 30 to grand jury or district court, and 2 change of venue.

20. State of Washington, *Constitution*, Article IV, Section 1 (1889).

21. Quentin Shipley Smith, *The Journal of the Washington State Constitutional Convention, 1889*, Beverly Paulik Rosenow, ed. (Seattle, Wash.: Book Publishing Co., 1962), 594-595; *Tacoma Morning Globe* (Tacoma, Washington Territory), July 19, 1889.

22. State of Washington, *Constitution*, Article IV, Sections 4, 6 and 10 (1889).

23. Ibid., Sections 10, 11, and 13.

24. *Tacoma Daily Ledger* (Tacoma, Washington Territory), July 19 and September 9, 1889; *Walla Walla Weekly Statesman* (Walla Walla, Washington Territory), July 29, 1889; *Walla Walla Union* (Walla Walla, Washington Territory), July 27, 1889; *Washington Standard* (Olympia, Washington Territory), July 19, 1889; *Post-Intelligencer* (Seattle, Washington Territory), July 20, 1889; James L. Fitts, "The Washington Constitutional Convention of 1889," M.A. Thesis, University of Washington, Seattle, Washington (1951), 50-51; Wilfred J. Airey, "A History of the Constitution and Government of Washington Territory," Ph.D. Dissertation, University of Washington, Seattle, Washington (1945), 462-463.

25. Theodore Stiles, "The Constitution of the State of Washington and Its Effects upon Public Interests," *Washington Historical Quarterly* 4 (October 1913):283; Airey, "Constitution of Washington Territory."

Afterword

1. George L. Haskins, "Reception of the Common Law in Seventeenth Century Massachusetts," *Law and Authority in Colonial America*, George Athan Billias, ed. (New York: Dover Publications, Inc., 1970), 17-31.

2. James Willard Hurst, Walker Ames Lecture, University of Washington, Seattle, Washington, May 3, 1973.

3. William N. Davis, Jr., "Western Justice: The Court at Fort Bridger, Utah Territory," *Utah Historical Quarterly* 23 (April 1955):104.

4. Recommendation of Henry Mahon as justice of the peace, Alabama Territory, July 4, 1818, in Clarence E. Carter, ed., *The Territorial Papers of the United States: The Territory of Alabama, 1817-1819* (Washington, D.C., 1952), XVIII, 365-366.

5. William Salter, *Iowa: The First Free State in the Louisiana Purchase* (Chicago: A. C. McClurg and Co., 1905), 173.

6. Thomas Perkins Abernethy, *From Frontier to Plantation in Tennessee: A Study in Frontier Democracy* (Chapel Hill: University of North Carolina Press, 1932), 64-90; Mirth Tufts Kaplan, "Courts, Counselors and Cases: The Judiciary of Oregon's Provisional Government," *Oregon Historical Quarterly* 62 (June 1961):117-163.

7. Frederick Jackson Turner, "The Significance of the Frontier in American History," *Annual Report of the American Historical Association for the Year 1893* (Washington, D.C., 1894), 200.

8. Ibid., 221-222.

9. Walter Prescott Webb, *The Great Plains* (New York: Grosset and Dunlap, 1931), 496.

10. Ibid., 500.

11. Philip D. Jordan, *Frontier Law and Order* (Lincoln: University of Nebraska Press, 1970), 1.

12. Fred Harrison, *Hell Holes and Hangings: The West's Territorial Prisons, 1861-1912* (New York: Ballantine Books, 1968), vii.

13. Jordan, *Frontier Law*, 1-17.

14. Anton-Hermann Chroust, *The Rise of the Legal Profession in America* (Norman: University of Oklahoma Press, 1965), II, 103.

15. Francis S. Philbrick, *The Rise of the West, 1754-1830* (New York: Harper and Row, 1965), 358.

16. Ibid., 357-358.

17. William Strong, MS, University of Washington Law Library, Seattle, Washington, 10.

18. Ibid., 36.

19. James G. Swan, *The Northwest Coast or, Three Years' Residence in Washington Territory* (Seattle: University of Washington Press, 1972 [first published by Harper and Brothers, 1857]), 278.

20. Ibid.

21. Ibid.

22. Ibid., 279.

23. Ibid., 279-281.

24. Ibid., 278-279.

25. Richard B. Morris, *Studies in the History of American Law, with*

Special Reference to the Seventeenth and Eighteenth Centuries (New York: Columbia University Press, 1930), 17; Thomas D. Clark, "Growing Up with the Frontier," *Western Historical Quarterly* 3 (October 1972):369-371; Francis S. Philbrick, ed., *The Laws of Illinois Territory, 1809-1818* (Springfield: Illinois State Historical Society, 1950), XXV, Law Ser. V, cccxlii-cccxliii; Philbrick, *Rise of West*, 358-360.

26. Philbrick, *Rise of West*, 370.

27. W. Eugene Hollon, *Frontier Violence, Another Look* (New York: Oxford University Press, 1974).

28. Glenn Shirley, *Law West of Fort Smith: A History of Frontier Justice in the Indian Territory, 1834-1896* (Lincoln: University of Nebraska Press, 1968), vii.

29. Charles L. Sonnichsen, *Roy Bean, Law West of the Pecos* (New York: Devin-Adair Co., 1958).

BIBLIOGRAPHY

In the first year of Washington Territory, Supreme Court Justice William Strong experienced a problem that has had direct ramifications on frontier legal history. Strong wrote: "I hereby certify that the records of the district court of the United States, within and for the third judicial district, were stolen and thrown into the Columbia."[1] Fortunately, Strong's records were retrieved, and although they were waterlogged, he was able to recopy them.

Finding legal records relating to justices of the peace and other local legal officials has been discouraged by the scattered distribution of records, the destruction of materials, and a general feeling among historians that local legal records do not exist. Indeed, more often than not, local legal records have been permanently destroyed. Negligence, time, and fire have frequently prevented historians from reconstructing the past. In Washington, fires at the repositories of such settlements as Spokane, Ellensburgh and Vancouver burned many records.

Nonetheless, substantial amounts of justice of the peace records for Washington Territory have survived. After contacting all county clerks and auditors, I found complete records for Island County (1854-1889), Walla Walla County (1872-1882), and King County (1885-1889) precincts; these have provided the bulk of the sources for Chapters 8, 9, and 10. JP records also exist in small amounts for Klickitat County (1886-1889) and Garfield County (1883-1889). In addition, individual justice diaries and journals, county histories, Washington Territory statutes, and Washington Territory supreme court records have provided a rich complement of excellent source material.

1. Arthur S. Beardsley, "Bench and Bar in Washington: The First Fifty Years, 1849-1900," MS, University of Washington Law School Library, Seattle, Washington, Ch. 2, 15.

Manuscripts

Coupeville, Washington. Island County Historical Society. Nathaniel D. Hill MS.

Seattle, Washington. University of Washington Law School Library. Arthur S. Beardsley, "Bench and Bar of Washington: The First Fifty Years, 1849-1900."

————. Walter Crockett MS.

————. Dubuar Scrapbooks.

————. "Family Records and Reminiscences of Washington Pioneers," typescript, 4 vols.

————. Benjamin Kizer, "History of the Spokane Bar and Bench."

————. Edmond S. Meany Pioneer File.

————. William Strong MS.

————. University of Washington Library. Isaac N. Ebey MSS.

————. University of Washington Library, Pacific Northwest Collection. Clarence B. Bagley Scrapbooks.

————. Washington Biography Pamphlet File. Walla Walla, Washington. Whitman College Library, Special Collections. William S. Clark Notebook.

Government Documents

Mississippi Territory. *Statutes.* 1798-1800.

Northwest Territory. *Statutes.* 1788.

Oregon Territory. *Statutes.* 4 Sessions, 1851-1853.

United States. *Congressional Globe.* 37th Congress, 1863.

————. *Congressional Record.* 46th Congress, 1880.

————. *Constitution.* Amendment VI.

————. *Eighth Census.* 1860.

————. *Eleventh Census.* 1890.

————. *Historical Statistics of the United States: Colonial Times to 1957.* 1960.

————. House. Committee on the Territories. *Report: Florida, Iowa, and Wisconsin, to Elect Certain Officers.* 1843.

————. *Inventory of the County Archives of Washington.* Vols. 8, 32. 1941-1942.

————. *Journals of the Continental Congress, 1774-1789.* Vols. 26, 32.

————. *Ninth Census.* 1870.

————. *Register of Debates in Congress.* 1929.

————. *Seventh Census.* 1850.

_____. *Statutes at Large*. 1804, 1805, 1812, 1815, 1829, 1830, 1834, 1836, 1844, 1853, 1856, 1883.

_____. *Supplement to Revised Statutes at Large*. 1880.

_____. *Supreme Court Reports*. 1803.

_____. *Tenth Census*. 1880.

Utah Territory. *Statutes*. 1855.

Washington. *Constitution*. Article IV.

Washington Territory. *Journal of the Council*. 1858-1861.

_____. *Journal of the House of Representatives*. 1858-1861, 1868-1869.

_____. Justice Court Records, Coveland Precinct, Island County. 1853-1888.

_____. Justice of the Peace Records, Newcastle Precinct, King County. Microfilm, University of Washington Library, Seattle, Washington. 1885-1889.

_____. Justice of the Peace Records, Walla Walla Precinct, Walla Walla County. 1872-1882.

_____. Justices' Docket, Island County. 1889-1911.

_____. Probate Records, Island County. 1860-1889.

_____. *Statutes*. 25 Sessions, 1854-1889.

_____. *Supreme Court Reports*. 1853-1889.

Newspapers

IDAHO TERRITORY

Bannock City. *Boise News*. 1863-1864.

Boise. *Capital Chronicle*. 1869-1870.

_____. *Democrat*. 1867-1869.

_____. *Idaho Tri-Weekly Statesman*. 1864-1870.

Idaho City. *Idaho Patriot*. 1864.

Lewiston. *Golden Age*. 1862-1865.

_____. *Journal*. 1867-1870.

_____. *North Idaho Radiator*. 1865.

Ruby City. *The Owyhee Avalanche*. 1866-1870.

Silver City. *Owyhee Bullion*. 1866-1867.

MONTANA TERRITORY

Deer Lodge. *Weekly Independent*. 1867-1870.

Helena. *Daily Gazette*. 1868-1870.

_____. *Herald*. 1866.

_____. *The Montana Post*. 1868-1869.

————. *Radiator*. 1865-1866.
————. *Tri-Weekly Republican*. 1866.
Virginia City. *Capital Times*. 1869-1870.
————. *Montana Democrat*. 1865-1869.
————. *The Montana Post*. 1864-1868.

OREGON TERRITORY

Salem. *Oregon Statesman*. 1863.

WASHINGTON

Pullman. *Herald*. 1938.
————. *Palouse Republic*. 1939.
Renton. *Chronicle*. 1938.
Seattle. *Post-Intelligencer*. 1914, 1916, 1919.
————. *Times*. 1958, 1961.
Stanwood. *Twin City News*. 1935.
Walla Walla. *Union*. 1896, 1934.

WASHINGTON TERRITORY

Bellingham [Whatcom]. *Whatcom Reveille*. 1883-1889.
Centralia. *News*. 1887.
Chehalis. *Bee*. 1888-1889.
————. *Lewis County Bee*. 1884-1888.
————. *Lewis County Nugget*. 1888.
————. *Nugget*. 1883-1888.
Ellensburg [Ellensburgh]. *Kittitas Standard*. 1883.
Goldendale. *Klickitat Sentinel*. 1883.
Kalama. *Beacon*. 1872-1873.
Olympia. *Columbian*. 1853.
————. *Daily Courier*. 1877.
————. *Daily Pacific Tribune*. 1867-1873.
————. *Overland Press*. 1861-1864.
————. *Pacific Tribune*. 1864-1865.
————. *Pioneer and Democrat*. 1854-1861.
————. *Puget Sound Daily Courier*. 1872-1873.
————. *Washington Democrat*. 1864-1865.
————. *Washington Standard*. 1860-1875.
Port Townsend. *Puget Sound Weekly Argus*. 1885-1889.
Seattle. *Daily Intelligencer*. 1876-1881.
————. *Post*. 1879-1880.

_____. *Post-Intelligencer.* 1881-1889.

_____. *Puget Sound Daily.* 1866.

_____. *Puget Sound Gazette.* 1867.

_____. *Puget Sound Semi-Weekly.* 1866.

_____. *Puget Sound Weekly.* 1866-1867.

Snohomish. *Northern Star.* 1876-1878.

Spokane [Spokane Falls]. *Chronicle.* 1881-1883.

Tacoma. *Daily Pacific Tribune.* 1873-1874.

_____. *Herald.* 1878-1880.

_____. *Ledger.* 1883-1889.

_____. *Morning Globe* [Globe]. 1888-1889.

_____. *Weekly Pacific Tribune.* 1873-1875.

Vancouver. *Independent.* 1875-1877.

_____. *Register.* 1865-1869.

Walla Walla. *Statesman.* 1865-1869, 1876-1881.

_____. *Union.* 1883-1889.

_____. *Washington Statesman.* 1861-1865.

Yakima. *Signal.* 1883-1884.

Theses and Dissertations

Airey, Wilfred J. "A History of the Constitution and Government of Washington Territory." Ph.D. Dissertation, University of Washington, 1945.

Dressler, John Barnes, Jr. "The Territorial System and the People: The Emergence of Factionalism in the Northwest Territory." M.A. Thesis, University of Washington, 1967.

Fischer, Thomas Covell. "A History of Territorial Government in Michigan, 1805-1837." M.A. Thesis, University of Washington, 1963.

Fitts, James L. "The Washington Constitutional Convention of 1889." M.A. Thesis, University of Washington, 1951.

Hamilton, William B., Jr. "American Beginnings in the Old Southwest: The Mississippi Phase." Ph.D. Dissertation, Duke University, 1938.

Hubbard, Greg Russell. "The Indian Under the White Man's Law in Washington Territory, 1853-1889." M.A. Thesis, University of Washington, 1972.

Hume, Richard L. "The 'Black and Tan' Constitutional Conventions of 1867-1869 in Ten Former Confederate States: A Study of Their Membership," I and II. Ph.D. Dissertation, University of Washington, 1969.

Wunder, John R. "The Mississippi Territory's First Experience with American Legal Institutions: Sargent's Code, Its Adoption and Abolition, 1798-1803." M.A. Thesis, University of Iowa, 1970.

Lectures

Hurst, James Willard. University of Washington, May 3, 1973.
Prosch, Thomas W. "Dr. D. S. Maynard, the Pioneer Physician of Seattle." Address to the King County Medical Society, Seattle, Washington, March 7, 1904 [typescript found in University of Washington Library, Pacific Northwest Collection].

Books

Abernethy, Thomas Perkins. *From Frontier to Plantation in Tennessee: A Study in Frontier Democracy*. Chapel Hill: University of North Carolina Press, 1932.
Adams, George Burton. *Constitutional History of England*. New York: Henry Holt and Co., 1921.
Alley, B. F., and J. P. Munro-Fraser. *An Illustrated History of Clarke County, Washington Territory*. Portland: Washington Publishing Co., 1885.
Alvord, Clarence W. *The Illinois Country*. Springfield: Illinois Centennial Commission, 1920.
Bagley, C. B. *History of Seattle*. Chicago: S. J. Clarke Publishing Co., 1916.
Bancroft, Hubert Howe. *Chronicles of the Builders of the Commonwealth*. Vol. 4. San Francisco: History Co., 1892.
_____. *History of the Pacific States of North America: Arizona and New Mexico, 1530-1888*. Vol. 12. San Francisco: History Co., 1888.
_____. *History of the Pacific States of North America: Oregon, 1834-1848*. Vol. 29. San Francisco: History Co., 1886.
_____. *History of the Pacific States of North America: Oregon, 1848-1888*. Vol. 30. San Francisco: History Co., 1888.
_____. *History of the Pacific States of North America: Utah, 1540-1886*. Vol. 21. San Francisco: History Co., 1889.
_____. *History of the Pacific States of North America: Washington, Idaho and Montana, 1854-1889*. Vol. 31. San Francisco: History Co., 1890.
Barnhart, John D. *Valley of Democracy: The Frontier Versus the Plantation in the Ohio Valley, 1775-1818*. Bloomington: Indiana University Press, 1953.

Blegen, Theodore C. *Minnesota: A History of the State*. Minneapolis: University of Minnesota Press, 1963.

_____. *Readings in Early Minnesota History*. Minneapolis: University of Minnesota Press, 1938.

Bloom, John Porter, ed. *The Territorial Papers of the United States*. Vol. 27. Washington, D.C.: U.S. Government Printing Office, 1969.

Buley, R. Carlyle. *The Old Northwest: Pioneer Period, 1815-1840*. Vol. 1. Bloomington: Indiana University Press, 1951.

Carter, Clarence E., ed. *The Territorial Papers of the United States*. Vols. 2, 3, 6, 9-12, 14, 15, 18, 23-25. Washington, D.C.: U.S. Government Printing Office, 1934, 1938, 1940, 1942, 1943, 1945, 1949, 1951, 1952, 1956, 1958, 1960.

Caruso, John Anthony. *The Great Lakes Frontier*. Indianapolis: Bobbs-Merrill Co., 1961.

Chroust, Anton-Hermann. *The Rise of the Legal Profession in America*. Vol. 2. Norman: University of Oklahoma Press, 1965.

Claiborne, John Francis Hamtramck. *Mississippi: As a Province, Territory, and State*. Jackson: Mississippi Historical Society, 1880.

Cole, Cyrenus. *Iowa Through the Years*. Iowa City: State Historical Society of Iowa, 1940.

Cook, Jimmie Jean. *"A particular friend, Penn's Cove," A History of the Settlers, Claims and Buildings of Central Whidbey Island*. Coupeville, Wash.: Island County Historical Society, 1973.

Dick, Everett. *The Dixie Frontier: A Social History*. New York: Alfred A. Knopf, 1948.

Downes, Randolph C. *Frontier Ohio*. Columbus: Ohio State Archeological and Historical Society, 1935.

Eblen, Jack. *The First and Second United States Empires: Governors and Territorial Government, 1784-1912*. Pittsburgh: University of Pittsburgh Press, 1968.

Eddy, John Percy. *Justice of the Peace*. London: Cassell and Co., Ltd., 1963.

English, William. *The Pioneer Lawyer and Jurist in Missouri*. Columbia: University of Missouri Press, 1947.

Farrand, Max. *The Legislation of Congress for the Government of the Organized Territories of the United States, 1789-1895*. Newark, N.J.: William A. Baker, 1896.

Fortier, Alcée. *A History of Louisiana, the American Domination, 1803-1861*. Vol. 3. New York: Manzi, Joyant and Co., 1904.

Friedman, Lawrence M. *A History of American Law*. New York: Simon and Schuster, 1973.

Gayarré, Charles. *History of Louisiana, the American Domination.* Vol. 4. New Orleans: F. F. Hansell and Bros., Ltd., 1903.

Gilbert, Frank T. *Historic Sketches of Walla Walla, Whitman, Columbia and Garfield Counties, Washington Territory.* Portland: Private printing, 1882.

Gilpin, Alec R. *The Territory of Michigan, 1805-1837.* East Lansing: Michigan State University Press, 1970.

Gleason, J. H. *The Justices of the Peace in England, 1558-1640.* Oxford: Clarendon Press, 1969.

Guice, John D.W. *The Rocky Mountain Bench: The Territorial Supreme Courts of Colorado, Montana, and Wyoming, 1861-1890.* New Haven, Conn.: Yale University Press, 1972.

Harrison, Fred. *Hell Holes and Hangings: The West's Territorial Prisons, 1861-1912.* New York: Ballantine Books, 1968.

Haskins, George Lee. *Law and Authority in Early Massachusetts.* New York: Macmillan Co., 1960.

Hawke, David. *The Colonial Experience.* Indianapolis: Bobbs-Merrill Co., 1966.

Herlihy, David, ed. *Medieval Culture and Society.* New York: Harper and Row, 1968.

Hines, H. K. *An Illustrated History of the State of Oregon.* Chicago: Lewis Publishing Co., 1893.

_____. *An Illustrated History of the State of Washington.* Chicago: Lewis Publishing Co., 1893.

History of the Big Bend Country. Spokane: Western Historical Publishing Co., 1904.

History of Skagit and Snohomish Counties, Washington. N.P.: Private printing, 1906.

Holdsworth, William S. *A History of English Law.* Vol. 1. London: Methuen and Co., Ltd., 1903.

Hollister, C. Warren. *The Making of England, 55 B.C. to 1399.* Boston: D. C. Heath and Co., 1966.

Hollon, W. Eugene. *Frontier Violence, Another Look.* New York: Oxford University Press, 1974.

Hooker, Richard J., ed. *The Carolina Backcountry on the Eve of the Revolution: The Journal and Other Writings of Charles Woodmason, Anglican Itinerant.* Chapel Hill: University of North Carolina Press, 1953.

Horsman, Reginald. *The Frontier in the Formative Years, 1783-1815.* New York: Holt, Rinehart and Winston, 1970.

Hull, Lindley M., ed. *A History of Central Washington.* Spokane, Wash.: Shaw and Borden Co., 1929.

Hunt, Herbert. *Tacoma: Its History and Its Builders.* Vol. 2. Chicago: S. J. Clarke Publishing Co., 1916.

Hurst, James Willard. *The Growth of American Law: The Law Makers.* Boston: Little, Brown and Co., 1950.

Illustrated History of Klickitat, Yakima and Kittitas Counties, State of Washington, An. N.P.: Interstate Publishing Co., 1904.

Illustrated History of Southeastern Washington, An. Spokane: Western Historical Publishing Co., 1906.

Illustrated History of Stevens, Ferry, Okanogan and Chelan Counties, State of Washington, An. Spokane: Western Historical Publishing Co., 1904.

Ireland, Robert M. *The County Courts of Antebellum Kentucky.* Lexington: University Press of Kentucky, 1972.

Jensen, Hazel Addie. *Across the Years: Pioneer Story of Southern Washington.* N.P.: Private printing, 1951.

Johansen, Dorothy O. *Empire of the Columbia.* New York: Harper and Row, 1967.

Jordan, Philip D. *Frontier Law and Order.* Lincoln: University of Nebraska Press, 1970.

Labaree, Leonard. *Royal Government in America: A Study of the British Colonial System before 1783.* New York: Frederick Ungar Publishing Co., 1930.

Lamar, Howard. *The Far Southwest, 1846-1912: A Territorial History.* New York: W. W. Norton and Co., 1966.

Lang, H. O., ed. *History of the Willamette Valley.* Portland: Himes and Lang, 1885.

Lyman, W. D. *An Illustrated History of Walla Walla County, State of Washington.* N.P.: W. H. Lever, 1901.

Maitland, Frederic W. *The Constitutional History of England.* Cambridge: University Press, 1926.

Malone, Dumas, ed. *Dictionary of American Biography.* Vols. 3, 7, 17. New York: Charles Scribner's Sons, 1935.

Meany, Edmond S. *History of the State of Washington.* New York: Macmillan Co., 1941.

Milton, Frank. *In Some Authority: The English Magistracy.* London: Pall Mall Press, 1959.

Morgan, Murray. *Skid Road.* New York: Ballantine Books, 1951.

Morris, Richard B. *Studies in the History of American Law, with Special Reference to the Seventeenth and Eighteenth Centuries.* New York: Columbia University Press, 1930.

Notestein, Wallace. *The English People on the Eve of Colonization, 1603-1630.* New York: Harper and Brothers, 1954.

O'Farrell, Mrs. V. J. *Eminent Judges and Lawyers of the Northwest, 1843-1955.* Palo Alto: C. W. Taylor, Jr., 1954.

Page, Leo. *Justice of the Peace.* London: Faber and Faber, Ltd., 1931.

Paul, Rodman W. *Mining Frontiers of the Far West, 1848-1880.* New York: Holt, Rinehart and Winston, 1963.

Pease, Theodore C., ed. *The Laws of the Northwest Territory, 1788-1800.* Vol. 17, Law Ser. 1. Springfield: Illinois State Historical Society, 1925.

Philbrick, Francis S. *The Rise of the West, 1754-1830.* New York: Harper and Row, 1965.

————, ed. *The Laws of Illinois Territory, 1809-1818.* Vol. 25, Law Ser. 5. Springfield: Illinois State Historical Society, 1950.

————, ed. *The Laws of Indiana Territory, 1801-1809.* Vol. 21, Law Ser. 2. Springfield: Illinois State Historical Society, 1930.

Plucknett, Theodore F.T. *A Concise History of the Common Law.* Boston: Little, Brown and Co., 1956.

Pomeroy, Earl S. *The Pacific Slope.* New York: Alfred A. Knopf, 1965.

————. *The Territories and the United States, 1861-1890.* Seattle: University of Washington Press, 1947.

Prucha, Francis Paul. *American Indian Policy in the Formative Years: The Indian Trade and Intercourse Acts, 1790-1834.* Lincoln: University of Nebraska Press, 1962.

Rowland, Dunbar. *Mississippi: The Heart of the South.* Vols. 1 and 2. Chicago: S. J. Clarke Publishing Co., 1925.

Rowland, Eron, ed. *Life, Letters, and Papers of William Dunbar.* Jackson: Mississippi Historical Society, 1930.

Salter, William. *Iowa: The First Free State in the Louisiana Purchase.* Chicago: A. C. McClurg and Co., 1905.

Scanlan, Peter Lawrence. *Prairie du Chien.* Menasha, Wis.: George Banta Publishing Co., 1937.

Shinn, Charles Howard. *Mining Camps: A Study in American Frontier Government.* New York: Charles Scribner's Sons, 1884.

Shirley, Glenn. *Law West of Fort Smith: a History of Frontier Justice in the Indian Territory, 1834-1896.* Lincoln: University of Nebraska Press, 1968.

Smith, Quentin Shipley. *The Journal of the Washington State Constitutional Convention, 1889.* Beverly Paulik Rosenow, ed. Seattle, Wash.: Book Publishing Co., 1962.

Smith, W. Roy. *South Carolina as a Royal Province, 1719-1776.* New York: Macmillan Co., 1903.

Sonnichsen, Charles L. *Roy Bean, Law West of the Pecos.* New York: Devin-Adair Co., 1958.

Sosin, Jack M. *The Revolutionary Frontier, 1763-1783.* New York: Holt, Rinehart and Winston, 1967.

Stevens, Hazard. *The Life of General Isaac I. Stevens.* Vol. 2. Boston: Houghton, Mifflin and Co., 1901.

Strong, Moses M. *History of the Territory of Wisconsin.* Madison: State of Wisconsin, 1885.

Swan, James G. *The Northwest Coast or, Three Years' Residence in Washington Territory.* New York: Harper and Brothers, 1857.

Tebeau, Charlton W. *A History of Florida.* Coral Gables, Fla.: University of Miami Press, 1971.

Thorpe, Francis Newton, ed. *The Federal and State Constitutions, Colonial Charters, and Other Organic Laws of the States, Territories, and Colonies Now or Heretofore Forming the United States of America.* 6 vols. Washington, D.C.: U.S. Government Printing Office, 1909.

Trevelyan, George M. *History of England.* New York: Longmans, Green and Co., 1928.

Trimble, William J. *The Mining Advance into the Inland Empire.* Madison: University of Wisconsin Press, 1914.

Webb, Walter Prescott. *The Great Plains.* New York: Grosset and Dunlap, 1931.

Wedgwood, C. V. *The King's Peace, 1637-1641.* New York: Macmillan Co., 1955.

Welch, William D. *A Brief Historical Sketch of Port Townsend, Washington.* N.P.: Private printing, 1956.

White, Lonnie J. *Politics on the Southwestern Frontier, 1819-1836.* Memphis, Tenn.: Memphis State University Press, 1964.

Wright, Louis B. *The Atlantic Frontier: Colonial American Civilization, 1607-1763.* New York: Alfred A. Knopf, 1947.

Articles

Andrew, Lyman B. "The Constitutional Convention of 1878." *Washington Historical Magazine* 2 (October 1900):17-20.

Bancroft, Hubert Howe. "Some Early Educational History." *The Washington Historian* 1 (September 1899):41-43.

Beard, Charles Austin. "The Office of Justice of the Peace in England in Its Origin and Development." *Studies in History, Economics and Law,* Vol. 20, No. 52-53, 1-184. New York: Columbia University Press, 1904.

Beardsley, Arthur S. "Compiling the Territorial Codes of Washington." *Pacific Northwest Quarterly* 28 (January 1937):3-54.

_____ and Donald A. McDonald. "The Courts and Early Bar of Washington Territory." *Washington Law Review and State Bar Journal* 17 (April 1942):57-82.

Bestor, Arthur. "Constitutionalism and the Settlement of the West: The Attainment of Consensus, 1754-1784." *The American Territorial System*, John Porter Bloom, ed., Athens: Ohio University Press, 1973, 13-33.

Blume, William Wirt, and Elizabeth Gaspar Brown. "Territorial Courts and Law: Unifying Factors in the Development of American Legal Institutions." *Michigan Law Review* 61 (November 1962):39-106 and (January 1963):467-538.

Brown, Richard Maxwell. "The American Vigilante Tradition." *The History of Violence in America*, Hugh Davis Graham and Ted Robert Gurr, eds., New York: New York Times Co., 1969, 154-226.

Burger, Warren E. "The State of the Federal Judiciary—1971." *American Bar Association Journal* 57 (September 1971):855-859.

Carson, James Milton. "Historical Background of Florida Law." *Miami Law Quarterly* 3 (February 1949):254-268.

Chafee, Zechariah, Jr. "Colonial Courts and the Common Law." *Proceedings of the Massachusetts Historical Society* 68 (1952):132-159.

Clark, Thomas D. "Growing Up with the Frontier." *Western Historical Quarterly* 3 (October 1972):361-372.

Davis, William N., Jr. "Western Justice: The Court at Fort Bridger, Utah Territory." *Utah Historical Quarterly* 23 (April 1955):99-125.

DeRosier, Arthur H., Jr. "William Dunbar: A Product of the Eighteenth Century Scottish Renaissance." *Journal of Mississippi History* 28 (August 1966):185-227.

"Extracts from the Diary of General A. V. Kautz." *The Washington Historian* 1 (April 1900):115-119 and (July 1900):181-186, 2 (October 1900):12-15.

Farquhar, Frank S. "Historical Sketches of Yakima County." *Washington Historical Magazine* 2 (July 1901):190-194.

Flandrau, Charles E. "Lawyers and Courts of Minnesota Prior to and During Its Territorial Period." *Collections of the Minnesota Historical Society* 8 (December 1896):39-101.

"Fragments of Early History." *Up-To-The-Times* 6 (May 1912):5060-5062.

Haskins, George L. "Law and Colonial Society." *American Quarterly* 9 (1957):354-364.

_____. "Reception of the Common Law in Seventeenth Century Massachusetts." *Law and Authority in Colonial America*. George Athan Billias, ed. New York: Dover Publications, 1970, 17-31.

_____. and Samuel E. Ewing. "The Spread of Massachusetts Law in the Seventeenth Century." *Essays in the History of Early American*

Law, David H. Flaherty, ed. Chapel Hill: University of North Carolina Press, 1969, 186-191.

Hassell, Mrs. Richard Burton. "A Whidbey Island Tragedy." *Washington Historical Magazine* 2 (April 1901):142-145.

Hennessy, Mary T. "Qualifications of California Court Judges: A Dual System." *Pacific Law Journal* 3 (July 1972):439-474.

Hicks, U. E. "Taking the Census in 1853." *Washington Historical Magazine* 2 (January 1901):78-83.

Izett, John M. "Whidbey Island History." *Washington Historical Magazine* 1 (July 1900):199-200.

Johansen, Dorothy O. "A Tentative Appraisal of Territorial Government in Oregon." *Pacific Historical Review* 18 (November 1949):485-499.

Kaplan, Mirth Tufts. "Courts, Counselors and Cases: The Judiciary of Oregon's Provisional Government." *Oregon Historical Quarterly* 62 (June 1961):117-163.

Kizer, Benjamin. "The Pioneer Lawyer." *The Pacific Northwester* (Winter 1962):1-8.

Kommers, Donald P. "The Emergence of Law and Justice in Pre-Territorial Wisconsin." *American Journal of Legal History* 8 (January 1964):20-33.

Lockwood, James H. "Early Times and Events in Wisconsin." *Collections of the State Historical Society of Wisconsin,* Vol. 2, 98-196. Madison: Wisconsin State Historical Society, 1855.

McGuire, J. E. "Newton and the Demonic Furies: Some Current Problems and Approaches in History of Science." *History of Science* 11 (March 1973):21-48.

Morgan, Dale, et al. "The State of Deseret." *Utah Historical Quarterly* 8 (April, July, and October 1940):65-239.

Moss, Henry L. "Last Days of Wisconsin Territory and Early Days of Minnesota Territory." *Collections of the Minnesota Historical Society* 8 (December 1896):67-88.

Pease, Theodore C. "The Ordinance of 1787." *Mississippi Valley Historical Review* 25 (September 1938):167-180.

Prosch, Thomas W. "The Pioneer Dead of 1914." *Washington Historical Quarterly* 6 (January 1915):11-20.

Provine, W. A. "Lardner Clark, Nashville's First Merchant and Foremost Citizen." *Tennessee Historical Magazine* 3 (March and June 1917): 30-46 and 115-125.

Putnam, Bertha Haven. "The Transformation of the Keepers of the Peace into the Justices of the Peace, 1327-1380." *Transactions of the Royal Historical Society* 12 (1929):19-48.

Shipton, Clifford K. "The Locus of Authority in Colonial Massachusetts."

Law and Authority in Colonial America, George Athan Billias, ed. New York: Dover Publications, 1970, 136-148.

Smith, Alice E. "Courts and Judges in Wisconsin Territory." *Wisconsin Magazine of History* 56 (Spring 1973):179-188.

Stiles, Theodore. "The Constitution of the State of Washington and Its Effects upon Public Interests." *Washington Historical Quarterly* 4 (October 1913):281-287.

Tharp, Marilyn. "Story of Coal at Newcastle." *Pacific Northwest Quarterly* 48 (October 1957):120-127.

Toulmin, George B. "The Political Ideas of Winthrop Sargent, A New England Federalist on the Frontier." *Journal of Mississippi History* 4 (October 1953):207-230.

Turner, Frederick Jackson. "The Significance of the Frontier in American History." *Annual Report of the American Historical Association for the Year 1893*. Washington, D.C.: 1894, 199-227.

"Walla Walla Pioneers." *Washington Historical Magazine* 2 (July 1901): 201.

Washburn, Wilcomb E. "Law and Authority in Colonial Virginia." *Law and Authority in Colonial America*, George Athan Billias, ed. New York: Dover Publications, 1970, 116-135.

Weir, Allen. "Roughing It on Puget Sound in the Early Sixties." *Washington Historical Magazine* 1 (April 1900):120-124.

Wunder, John R. "American Law and Order Comes to Mississippi Territory: The Making of Sargent's Code." *Journal of Mississippi History* 38 (May 1976):131-155.

_____. "Constitutional Oversight: *Clarke v. Bazadone* (1803) and the Territorial Supreme Court as the Court of Last Resort." *The Old Northwest* 4 (September 1978): 259-284.

_____. "Tampering with the Northwest Frontier: The Accidental Design of the Washington/Idaho Boundary." *Pacific Northwest Quarterly* 68 (January 1977):1-12.

Zobel, Hiller B. "Law Under Pressure: Boston, 1769-1771." *Law and Authority in Colonial America*, George Athan Billias, ed. New York: Dover Publications, 1970, 187-205.

INDEX

ABOUT THE AUTHOR

John R. Wunder is assistant professor of history at Texas Tech University in Lubbock, Texas. He has edited such works as *Pacific Northwest Sourcebook* and *Toward an Urban Ohio*, and his articles have appeared in scholarly journals.